D0609527

THE VOICE OF BUSINESS

THE
LUTHER
HARTWELL
HODGES
SERIES

ON
BUSINESS,
SOCIETY,
AND THE
STATE

William H. Becker, Editor

The Voice of Business

Hill & Knowlton and

Postwar Public Relations

KAREN S. MILLER

The University of North Carolina Press

Chapel Hill and London

The paper in this book meets the guidelines for
permanence and durability of the Committee on
Production Guidelines for Book Longevity of the
Council on Library Resources.

Library of Congress Cataloging-in-Publication Data
Miller, Karen S.
The voice of business: Hill & Knowlton and postwar
public relations / Karen S. Miller.
p.   cm.—(The Luther Hartwell Hodges series on
business, society, and the state)
Includes bibliographical references and index.
ISBN 0-8078-2439-9 (alk. paper)
1. Hill and Knowlton, Inc.—History. 2. Public
relations firms—United States—History. 3. World
politics—1945—Public opinion. 4. Public opinion—
United States. I. Title. II. Series.
HD59.6.U6M548   1999   98-11935
331.7′616592′0973—dc21   CIP

03 02 01 00 99   5 4 3 2 1

To Clairsa and Walter Heigel

and Rosetta and Allyn Miller

CONTENTS

Writing a book is hard work, but without the assistance of many friends and colleagues it would have been impossible. I owe my greatest debt to James L. Baughman, my dissertation adviser, and committee members Colleen A. Dunlavy, Jack M. McLeod, Diane Lindstrom, and William B. Blankenburg at the University of Wisconsin–Madison. I thank them all for their time, guidance, and friendship.

A special thanks to my colleagues and students at the University of Georgia's Henry W. Grady College of Journalism and Mass Communication and to the reviewers, staff, and editors at the University of North Carolina Press, especially Lewis Bateman and Pamela Upton. They made my job both easier and more fun.

A number of librarians and archivists also provided invaluable assistance. First and foremost was the staff at the State Historical Society of Wisconsin, particularly Harry Miller. At the Truman library, Elizabeth Safly and Dennis E. Bilger; at Washington University, Paul Anderson; and at Catholic University, Lynn Conway—all have my appreciation. Senate historian Donald Ritchie also offered good advice on the Library of Congress, and the librarians at the University of California–San Francisco are to be commended for putting the Brown and Williamson papers online.

My thanks to Charles T. Salmon for introducing me to the social problems literature that provided a framework for understanding public relations; Richard Pollay, for his *Ad Age* index and advice on tobacco industry research; Roland Marchand, Scott M. Cutlip, and Roger Olien for reading and commenting on my dissertation; Laura Sutton, the best graduate assistant ever, and Paula Smith, computer genius; and discussants at the Business History Conference in Fort Lauderdale and Association for Education in Journalism and Mass Communication meetings in Boston, Stone Mountain, Tuscaloosa, and Madison. Thanks to AEJMC for allowing me to reprint parts of "Smoking Up a Storm," which appeared in *Journalism Mono-*

graphs in December 1992, to *Business History Review* for permission to reprint portions of "Air Power Is Peace Power" from its autumn 1996 issue, and to the editors and anonymous reviewers of both journals.

Several of John Hill's colleagues and competitors allowed me to interview them or responded to my questions in writing. My thanks to Chester Burger, Harold Burson, Howard Chase, Robert Gray, George Hammond, and Farley Manning for their time and insight. Two small but invaluable grants from the Harry S. Truman Library Institute and the Institute for Public Relations Research and Education helped to finance trips to archives and to New York for interviews.

My undying gratitude goes to the Atlanta Braves, especially for 28 October 1995; the Wisconsin Badgers, especially for 1 January 1994; the Green Bay Packers, for being back; and the UGA basketball teams, whose day will come.

Finally, thanks to my family and friends, with love.

AAF	Army Air Force
ACS	American Cancer Society
AIA	Aircraft Industries Association
AISI	American Iron and Steel Institute
AWA	Aviation Writers Association
BCCI	Bank of Credit and Commerce International
CFK	Citizens for a Free Kuwait
CIO	Congress of Industrial Organizations
CR	community relations
CTR	Council for Tobacco Research
ERP	employee representation plan
H&K	Hill and Knowlton, Inc.
NAM	National Association of Manufacturers
NAMM	National Association of Margarine Manufacturers
NGORC	Natural Gas and Oil Resources Committee
NIRA	National Industrial Recovery Act
NLRB	National Labor Relations Board
SAB	Scientific Advisory Board
SWOC	Steel Workers Organizing Committee
TIRC	Tobacco Industry Research Committee
USWA	United Steelworkers of America
VFW	Veterans of Foreign Wars
WCA	Wisconsin Creameries Association
WSB	Wage Stabilization Board

THE VOICE OF BUSINESS

"Every morning, John W. Hill, a lean and wiry man with soft, blue eyes can be observed walking from his home at 74th Street and Park Avenue to his office and 42nd Street and Third Avenue," a biography produced by his public relations agency declared in 1961. "He walks at least five miles a day and spends eight hours daily at his job, and often is required to put in more time. At 72 years of age, when many men are content to spend their time idling in the sun or beside a fireplace, he is actively overseeing one of the busiest and most successful enterprises in the nation."[1]

The agency exaggerated. But John Hill could justifiably have claimed to head the most important public relations agency ever: Hill and Knowlton, Inc., of New York. Its clients included the steel, tobacco, and aviation industries' trade associations, Procter and Gamble, Texaco, Gillette, and Avco Manufacturing—some of the biggest corporations and most basic sectors of industry in the largest and most productive economy in the world. Agency executives boasted that the combined sales of its clients in 1959, exceeding $50 billion, amounted to 10 percent of the gross national product. Hill and Knowlton had expanded internationally, which brought both clients and prestige and gave the agency a payroll of 250 employees in New York, Washington, Los Angeles, Chicago, Pittsburgh, Cleveland, Nassau, Geneva, The Hague, Düsseldorf, and Sydney. Annual billings topped $3 million plus out-of-pocket expenses, making it either first or second among agencies, and in surveys of public relations practitioners and journalists alike H&K ranked first and best.[2]

Participation in client policy making increased the public relations executives' influence. H&K's founder, a conservative ideologue who held many of the same views about government and labor as his corporate clients, routinely participated in board and executive meetings of the agency's largest accounts, as did many of his top managers. The agents thus had regular opportunity for input on decisions made at the highest levels of the nation's leading industries. The only similar practitioners of the day, Earl Newsom and T. J. Ross, had smaller agencies with staffs of less than twenty-five, while Hill and Knowlton's biggest competitor, Carl Byoir and Associates, was known primarily as a publicity house.[3]

Despite the size and significance of Hill and Knowlton's clients and its stature in the field of public relations, little scholarly work has examined its history—or that of any other agency. Although many have considered the lives of individual PR practitioners and others document the growth of public relations generally, few scholars have attempted to describe an agency's development over time.[4] This lack of information is troubling because recent histories of postwar opinion management have overestimated the power of public relations. In discussions of the Taft-Hartley debate, for instance, Kim McQuaid asserts that because people wanted something done about strikes, "propaganda proved particularly important in the Truman era because masses were easy to sway," and Elizabeth Fones-Wolf states that "a compliant press aided business in mobilizing public opinion" about the bill. An examination of Hill and Knowlton's history creates a more accurate picture of public relations by describing the ways that one firm operated with and for its clients and by locating the limits of PR's impact.[5]

Because the scholarly record on the history of public relations is so slim, Part I of this book reviews the agency's policies and practices. Chapter 1 discusses John Hill's background and the founding of the agency based on its steel industry account, documenting the relationships between client and agent, the development of Hill's political and public relations philosophy, and the refinement and institutionalization of techniques basic to the agency's operation. Hill's belief in free enterprise and the relationship between government, labor, and industry emerge as particularly important to the agency's development. Chapter 2 reviews a typical Hill and Knowlton campaign of the middle decades of the twentieth century, the program for the Aircraft Industries Association (AIA) after World War II, which was characteristic of H&K's work because it focused on the relationship between government and business for a trade association and because, although the campaign had effects, the agency's influence on people and events was complex and indirect. Chapter 3 describes how the relationship between client and agent affected the development of the steel industry program in 1947–48.

Part II assesses the ability of the public relations agents to direct political, public, and media discourse relating to their clients. The butter-versus-margarine controversy of 1948 to 1950, discussed in Chapter 4, reveals that although H&K did influence political discourse about the issue, most citizens desired an end to regulation of margarine, and Congress complied with their wishes. Chapter 5 investigates the role of public discourse and opinion in the steel strike of 1952, when President Harry S. Truman seized the mills during the Korean War. A massive public relations campaign did affect how people talked about the problem, but that did little to change anyone's opinion about the situation. Still, the ability of the firm to focus and rally conservative elite opinion around the issue was significant. Despite lackluster public support and the powerful opposition of labor and government, steel executives got what they wanted when government price controls were broken. Chapter 6 explores media discourse about an issue of great public interest, cigarette smoking. Hired during the mid-1950s health scare, Hill and Knowlton resolved the crisis by communicating with cigarette smokers through the news media, gaining control of the issue by arguing that there existed a medical controversy about the safety of tobacco smoking.

Part III examines the ways that Hill and Knowlton's philosophy and tactics changed over space and time. As the first international public relations agency, Hill and Knowlton holds a special place in public relations history, discussed in Chapter 7. H&K's main goal was, as in domestic campaigns, to spread the client's messages, but it also sought to promote American business and values internationally. Chapter 8 provides a summary of some of Hill and Knowlton's work since 1955, including a review of events in the 1990s that made the agency a pariah in the world of public relations. Founder John Hill's approach to PR endured only as long as his handpicked and personally trained successors remained at the helm. Although he built the biggest and one of the most reputable agencies in the world, Hill's legacy must be viewed as mixed. The concluding chapter summarizes the ways that the public relations agency was at times able to influence news media, public, and political discussions about issues, and it describes how that in turn affected social and political action. Although H&K's manipulation of information regarding powerful industries influenced both the content and the quantity of public discussion about important issues, the agency's biggest impact was not on the general public but on its own clients and people who already thought like they did.

Influencing the Client and the Like-Minded

Hill's relationship with traditionalist clients and his political views put into practice meant that Hill and Knowlton's messages to the public came with a uniformly conservative point of view. They insisted that the federal government and organized labor should not be allowed to intrude on big business's decision-making territory. At times, the agency's client choices seemed to contradict Hill's free-enterprise position, as when the agency argued for oleo regulation to protect farmers or for a special relationship between the government and aircraft manufacturers. But the agents found ways to rationalize special circumstances for these clients and presented their cases in ways that remained consistent with the free-enterprise message.

The public heard the agency, but that does not mean that people were necessarily convinced by its messages. H&K served an information-providing role in its product promotion for its many trade association and corporate accounts, as when it made people aware of Crosley refrigerators on behalf of Avco Manufacturing. But educating the public about free enterprise and the role of industry in American society proved a more difficult task. "I am forced to wonder," Hill wrote in 1963, "why seemingly so little progress has been made in the economic education of Americans." Large portions of the public continued to disagree with some of the steel industry's educational tenets, even basic messages regarding steel's safety record and industrial relations, although the agency hammered at these points for years. Hill apparently never considered that the American public might have understood but simply disagreed with industry on such fundamental questions.[6]

That the American Iron and Steel Institute (AISI) remained with Hill and Knowlton despite its uneven record in improving public attitudes is testament to John Hill's strength as a public relations counselor, his ability to say what the client wanted to say. H&K amplified the voice of business, as opposed to fostering dialogue between competing groups. As Hill wrote in 1968, "The role of public relations in the opinion forming process is to communicate information and viewpoints in behalf of causes and organizations. The objective is to inform public opinion and win its favor." Given that reasoning, it makes sense that, for instance, in strike-year programs for the steel industry, the agency did not seek resolution of basic disagreements between labor and management but public support for management's perspective. It was as though clients expected to defeat unions, federal regulation, or a disapproving public by yelling louder than anyone else.[7]

But Hill did not allow or encourage his staff to say anything the client wanted. Quite to the contrary, his reputation among public relations executives as a highly ethical professional was based on his willingness to turn down or let go clients who refused to act in what he regarded as the public interest, most spectacularly when the agency dropped the Tobacco Institute account in the late 1960s. Edward W. Barrett, dean of the Columbia School of Journalism and a former Hill and Knowlton vice-president, wrote, "I have seen John Hill decline an exceedingly lucrative new account because the would-be client impressed him as wanting to shade the truth"; support subordinates "in disputes with major clients" over what was right; and convert "top management to his point of view—which is essentially: Be sure your policies are right and fair, then stand up on your hind feet and tell about them forthrightly and repeatedly." For Hill, then, client selection and participation in client policy making were foremost in public relations ethics.[8]

However, when client and executive agreed on the cause, the agency's campaigns said well what the client believed. H&K's campaigns rang true for clients and people who were like them. Roland Marchand, in a study of advertising agencies, found that quite often in designing an ad, an executive's most important audiences were not the consumers, but such secondary groups as clients, critics, and colleagues. This holds true for the public relations agency. The firm's campaigns resonated most, and most often, among those in Hill's own circle. Hill's H&K successor made this same point in 1966, when he observed, "too often businessmen spend large sums of money and great amounts of valuable time to talk to themselves." Industrial executives, certain journalists, conservative members of Congress, and others composed a powerful although unorganized group that did not need to be converted to Hill's position.[9]

The most important effects of the agency, then, were not on clients' competitors like labor unions, or even on the general public, although these groups were affected indirectly. As management-level counsel, dealing with top industrial and government authorities, Hill and Knowlton had the powerful effect of echoing the beliefs of such influential leaders as United States Steel president Benjamin Fairless, Avco's Victor Emanuel, Senator Robert A. Taft, and members of the National Association of Manufacturers. Over time this reinforced and perhaps even strengthened the conservative views held by both John Hill and his clients, with significant consequences for the public. If these powerful business leaders became convinced, for instance, that federal control over steel wages and prices during the Korean War was a step toward socialism at home, they might be willing to do anything to challenge that control, even if it meant losing a great deal of money—which they did, in a showdown with the government in 1952. The agency's campaigns expressed a feeling of defensiveness among some in the business community, provided a rationale against what they saw as unfair criticisms, unified the many opinions held by trade association members into what Hill called "the common voice of corporations," and gave them the mettle to withstand public and governmental reproach for a position they saw as not only economically but morally correct—with significant consequences for the public.[10]

PART ONE

Policies and Practices

CHAPTER ONE

Forged in Steel

Founding Hill and Knowlton

W hen John Hill opened a "corporate publicity" office in 1927 in Cleveland, Ohio, he embarked on a long, distinguished career in public relations. Hill would take a partner, Don Knowlton, in 1933, creating an agency that was grounded in the reputation, ideology, and public relations philosophy that Hill developed during this formative stage of his life and work. H&K's approach to public relations was strongly influenced by the Depression and the New Deal, watershed events for the agency and its first clients.

Hill's early career, especially his work for the steel industry, indicates that he was a conservative who wholeheartedly believed in the free-enterprise system and resented organized labor and an active federal government. In his view only public understanding of corporate responsibility could halt the intrusion of government and labor into industry's territory. His job as public relations counsel, then, was to encourage industry to behave in the public interest and to publicize those actions and business leaders' opinions as widely as possible. Hill's professional and personal relationships with his clients, a handful of influential steel, oil, and aircraft executives, made him a respected equal, setting him apart, at least by reputation, from much of his competition when he moved to New York to open shop.

Hill and Knowlton of Cleveland

John Wiley Hill was born on a farm near Shelbyville, Indiana, on 26 November 1890. He was the third of the four sons born to T. Wiley and Katherine (Jameson) Hill. Although his grandfather had been wealthy, his father's Wichita, Kansas, grain elevator failed, his Indiana farm fared little better, and Hill later recalled that his father "was a first rate farmer but a poor business manager and died poor." After his high school graduation in 1909, Hill worked for the local newspapers and then got a job at the *Akron (Ohio) Press*. In 1911 he left the paper to study journalism and English at Indiana University, but after two brief stints there he quit school and returned to Akron, this time to work for the *Beacon-Journal*. Hill and a friend founded in 1913 the short-lived *Chicago Daily Digest*, and a few months later he and another friend founded a paper in Shelbyville that also folded. In 1915 he moved to Cleveland, where he reported for the *Press* and then the *Plain Dealer*. He remained there, holding various newspaper positions, for several years.[1]

Hill took his first steps toward a career in public relations in 1920. He began by creating a newsletter for local executives for Cleveland's Union Trust Company, while also serving as financial editor for the *Daily Metal Trade*. These activities exposed him to executives who had no desire to deal with the press and to reporters who relayed financial news with "incredible ineptitude," while also providing him with important connections in both communities. Thus, Hill both saw the need and knew the right people, enabling him to open a "corporate publicity office" in April 1927 (the term public relations was not yet commonly in use). That month, the head of Union Trust, John Sherwin Sr., offered to retain Hill for $500 a month. Hill replied that he would accept the offer provided that the banker would help him obtain more business. Sherwin called the president of Otis Steel, securing Hill's second account. As clients spread the word, the publicist added United Alloy Steel, Standard Oil of Ohio, and Republic Steel.[2]

Hill and his first client were not alone in recognizing a need for public relations during the 1920s. The first public relations counseling firm, Parker and Lee, had been founded in 1904, but the first period of rapid growth occurred after World War I. A number of men—and a few women—who had worked for the federal government's Committee on Public Information and for such civilian organizations as the Red Cross transferred their experience from the war effort to the corporate sphere in the 1920s. Carl Byoir, Edward Bernays and his wife Doris Fleischman, John Price Jones, and William Baldwin all established influential agencies in New York after the war. Public relations also moved into industrial centers like Pittsburgh and Cleveland, where Carlton Ketchum and Edward D. Howard opened agencies in 1919 and 1925.

The Depression quite literally made Hill and Knowlton. No one, least of all business leaders, understood the economic calamity. Only recently have economic historians pinpointed the multifaceted causes of the Depression, including the international return to the gold standard, contradictory fiscal and monetary policies in the United States, and the imbalance of world wealth caused by World War I and postwar reparations. But lack of understanding only increased the desire to find a scapegoat. The historian William Leuchtenberg argues that because publicists had spent the 1920s trumpeting the genius of business leaders as the cause of prosperity, many Americans blamed them for poverty as well. Business and financial leaders were as bewildered as anyone else, and they wanted to explain that it was not their fault, thus creating an opportunity for public relations. For a few, like John Hill, the Depression brought success. Among the victims of the banking crisis was Hill's first client, Union Trust. When the bank went under, Hill invited its director of advertising and publicity, Don Knowlton, to join him in a partnership in March 1933 — by which point he was already grossing $100,000 on Republic Steel and six other accounts. Moreover, Republic's Tom Girdler secured for the new firm its most important client, the American Iron and Steel Institute, in 1933.[3]

Hill and Knowlton's most important account, the AISI requested that the agency open a branch in New York, where it made its headquarters in the Empire State Building. The institute had been made the steel code authority, given the power to write and enforce National Industrial Recovery Act–mandated regulations on what Hill called "ruinous price cutting" and "fair practices with regard to wages, hours of work, and collective bargaining." Although industry generally opposed regulation, steel executives realized that drastic action must be taken to halt the grinding deflation of unemployment, output, and prices that marked the economic slump, and they favored composing their own codes to having rules written for them. The institute hired a public relations agency because only four of its members—Bethlehem, Armco, National Steel, and Jones and Laughlin—had their own PR directors in 1933, and because hiring outside counsel freed its administrators, according to Hill, "of the burden of selecting and supervising people in the specialized work of public relations."[4]

From 1933 to 1946 John Hill traveled between Cleveland and New York, working at both the headquarters and the new branch. Because almost none of the agency's papers from this era survive, little is known about its growth, clients, or programs, but in a few instances the agency's work is part of the public record. H&K wrote an institutional advertisement for Standard Oil of Ohio during FDR's "first hundred days," to "allay the feeling of panic and to bolster confidence" in business and the new president. In 1934 the agency began publication of a bulletin called *Steel Facts*, which became the authoritative source of steel data for the press and the government. It also prepared pamphlets such as *The Men Who Make Steel*, which described what it saw as the harmonious relationship between management and labor, due to the implementation of employee representation plans; the high wages and standard of living enjoyed by American steelworkers; and the exorbitant cost of running a steel mill.[5]

The glory years of the 1920s far behind them, business managers like Hill's clients found that "there are no longer any laurels for the corporate manager," according to *Fortune*. The people now turned to the political manager "for an improvement in their condition." Executives by contrast believed that the conditions of business should be determined by owners and managers exclusively. Although many business leaders initially favored the New Deal, this public faith in government intervention left industrialists—and John Hill—shocked and horrified. "It is one thing for the public to have the power of evaluating dollars in terms of *products*, as it chooses this or that in a free market," Hill later wrote of the New Deal. "It is enormously different for Public Opinion, *via* government, to emerge as the sole standard back of the dollar system by which corporate management computes the value of goals, measures the efficiency of work, and judges the worth of its enterprise." Such concerns occupied the firm until its first major crisis, the Little Steel strike of 1937.[6]

The New Deal and Labor
Relations in the Steel Industry

The steel industry had a long history of repressing unionization, an obsession that peaked in 1937. The mere size of the industry made it a target for unionization. At its founding in 1901, United States Steel was the largest corporation, the biggest employer, and the first company worth $1 billion in the United States. Together with the many smaller companies, it propelled the nation to preeminence in world steel production. Steelmakers considered themselves a bulwark against industrial unionism, and steelworkers refused to give up their attempts to organize, so throughout the history of the American labor movement, steel conflicts stand among the most protracted and vicious of all. Attempts to unionize were defeated time and again by the immense political and economic power of the steel magnates and in 1919 by the Red Scare, an effective weapon against collectivism of any kind.[7]

The upheaval of the Depression and the encouragement of New Deal reforms spurred the labor movement to take on steel yet again. Passage of the National Industrial Recovery Act (NIRA), which had been such a boon to Hill and Knowlton's business, provided the primary stimulus to labor organization. The act's sections 7(a) and (b) guaranteed workers the right to organize without employer domination, which, together with the Wagner Act of 1935, created an environment that workers believed was conducive to unionization. The Committee of Industrial Organizations formed a Steel Workers Organizing Committee (SWOC) in June 1936. By the end of the year, Philip Murray, who headed the effort, announced that 125,000 steelworkers had joined the union in 154 lodges. Employees were not content, and their organization with the apparent support of the government seemed to threaten managerial control within the firm, something manufacturers refused to tolerate.[8]

Executives in all industries sprang into action. Some criticized the Wagner Act, the NIRA, and other aspects of the New Deal for assuming that labor and management held opposing interests, but many also did what they could to discourage unionization. Some companies redoubled their efforts in welfare capitalism, sponsoring corporation choruses, athletic teams, and picnics to build loyalty. Others granted wage concessions and offered to negotiate with company unions (employee representation plans, or ERPs) to identify and address grievances before unions could act, in an attempt to ward off CIO-inspired drives. Company unions had been successful, as ERPs represented over 90 percent of workers in 1934. However, a study of rubber workers indicated that employees remained unsold on ERPs, because representatives were identified not with the workers but with their employers. Perhaps not surprisingly, therefore, workers like those at U.S. Steel in Chicago ignored the company unions to form their own groups that affiliated with the CIO, or even used the ERPs to organize companies from within. More serious employer resistance to the CIO appeared in concerns that employed industrial espionage and private police systems and invested heavily in munitions, notably Republic Steel.[9]

Industrialists also turned to public relations. The National Association of Manufacturers' (NAM) program of the 1930s is the best-known example of Depression-era corporate public relations. The campaign's principal tenet was that the profit motive was a vital part of American business, and therefore government regulation was damaging. The crusade included motion pictures and film strips, print and outdoor advertising, direct mail, a speakers bureau, and a radio program, *The American Family Robinson*. In large part because of these campaigns—NAM's public relations budget grew from $36,000 in 1934 to almost $800,000 in 1937—public relations was one of the few growth industries of the era; or, as a contemporary critic wrote, "the propaganda of big business is itself a big business."[10]

Institutional advertising like NAM's became an increasingly popular medium to advocate managerial opinions during the Depression. "Strikes, racketeering, impending legislation, bank crises, equipment breakdowns, harassing politics, whispering campaigns—these are some of the causes from which spring special campaigns to meet the emergency created," a *Printers' Ink* editor wrote. A trade publication for advertisers, *PI* made frequent reference to antiunion copy during the early 1930s. For instance, one story praised a Cleveland auto manufacturer for an ad that threatened workers with a factory shutdown if unionization occurred. According to the historian Roland Marchand, advocacy ads were used for many other reasons, including boosting employee and business community morale. Public relations agents like Hill favored the ads because, he later explained, "the 'public relations message' can be placed before the desired audiences in exactly the desired phraseology."[11]

Such advertisements constituted a new weapon in steel's antiunion arsenal. On the last day of June and the first of July 1936, the AISI sponsored full-page ads in 382 newspapers in thirty-four states, spending almost $115,000—more than one-fifth of the entire SWOC budget. Hill and Knowlton's broadside suggested that outside agitators had coerced employees into joining the union; that the closed shop (employment of union members only) amounted to forcing a worker to pay for a job; and that the industry, and therefore its employees, would be irreparably harmed by a work stoppage during the recovery from years of depression. Lauded by the advertising community and much discussed on editorial pages, the manifesto did little to redress labor's grievances, and, according to the steelworkers' union, it actually propelled the SWOC into public consciousness.[12]

The most fantastic response among steel manufacturers was that of U.S. Steel, which on 2 March 1937 capitulated without a strike, starting a chain reaction of negotiation with the new union. Chairman Myron Taylor recognized the SWOC, granted a 5 percent wage increase and a forty-hour week with overtime pay, and agreed to develop an employee grievance procedure. Taylor chose to negotiate rather than endure a sit-down strike like the one that had paralyzed General Motors, particularly when European orders for steel had begun finally to pull the company out of the Depression. The amount of raw steel produced, which had fallen to a low of about 15 million tons in 1932, had risen to almost 57 million tons in 1937, and seeing that the recovery was in jeopardy, more than forty other companies likewise settled contracts within a month, for a total of 260 within a year of the SWOC's founding. Soon afterward, the Supreme Court ordered Jones and Laughlin to permit union organization without company interference, allowing the SWOC to negotiate a contract that made the CIO seem unstoppable.[13]

However, holdouts were notable. Workers' successes angered antiunion leaders of the Little Steel companies—Republic, Bethlehem, Youngstown Sheet and Tube, National, Armco, and Inland, which employed more than 185,000 workers and were "little" relative only to U.S. Steel. These and other executives believed New Deal trends deprived industry of its own property. Managerial ideology held that management was the trustee for other groups with an interest in business, such as state, consumer, community, and employees. Management's responsibility was to maximize profitable production. It perceived no room for democracy in the production process; rather, hierarchy led to efficiency. Eugene Grace, in his annual address as president of the AISI, made this philosophy clear. In an industry that directly or indirectly employed 450,000 with a payroll of $12 million annually and investments of $4.5 billion, he said, "we have a tremendous responsibility to conduct this great enterprise in a manner eminently and jointly fair to the workmen, to the investors and to the public." Managers, not workers, should make business decisions.[14]

Little Steel thus became the lone obstacle to industrywide unionization for the first time in history. "I won't have a contract, verbal or written," Tom Girdler reportedly said in 1937, "with an irresponsible, racketeering, violent, communistic body like the CIO." The CIO was "utterly irresponsible," its leader, Philip Murray, a "liar." The president of Republic, darling of the business press for bringing the corporation through the Depression, would do anything to maintain complete control of his company. Hill described his client as "sharp-witted, fearless, decisive and ruthless." But Girdler's determination was matched by that of CIO president John L. Lewis, who saw the organization of steel as his most urgent task.[15]

Tom Girdler took action. Little Steel companies seized control of the AISI when Girdler was elected president of the association on 27 May 1937. At the same time, his company spent $49,439 in two months for munitions for a police force of 370 men, and more for the publicity expertise of Hill and Knowlton. Later, Republic reported having 552 revolvers, 64 rifles, and 245 shotguns with 2,702 gas grenades. Lewis perhaps understandably described Girdler as "a heavily armed monomaniac, with murderous tendencies, who has gone berserk."[16]

In retrospect it seems inevitable that the Little Steel strike would result in violence. The strike began 26 May 1937, and four days later open combat broke out at Chicago's Republic Steel plant, when strikers and some of their family members held a meeting and then walked to the plant to demonstrate. As they approached the building, possibly throwing stones and brandishing bats or sticks, one police officer fired his gun into the air as two others threw tear gas bombs. In the ensuing panic the police fired into the crowd, killing ten and injuring many others, then they began to hit people with clubs, injuring scores more. The SWOC held a mass funeral, attended by hundreds of Chicago working-class people, and showing the newsreel footage of the "Memorial Day massacre" to meetings of its strike forces across the nation. Another riot on 19 June at the Republic plant in Youngstown, Ohio, ended with two dead and forty-two injured. In Massillon, Ohio, a Republic Steel police officer led citizens' committee volunteers in a bloody attack on union headquarters, and in Warren agitators fired guns at planes attempting to drop supplies to men who had stayed in the mill.[17]

Ultimately the steelworkers settled for a moral victory, the industry a hollow one. The union lacked the resources to support the workers for any length of time, and in Ohio the governor called in the state militia to protect those who wanted to go back to work. By early July plants had resumed full production. However, on 18 October the National Labor Relations Board (NLRB) ordered the Little Steel companies to reinstate more than 7,000 workers with back pay. Additionally, Senate investigations revealed the employers' unsavory and illegal practices, publicly shaming the industry. Little Steel halted an impressive advance for CIO organization, but if it had set out to break the CIO, it, too, had failed. Despite the setback, thousands of workers in other industries had joined the CIO, and the SWOC was administering 439 collective bargaining agreements and had over 1,000 locals. World War II rendered the outcome of the strike moot, because the steel companies were forced to unionize anyway.[18]

Other than preparing the advertisement announcing Little Steel's position, Hill and Knowlton's role in the Little Steel strike is unknown. John Hill undoubtedly attended the AISI meeting when Girdler became president. He later said he had counseled the steel magnates to accept unionism, explaining that the institutional advertisement he helped to write "as finally run made no reference to the point we had urged; that there be a declaration of the principle that employees were 'free to choose to join or not to join a union.'" At the same time, however, Hill said he believed the company-sponsored unions could serve as fair collective bargaining agents, a point that Hill and Knowlton press materials made throughout the 1930s.[19] Agency press materials for Republic Steel, which had no public relations department of its own, emphasized several themes—the "real issues," according to one booklet. These included opposition to the closed union shop, because it "denies the right of the individual worker to make his own choice as to whether he wishes to belong to a union," and to the check off (deduction of union dues from the worker's paycheck), because "we believe a worker's money is his own personal property to do with as he chooses." The agents reported that Republic's hourly wages ranked as high as any in the industry and above the average for industrial workers generally. Its employees enjoyed the forty-hour week and vacations with pay. The easiest thing would be to sign with the CIO, avoiding a strike, the pamphlet acknowledged, "but that doesn't make it the right thing." [20]

Hill and Knowlton also participated in the Little Steel episode by counseling Girdler and others during the Senate committee hearings that followed the strike. Hill, together with Republic's general counsel and others, helped to prepare Girdler's opening statement to the Senate Post Office Committee, which investigated the CIO's stoppage of the mails during the strike. Girdler testified that, along with stopping mail delivery, union agitators had dynamited railroad tracks and threatened and stoned families of men still in the mills. Flagrant defiance of law and order, he said, had led in some communities to the complete collapse of law enforcement. Hill also took part in preparation for testimony before a more visible congressional committee. [21]

The subcommittee of the Senate Education and Labor Committee, comprised of Senators Robert M. La Follette Jr., Elbert D. Thomas, and Louis Murphy, began investigation of industry's record of suppression of labor's civil rights in June 1936. Its purpose, ostensibly to protect labor under the new provisions guaranteeing the right to organize, coincided with "the cutting edge of the CIO's effort to muster public support for its campaigns and tactics," the historian Jerold Auerbach concluded. "The Committee served the CIO by exposing four antiunion practices which had frustrated labor organization for decades: espionage, industrial munitions, strikebreaking, and private police." Republic had employed all four, and Hill and Knowlton's job was to help the company explain why. [22]

During the hearings and after, Girdler and other Republic managers said the corporation's actions had been taken entirely for the benefit of its employees. Company vice-president Charles M. White testified that management would meet and bargain with any person or organization on the local level, according to its industrial relations policy; that the workers did not want CIO representation, preferring the company union; and that the procurement of industrial munitions had occurred because "our general experience has been that during these strikes it is well to have your plants sufficiently armed and in proper shape to repel an invasion." Girdler emphasized the rights of employees who did not wish to join the new steel union, saying he realized that there might be a strike if he did not sign with the SWOC, but that if he did sign a strike would definitely occur. He blamed outside agitators for the Memorial Day incident, insisting that the company had enjoyed "industrial peace until reckless and selfish union organizers made unprovoked war on our workers." They had refused to surrender "because we were resolute men who understood not only our duty to our stockholders, but our duty to our workers and likewise our country."[23]

Hill and Knowlton took part in the controversy in a more general way by sponsoring antiunion messages appearing in the news media, which embroiled John Hill in the La Follette hearings. La Follette revealed that George Sokolsky received $28,599 from Hill and Knowlton from June 1936 to February 1938, chiefly for consultation to the American Iron and Steel Institute. Sokolsky, a columnist for the *New York Herald Tribune*, frequently wrote about free enterprise and antiunionism in such periodicals as the *Atlantic Monthly*. In September 1937, for instance, he wrote that "it will probably never be settled to everyone's satisfaction who started the riots in Chicago. . . . But violence in Monroe, Niles, Canton, Youngstown, and Johnstown may be placed definitely at the door of the CIO." The article failed to mention his connection to Hill and Knowlton or the institute.[24]

The agency's advertising practices also came under scrutiny. A memorandum prepared by an employee, Ed Bowerfind, suggested using pressure from advertisers to procure newspaper support for the Little Steel line. Of the incident Hill later wrote that the committee had twisted an unfortunately phrased sentence ("some pressure might also be judiciously exerted through the advertisers in Birmingham"), and that the procedure "would have violated the principles and practices of our firm." Bowerfind, however, remained at Hill and Knowlton in Cleveland until Republic dropped the agency and retained him as in-house counsel in 1948. La Follette also accused Hill of placing the institutional advertisement in 1936 simply to curry favor with editors. Hill denied that strategy, doubting a single insertion would have an effect even if that had been the intention.[25]

Hill and Knowlton interested La Follette most in relation to the various citizen's committees that sprang up in many Ohio steel towns promoting back-to-work movements. The Wisconsin senator questioned H&K's work for the Greater Akron Association, which paid the agency over $32,000 between August 1936 and December 1937, for such activities as placement of an advertisement that carried the skimpily veiled threat that "no new industry will settle, nor will present industry long remain, in a city torn by internal strife and dissension." La Follette also returned several times to a mysterious fund Hill and Knowlton had created during the strike period. Six corporations hired the agency to describe the history of the strike, trends and characteristics of the labor movement, British labor laws, and NLRB hearings, and to provide a weekly digest of news articles and comment. The agency collected $1,500 per month from each corporation and kept track of those funds in a separate account book. The project began in July 1937 and involved hiring five new employees. Yet, one year later, none of the corporations had received anything from the agency. Girdler, in a statement prepared with Hill's assistance, claimed, "I have been advised of the progress of the work at all times, and I am satisfied that it will prove of real value," but La Follette remained skeptical. "What happens to this valuable service for which you paid $13,499?" he asked a Youngstown Sheet and Tube representative, who responded that the company got a newsletter from the agency. But all of the agency's clients received it, and La Follette snapped, "You don't have to pay $13,499 to get that." The senator never found a smoking gun to connect that money or H&K to anything underhanded, and agency activities returned to normal.[26]

Hill and Knowlton Expands; John Hill Outgrows Cleveland

It was said that John Hill never met a millionaire he didn't like (although friends added that he liked everyone). Even so, Victor Emanuel was a millionaire Hill liked especially. Emanuel, president of Avco Manufacturing, became the first industrial company client of Hill's New York office, the beginning of a long and, for Hill at least, profitable relationship. Tom Girdler introduced Hill to Emanuel in 1939, and Emanuel hired Hill to write his company's annual report and offer counsel to the financier. Promotion of the B-24, the Liberator, constituted Hill and Knowlton's first major job for what was then called the Aviation Corporation. Hill went to San Diego in January 1942 to visit Emanuel's Consolidated Vultee plant, which had 5,000 employees. By the end of the war, there were 100,000 employees, and Hill was responsible for staffing and directing the entire public relations operation, amounting to seventy people in thirteen plants across the United States. Eventually, the agency took over all national public relations for the entire conglomerate, including its appliance and farm equipment subsidiaries—the corporation had no PR department of its own.[27]

Emanuel looked to Hill for much more than publicity. He sought Hill's advice on everything from political questions to speaking engagements to predictions on the future of business. Emanuel sent Hill and other associates a steady stream of correspondence, including newspaper clippings, mimeographed copies of speeches, and requests for information. Their alliance lasted until Emanuel's death in 1960, and it resulted in important contacts for Hill and new clients for the agency, including the Aircraft Industries Association, for which Emanuel served as a director, and the National Retail Dry Goods Association, whose chairperson sat on Avco's board. Emanuel also introduced Hill to George E. Allen, who likewise brought the agency new clients. Not surprisingly, then, Hill would later refer to Emanuel as "one of the very best friends this firm has ever had."[28]

George Allen, friend of President Harry S. Truman and head of the Reconstruction Finance Corporation, had long-standing relationships with both Emanuel and Girdler, serving on the boards of both of their corporations. In 1947 he entered formal association with Hill and Knowlton as well, becoming a member of its board and later its chairman, serving as the firm's legal counsel, and advising H&K and its clients on political problems. Allen's job also included bringing in new business. For example, when William Robinson, partner in the public relations firm Robinson-Hannagan Associates, expressed a desire to sell the firm, Allen advised him to contact Hill. Hill and Knowlton bought the firm in 1955, adding to the agency's list of blue-chip accounts such clients as Coca-Cola, Electric Auto-Lite, Gillette, and Owens-Illinois. Between Emanuel and Allen, Hill and Knowlton's future was assured.[29]

Hill and Knowlton of Cleveland began to expand even before it had any major New York clients beyond the AISI. It opened a separate New York branch in 1938—Manhattan was quickly becoming the center of public relations, with over 100 counselors listed in the telephone directory there by 1944. Hill, who ran the office wholly without Knowlton, began adding to the staff to work on the AISI account in 1933, when he hired an assistant. The following year he hired John G. Mapes, former director of public relations of the American Society for Metals and assistant editor of *Metal Progress*, whose background made him a natural for the steel account. In 1944 H&K opened a Washington, D.C., office, and the agency hired Bert C. Goss to work with its newest account, the Aeronautical Chamber of Commerce, which was headquartered in the nation's capital. Goss, formerly a university professor and business editor of *Newsweek* magazine, Mapes, Avco's Kerryn King, and Glenn L. Martin's Richard W. Darrow would become Hill's most trusted executives.[30]

H&K's Washington office did not have its own accounts but existed solely to handle government relations for the New York and Cleveland clients, work that grew especially heavy during World War II. The beleaguered steel industry, running full for the first time in a decade, was repeatedly charged with war profiteering, and Little Steel was forced to submit to union

John Wiley Hill in the 1940s,
at about the time he founded
Hill and Knowlton, Inc., in
Manhattan. (Courtesy of the
State Historical Society of
Wisconsin)

contracts to keep the mills operating. In 1942, to control inflation, the War Labor Board devised guidelines for pay hikes relating to the cost of living. Known as the Little Steel formula, the guidelines included measures to protect union security with a modified union shop, anathema to the industrialists but a necessary measure as part of the war effort. The Washington office maintained close contact with legislators and regulators about all such issues.[31]

So successful was Hill's work for steel and other accounts that the New York branch had doubled the headquarters in billing by November 1945. Hill's future was clearly in Manhattan. In 1947 he turned over all but 5 percent of the Cleveland firm to Don Knowlton and established a separate agency, Hill and Knowlton, Inc., in the nation's largest city. Several of the Cleveland accounts elected to transfer along with Hill, so H&K continued to represent Standard Oil of Ohio, Warner and Swasey, and the Austin Company into the 1950s. Knowlton owned a small share in the New York firm, but the agency was essentially Hill's, and it would dominate public relations.[32]

John Hill and the Rise of a
Major Public Relations Firm

Much of Hill and Knowlton, Inc.'s success grew from the lessons that Hill took away from his earliest years of opinion management. Close association with Emanuel, Girdler, and other conservative business leaders meant that Hill's recommendations, spoken, according to colleague Pendleton Dudley, in "the language, or lingo, of business," rang true to his clients; they were words the client might have used himself. Long relationships with such men also fostered a measure of conservatism in the PR agent. This is not to suggest that Hill was not essentially a conservative individual. His upbringing in rural Indiana also suggests an affinity for the status quo. Whatever the reason, Hill held many of the characteristics and beliefs of his clients.[33]

Hill developed an executive demeanor and his agency a subdued decorum that separated H&K from its often showman-like rivals. While other public relations practitioners spent as much time promoting themselves as their clients, John Hill stayed in the background. A 1950 *Harper's* profile of PR man Benjamin Sonnenberg, for instance, opened with the statement that he "may not be the richest or the most powerful man in his trade, but he is certainly the most successful in giving that impression." Hill, whose appearance reminded people of a financier or a statesman, sent a copy of the article to colleague Tommy Ross, with a mocking note about "the many valuable hints it contains on how to be a successful public relations man (after reading it I have decided to go in for elongated sideburns and a sailor suit)." Hill might also be contrasted with the most famous practitioner of his day, Edward Bernays, best known for such stunts as having a group of debutantes smoke cigarettes while they marched in New York City's Easter parade in 1926 to break the taboo against women's smoking. Building on a pattern first established by Ivy Lee (who had died in 1934), Hill found that business executives were drawn to the agency by its calm proficiency, not by his personal fame or frivolous public displays. "We at Hill and Knowlton," a senior manager explained later, "don't do the fast and flashy thing." In fact one of the few big clients ever to leave H&K, Coca-Cola, did so in 1960 because it lacked the flair of the agency it had previously retained.[34]

Participation in the policy making of his corporate clients, an alien concept for many other public relations firms before or since, was natural for a man with what *Fortune* described as Hill's "banker-like affability." Other agencies, California's Whitaker and Baxter or Byoir or Bernays, may well have been more adept than Hill and Knowlton at securing publicity for their clients, but few others could consider themselves the client's equal. To take

Although best known for its high-level counsel, Hill and Knowlton also conducted product publicity for its clients. Agents arranged this tour of the Crosley Talking Kitchen, which displayed the Avco subsidiary's state-of-the-art appliances to large crowds around the United States during the 1950s. (Courtesy of the State Historical Society of Wisconsin)

just one example, Whitaker and Baxter's political campaigns, such as the 1948 American Medical Association program, consisted mostly of wide dissemination of slogans like "The Voluntary Way Is the American Way" to defeat Truman's proposed "socialized medicine." The client informed the agency of the policy, and the practitioners publicized it. Hill, on the other hand, sat in on every meeting of the directors of the American Iron and Steel Institute and Avco Manufacturing for decades, and other executives also worked intimately with clients. Bert Goss for example was an H&K vice-president but he also held the position of public relations director for the Aircraft Industries Association.[35]

Like his clients, Hill grew to detest big labor and big government. As if his job educating the public about business were not difficult enough, he bemoaned, "it is made a thousand times more difficult in the face of phoney economics and class hatred preached by some labor unions and, in the late years, by government itself." Long fraternization with his clients made him sympathetic with big business and myopic toward the problems of the consumer and the laborer. Harold Burson, a friend of Hill's in later years, believes Hill was greatly influenced by his early clients. "Most of those people were very much opposed to what was going on in the New Deal," Burson said. "I think that John, a relatively young man at the time, was shaped to some considerable extent by that experience." Although his attitudes moderated in later years, Hill throughout his career supported many measures and individuals seeking to curb the power of big labor, organizing, for instance, a group of New York public relations executives to promote the nomination of Senator Robert Taft of Ohio as the Republican candidate for president in 1952. H&K executive Merrick Jackson remembered Hill as a "virulent" Republican who, after Taft's loss, "was grouchy for weeks."[36] Hill, like many citizens after World War II, tended to see the danger of socialism in every aspect of American life. The story of the early years of his agency cannot be told without attention to the anti-Communist subtext that runs through so many of the news releases, brochures, and advertisements prepared by Hill and Knowlton. Of course, he was not alone. National Association of Manufacturers spokespersons and many other business leaders often resorted to red-baiting the union movement. But Hill did not make these claims idly, or simply because his clients wished it. The historian Richard Tedlow asserts that unlike Bernays or Byoir, who apparently would work for any client, "Hill was a genuine ideologue of the right." Constant alarms about socialism's threat were not made for malevolent purposes, because John Hill had only good intentions.[37]

To Hill's credit, he favored education rather than coercion to halt the spread of communism. During the earliest years of his career, he gained an appreciation for the power of public opinion. He believed that many of the measures of the New Deal were destined to pass, not necessarily because they were right, but because "they had the solid backing of public opinion." Moreover, some of the industries that "bitterly fought union organization of their employees, in a fight foredoomed to failure, succumbed only at huge cost," he concluded.[38]

This regard for public opinion led Hill to develop a philosophy of and justification for good public relations. His rationale, to quote from Justice Oliver Holmes's description of the marketplace of ideas, held that "the ultimate good desired is better reached by free trade in ideas," and that "the best test of truth is the power of the thought to get itself accepted in the competition of the market." Starting with the premise that rational people rule a democracy through common consent, Hill asserted that "public opinion is entitled to the facts in matters of public concern." Success in building goodwill for a corporation or industry had three requirements: integrity, sound policies "viewed in the light of the public interest," and "the use of facts that are understandable, believable, and presented to the public with imagination." By informing the public about the facts of big business, corporate public relations aided the client while serving the public.[39]

Hill's thinking was greatly influenced by Ivy Lee, whose book Hill read and whose ideas he repeated and refined over the years. Lee assigned two roles to public relations: publicity and counsel. "The great publicity man," Lee said in his 1934 collection of speeches titled *Publicity*, "is the man who advises his client as to what policy he shall pursue, which, if pursued, would create favorable publicity," and then promotes the policy. And again, "unless the policy is sound intrinsically no amount of propaganda will make it appear to be so," Lee told a group of British citizens. Hill likewise adopted a philosophy of public relations that emphasized counseling the client on public desires as part of the policy-making process. Public opinion would then judge the worthiness of the client's positions and products. Although the historian Stuart Ewen argues that conceptions of the public swung between rational and irrational during the twentieth century, Hill maintained a belief in the sovereignty of public opinion throughout his lifetime.[40]

Hill's concept of public opinion was closely tied to his beliefs about the government. "Corporate enterprise operates under franchise from public opinion," he wrote in the mid-1960s, "and that franchise can be modified or withdrawn by the people's representatives in government at any time they so wish." Hill and Knowlton's trade association work consistently reflected this idea. Public relations used the tools of opinion management to forestall government regulation by persuading the public that business leaders were best equipped to make economic decisions for the nation. As H&K's Bert

Goss explained, "The question is not . . . whether a business problem should be in politics or not. . . . The only question for today's corporation is how to be in politics effectively."[41]

Examination of Hill's speeches and articles shows the extent to which his professional ideals formed while he worked for the steel industry in New York and Cleveland. A 1931 article by the "industrial and financial publicity" expert explained why companies needed assistance. "We have a growing public demand for the news of corporations and general industrial developments" stemming from the growing public dependence on industry, Hill said, and "we have the corporations themselves with every reason of self[-]interest to co-operate in responding to this demand." Industry depended on goodwill toward the institution and its products by millions of stockholders, consumers, and employees. The publicist served as an intermediary, because even the most skilled business journalist could not keep track of all the affairs of all companies, while a publicist could follow the affairs of a single corporation and disseminate that information with relative ease. Hill added that corporate publicity also involved "counseling in matters of public relations," which he did not define. He apparently considered his job mostly gathering facts about industry and placing them "before the public in legitimate ways and through legitimate channels." This is consistent with Hill's practice at the time. One of his first actions for the AISI was creation of the magazine *Steel Facts*, which, although it did place inordinate emphasis on the benefits of company unions, remained a useful source of data even during the Little Steel strike, a subject never addressed in its columns.[42]

By 1938 Hill's job description had broadened and his focus on free enterprise deepened considerably. In a talk given in June, he explained that industrialization had put distance between people — owner and management, customer and manufacturer, employee and owner — and that, unfortunately, "industrial leaders gave little thought to the job of explaining the achievements and purposes of industry to the public." People therefore got information from "demagogues and crack-pots," who seemed proven correct when the Depression hit and "the mistakes and failures of capitalism were magnified and exploited." The result: "private industry finds itself on trial for its life" before the bar of public opinion. Rebuilding confidence required "the shaping of basic policies in keeping with the social and economic responsibilities of a changing world," and "the patient, persistent and never-ending telling of industry's story, over and over again, to the public." Thus, the public relations practitioner must make factual, responsible statements about the client and make "the average citizen realize what contribution private enterprise has made to American society, and how important its preservation is to the material and spiritual welfare of all the people."[43]

Within a few years, Hill had gone even farther in defining the practitioner's role with a discussion of public relations at the policy-making level. His November 1942 speech before the National Association of Manufacturers focused on policy, he said, because "if policy is lacking or deficient . . . there is trouble in store." Therefore, "it is of first importance that the place of policy be recognized and provided for in any public relations plan," calling for "a high degree of management understanding of the requirements of public relations, and for a full measure of management cooperation." Management must recognize public relations as part of its job and should understand that, "in a majority of matters coming before management for decision, some measure of public relations is involved." Whenever management meets to discuss problems and make policy, Hill asserted, "there should always be a chair reserved for public relations counsel," as was true for legal counsel in many organizations.[44]

Hill therefore embraced what James Grunig and Todd Hunt call the "two-way asymmetrical" model of public relations. This contrasts with the two-way symmetrical model, which serves as an ideal for scholars who see PR as the liaison between an organization and its publics. Hill and Knowlton did not seek the role of mediator between conflicting groups, instead privileging one point of view, that of the client. The agency conducted research on public opinion not to foster mutual understanding but to increase the efficacy of its persuasion efforts, a textbook example of the asymmetrical model. Strike advertisements, for example, have been held up as the antithesis of the symmetrical model because they all too often antagonized rather than creating dialogue. Steel ads proclaimed the institute's point of view, but people who wanted to respond could do so only by writing to the AISI or, to reach the same audience, by buying similar space. In no sense did the agency create a channel for discussion, nor did it seek to do so. Hill believed that if the client's policies were in the public interest, then the most ethical behavior was to present that position to the public in a persuasive manner.[45]

In addition to developing a philosophy and theory of public relations, Hill also learned during this formative period that pleasing clients not only made for long relationships but also attracted new business. Serving as what PR pioneer Averell Broughton called "the voice and interpreters of business to politicians and public," Hill and his top executives developed lasting relationships with leading industrialists whom he greatly admired. The respect was mutual. Industrialists began to take Hill's advice as a confidant, as much as paid consultant, solidifying his place at the directors' table. No mere publicity flack, John Hill had been a respected associate, in some cases even a friend, of his Cleveland clients. Because of these close relationships, finding new clients came relatively easy to Hill and Knowlton. Hill prided himself on the agency's policy of not soliciting new business, although he certainly encouraged third parties like Emanual and Allen to cultivate prospects for him. Most new accounts, however, seemed to come on the recommendation of satisfied customers.[46]

Hill's development as a public relations practitioner culminated when he placed himself at the forefront of his field by plugging into a network of leading public relations agents. In November 1938, following a dinner at his New York apartment, he and a group of fifteen practitioners started a series of monthly invitation-only meetings. Among the members of this prestigious assembly, who called themselves "the Wisemen," were Tommy Ross, who had been Ivy Lee's partner; Claude Robinson, a public opinion pollster; Pendleton Dudley, then the dean of practitioners; Paul Garrett of General Motors; Howard Chase of General Foods; and two of steel's leading PR men, John Long of Bethlehem and Carlisle MacDonald of U.S. Steel. The coterie carried such respect that when he was asked to join in December 1938, Jim Irwin, stationed in St. Louis for Monsanto, secured permission from Edgar Monsanto Queeny to "make every meeting barring some serious emergency," and the requirement that he attend the chemical company's board meetings would be waived if the dates conflicted. Such was the influence of the group that the Public Relations Society of America, founded in 1948, sprang from a discussion at one of the Wisemen's meetings.[47]

Thus, by the time Hill and Knowlton, Inc., opened its New York office, with the steel and aviation industries and Avco its major accounts, the agency and the agent had already been established as standard-bearers. The office, located on the thirty-third floor of the Empire State Building, was el-shaped, with the longer line facing Fifth Avenue and the shorter one, 33rd Street. At the corner sat John Hill's office, walls filled with photographs of clients and other dignitaries, mostly, by one employee's memory, "corporate executives. Oh, yes, and Republicans." In a matter of months a small stream of important clients began knocking on H&K's door, seeking advice on public relations. John Hill stood ready.[48]

CHAPTER TWO

Air Power Is Peace Power

Postwar Trade Association Public Relations

I f investors in aircraft manufacturing companies had any doubts about the meaning of the end of World War II for their portfolios, those misgivings were quickly confirmed. Letters such as one that began, "To the Stockholders: The fiscal year 1946–47 was an extremely difficult one for your company," made the situation all too clear. Like many aircraft manufacturers, All-American Aviation, Inc., found itself approaching financial straits after the war, when the drastic drop in government contracts, together with labor difficulties and the unavailability of raw materials, spelled disaster. All-American explained to its stockholders that it would develop an air transport service in place of its former emphasis on manufacturing and engineering. Other aircraft makers likewise scrambled to find ways to survive, as military aircraft production dropped by more than 98 percent.[1]

Military officials had caught no one in the aircraft industry by surprise when they terminated $9 billion worth of contracts in August 1945. Demobilization after World War I had produced an almost complete collapse of aircraft manufacturing. This experience had made deep impressions on people in the industry and the government, and they all expected similar conditions after World War II. But they hoped to make the process less disastrous than it had been after the Great War, and they went to work on these efforts even before the end of World War II. The manufacturers turned to

Hill and Knowlton,[2] and the agency spent the next years championing the cause of air power and the need for a strong aircraft industry. Although H&K representatives at times directly lobbied members of Congress, they focused most on a grass-roots public relations program designed to sway public opinion, which they hoped would in turn pressure the government to support air power. Devoting as much as half of their annual budget to public relations, the manufacturers embarked on the most extensive campaign for public support ever undertaken by the industry.[3]

This chapter documents the anatomy of a postwar public relations campaign conducted by Hill and Knowlton for a large trade association, examining the aircraft industry's approach to the business-government dynamic from a public relations perspective. A review of the campaign through the lens of social science theory indicates that the effects of the air power program were complex and indirect. Although the industry's public relations program did not lead directly to increased procurement or shifts in public opinion, it did bring together many groups that were interested in air power. By linking these groups to create one unified voice and by capitalizing on the domestic and international situation, Hill and Knowlton helped to create a climate in which air power was an acceptable solution to national defense and budgetary problems. By introducing the issue of air power into public discussion, H&K offered all groups an opportunity to debate the problem, and the pro-aircraft side won.

Hill and Knowlton, the Industry, and Aviation Policy after the War

The 175-member Aircraft Industries Association included a dominant group of twenty-one airframe and engine manufacturers, dozens of makers of accessories and parts, and various affiliates and individuals.[4] The AIA was not the only private agency interested in aviation after World War II. Others included the Air Transport Association, the National Aviation Trades Association, the Air Force Association, and the Air Line Pilots Association. But the AIA and its predecessors had served as the primary trade association for manufacturers since World War I. Formed in February 1917, the Aircraft Manufacturers Association dealt mainly with patent issues. In 1922 it reorganized as the Aeronautical Chamber of Commerce, which included not just manufacturers but operators, distributors, and trade publishers. In 1934 the airlines formed the Air Transport Association, and the chamber focused more sharply on the manufacturers. World War II forced still another reorganization, with the creation of the Aircraft War Production Council. This organization hired Hill and Knowlton in late 1943. In June 1945 the council reformulated as the AIA, with a board of governors consisting of the chief executives of twenty-one major companies. Eugene Wilson, who had been affiliated with the Navy and United Aircraft, chaired the association through the end of World War II, after which Oliver Echols, chief of procurement for the Army Air Force during the war, took over.[5]

The numbers tell a simple story of rapid postwar decline. Instead of encountering pent-up civilian demand that many other industries enjoyed, aircraft makers faced overwhelming surplus. Including subcontractors, aircraft manufacturing employment had risen to over 2 million during the war, but fell to 567,000 by war's end and to 237,700 by 1948. In 1944 the manufacturers produced 96,318 planes, all for the military, and the following year, they made 49,761 planes, of which all but 2,047 were procured by the military. This drop in procurement showed up dramatically at the bottom line. An AIA analysis of the profits of twelve major airframe companies indicated that in 1945 company profits totaled $67.4 million on sales of almost $4 billion. But in 1946 the companies lost $10.7 million on sales of $519 million—and this, according to the AIA, "despite use of the reserves that had accumulated during the war" and favorable tax laws—and 1947 proved even worse.[6]

There were several sources of pressure to keep military spending down after the war. President Harry Truman and Secretary of Defense James Forrestal both considered high military expenditures a major contributor to postwar inflation, and both subscribed to the notion that a "balanced military" (balanced, that is, among air, land, and sea forces) offered the best protection. "Old isolationists" of the Republican Party and "old Progressives" in Congress composed two more groups who wanted to limit military spending, the former for economic and strategic reasons, the latter for ideological ones. Many Americans, while shunning isolationism per se, demanded demobilization. "Bring-Daddy-Home" clubs, letter-writing campaigns, and pleas of servicemen rang in the ears of government officials. The clamor was hard to ignore, even though national defense issues were equally pressing.[7]

The debate over national security after the war encompassed much more than simply the plight of the aircraft industry. During the war, recalled General Ira C. Eaker, the Army Air Force felt equal to the Army and Navy, "but we were so busy with the war that we didn't jeopardize the war effort by launching a campaign" for an independent U.S. Air Force. For this reason, only after the war did AAF officers, as Eaker put it, "lay plans pretty rapidly to get legislation enacted to implement coequal status." Unification of the armed services and independence for the aerial arm formed a central point of contention during the early years of the Truman administration.[8]

The unification question forced Hill and Knowlton to walk a fine line between Army and Navy desires regarding air power. Neither the agency nor the manufacturers could afford to antagonize any element of the military or of Congress during the unification debate. Certainly an independent air force would work to the industry's benefit, and H&K had close ties with top Army Air Force officials through former procurement chief Echols. But, according to the historian John B. Rae, the Navy, an important aircraft customer in its own right, disliked "what it considered an excessive commitment of the nation's military resources" to a strategy that "relied on long-range aerial bombardment with nuclear weapons at the expense not only of surface forces but of the tactical employment of air power." The Navy opposed unification, particularly if it meant any loss of what it called "sea air power." H&K's position was complicated further by the fact that the Shipbuilder's Council of America was another of its clients, for which it created a similar although more modest program. Although the Army-Navy debate could have been divisive, H&K executives maintained a unified voice for the industry by refusing to take sides, avoiding public comment on unification, and focusing instead on the need for an improved procurement policy. This precarious situation eased with unification of the services in the National Defense Act of 1948, and with the 1949 election of a new AIA president, Admiral DeWitt C. Ramsey, the newly retired naval commander in chief of the Pacific.[9]

Manufacturers responded to the postwar calamity in numerous ways. Strategies to return to peacetime status ranged from diversification into nonaeronautical fields, to development of passenger and cargo transport capabilities, to research on new technology such as guided missiles and jet propulsion. Some companies tried to develop a civilian market. According to the AIA, manufacturers sold 35,001 airplanes to nonmilitary buyers in 1946. But that number could not be sustained. In 1947 only 15,617 and in 1948 just 7,302 planes were sold to civilians. During those three years the number of planes sold to the military averaged just over 2,000.[10]

While individual companies' responses to the crisis varied, the approach of the industry as a whole was clear: seek government assistance. Even in 1943 aircraft makers had assumed that reconversion would be difficult and that the government held the key to the industry's survival. The AIA's first staff report, for 1945, indicated that the board of governors had two primary goals: "solve survival problems" and "deal with long-term problems." Survival problems included surplus disposal, export promotion, an airport bill, labor relations, and "public appreciation of aircraft problems," meaning "strong editorial support, favorable radio and press, [and] public and congressional support of air power." In the long term, the report added, "Continuation of Government-Science-Industry partnership is essential to our military and economic security and to world peace," the AIA being "the medium through which the industry operates within the team." [11]

But government assistance was carefully defined. The AIA called for a national air policy that would provide for research and development, military procurement, and revision of restrictive legislation on air transport and personal flying. It devoted large portions of its budget to H&K's public relations campaign to convince America taxpayers of the importance of such a policy. But the manufacturers wanted to control government intervention by maintaining a free-enterprise system of private companies seeking government contracts, not a nationalized aircraft manufacturing system. As the historian David Vogel has noted, business executives have supported many government initiatives, but, "for the most part, government policies that merit business approval do not interfere with management prerogatives." [12]

Primary sources on the earliest years of Hill and Knowlton's air power campaign, 1943–46, are very sparse, but other sources indicate that the program was both extensive and unsuccessful. The April 1944 policy statement of the AIA was presented to Congress and such agencies as the War Production Board. The AIA also sponsored speakers, publicity, and a radio program. In 1945 AIA published seven different booklets, distributed reprints from the *Congressional Record,* and developed press contacts, while company officials spoke over the radio and before large audiences. H&K assisted in the preparation of statements that AIA officials made before numerous commissions and Congress with members appearing before six different committees in 1945. The slogan "Air Power Is Peace Power" was in use, although apparently not universally. None of this activity resulted in maintenance of appropriations, as canceled contracts remained the rule. [13]

Military and industry leaders alike agreed that a more substantial program was needed. During a 1946 meeting of industry, government, and military officials, leaders of the armed services concluded, in the words of John Hill, "our air power was facing extinction," and urged the industry to "arouse Americans to the danger they were courting." The AIA's board of governors therefore instructed its Public Relations Advisory Committee, composed of company PR directors, to work with H&K to develop an air power program. According to Hill, they developed a program in twenty-four hours, and the board adopted it and tripled the PR budget for two years. From a long list of suggestions the PR directors selected "Air Power Is Peace Power" as the campaign's theme. [14]

The aircraft industry's turn to public relations represented an important departure from previous strategies. The historian Jacob Vander Muelen analyzed the period from the beginning of World War I to the end of World

War II and concluded that "the key to understanding why most aircraft look and perform the way they do is the way they were understood in terms of national security." Congress, Vander Muelen argues, dominated the industry because of aircraft procurement for the military: contracting rules shaped the industry as national security needs shaped the airplane. The post–World War II campaign was an attempt to introduce another voice, the public's, to the debate. The industry hoped to use public opinion as a lever to pry open the door to the federal vault.[15]

Hill and Knowlton's Campaign

H&K's campaign was directed out of AIA's Washington office by Bert Goss, who had been a vice-president of the firm since 1945. A competitor recalled Goss as a "sort of homespun, disarming" man "with a very deep, Texas southern accent." He had a doctorate in banking and finance and taught finance at New York University before becoming associate editor of the *New York Journal of Commerce*, then *Newsweek*'s business, labor, and agriculture editor. Goss's staff included both AIA and H&K employees, and an H&K executive attended all AIA board and committee meetings, participating even in a conference involving AIA's president, executive director, and Assistant Secretary of War for Air Stuart Symington. The account was important to H&K's quest for growth, giving the agency a reason to open a Los Angeles office to accommodate the large number of West Coast manufacturers and allowing it to expand beyond steel.[16]

The AIA program was not limited to the battle for military appropriations. Agents also promoted air safety, travel, and other aspects of civil aviation. But the military element was by far the most public, and controversial, aspect of H&K's work. And even the military emphasis came to focus on strategic bombing at the expense of other functions. Former AIA chairman Eugene Wilson despaired in 1950 that, to the public and even to many in aviation circles, "air power" meant "strategic bombing," even after successful peacekeeping missions such as the Berlin Airlift.[17]

Fortunately for H&K, the aircraft industry already had numerous political, media, and public allies at the end of World War II. Hundreds of thousands of individuals across the United States found airplanes fascinating. Many considered national security a top priority and viewed air power as a cheap way to defend their country while keeping government spending to a minimum. If H&K could align these groups behind a central message, the industry's constituency would be formidable. The agency began to focus its efforts on elected officials, journalists, and civic organizations. Hill and

Knowlton's strategy coincides with Stephen Hilgartner and Charles Bosk's arenas model of the rise and fall of social problems. Hilgartner and Bosk suggest that any number of issues is available for public attention at a given time. Actors in the media, public, and political arenas, where discourse about public issues occurs, serve as advocates who try to convince people that one particular issue deserves more attention and resources than the others. According to Hilgartner and Bosk, this element of competition means that advocates must be highly skilled to make their issue a problem while others are ignored. Public relations practitioners can be considered specialists in the construction of social problems because they attempt to influence social and political action by directing how people think about and what they say about issues that affect their clients. This direction is accomplished through what sociologists call "framing." The sociologist Todd Gitlin defines frames as "persistent patterns of cognition, interpretation, and presentation, of selection, emphasis, and exclusion, by which symbol-handlers routinely organize discourse, whether verbal or visual." The remainder of this chapter, then, explores Hill and Knowlton's role as an advocate for air power as a social problem, developing a vocabulary for discussion about the role of public relations in the political, media, and public arenas.[18]

H&K Seeks a Federal Air Policy

The first goal of H&K's campaign was, according to John Hill, to get a federal "audit of our air power problems." In essence the agents hoped to set the political agenda, which political scientists Roger Elder and Charles Cobb define as a general set of controversies that fall within the range of legitimate concerns meriting the attention of the polity, or a set of concrete, specific items that are scheduled for active consideration by institutional decision makers. Elder and Cobb assert that, with a multiplicity of possible definitions of a problem, what matters is not which definition is "correct," but which is most acceptable politically. They therefore argue that the way to place an issue on the political agenda is to evoke a response at a mass level with a problem definition that has implications for as many people as possible, using language and symbols that are simple and resonant with the majority. Political action is shaped by the discourse, including the interpretive frames of understanding used, that takes place in the political arena.[19]

Hill and Knowlton sought a federal review of air policies because the agents hoped that such a review would place the issue of air power on the political agenda. By 1947 federal authorities began to show increased interest in developing an air policy. President Truman had already authorized an Air Coordinating Committee to gather information from all government agencies with a major interest in aviation, but when a pro-aviation senator began to push for a congressional review of policies, Truman appointed his own high-profile board to short-circuit this move. In July 1947 Truman appointed an Air Policy Commission and Congress sponsored a joint Aviation Policy Board. Each group was instructed to study aircraft industry problems and civilian and national defense needs.[20]

Chaired by Thomas K. Finletter, the President's Air Policy Commission made its report on 1 January 1948, later published under the title *Survival in the Air Age*, after five months of exhaustive hearings.[21] Its recommendations delighted the industry. The commissioners set an "A-day," 1 January 1953, the earliest date they believed an atomic attack on the United States could occur. They based the entire report on estimated war requirements, projecting appropriations, research and development, and industry needs according to those estimations. The United States, said the commission, "must be ready not for World War II but for a possible World War III." This meant maintaining "a force in being in peacetime greater than any self-governing people has ever kept." While ground and sea forces must be maintained, "our military security must be based on air power." The commission recommended an Air Force of 70 groups plus 22 special squadrons with a total of 12,400 modern planes, as advocated by first Secretary of the Air Force Stuart Symington, although the Air Force initially had wanted 105 groups. Even 70 groups exceeded the Truman administration's official request, however, for 55 groups with 10,800 planes, a plan that industry officials and Symington opposed because it required no new appropriations.[22]

The Joint Congressional Aviation Policy Board's report closely mirrored the Finletter commission's findings. The board's chair and vice-chair, Senator Owen Brewster of Maine and Representative Carl Hinshaw of California respectively, both vigorously supported enhanced air power. Brewster's speeches went further than most by naming the Soviet Union as the potential enemy and the reason for a strong aviation policy. Hinshaw supported the industry without hesitation, perhaps in part because so many manufacturers had located plants in his district. The board, with an advisory council that included such air power supporters as Victor Emanuel and Hap Arnold, not surprisingly concluded that "the United States has no other course to follow but to maintain such a military air force and civil air effort that no sudden attack upon the American people can succeed—and that any such attack will prompt swift and awful retribution." It supported the Finletter report, advocating the seventy-group plan.[23]

The reports of the Finletter commission and the congressional board gave the AIA's campaign, which had not garnered significant support, a much needed boost. Hill and Knowlton worked vigorously to publicize both reports. AIA's magazine, *Planes*, which was modeled after AISI's *Steel Facts*, devoted an entire issue to the Finletter report. Companies ordered enough copies to give one to every employee. H&K sent bulk quantities to the American Legion and the military, giving the issue a run of over 150,000. The agency planned another special issue for the congressional board findings in March. In fact, Goss thought that, because Congress controlled the purse strings, the second was "the important report and the one that must be promoted with every available resource."[24]

H&K's work involving the commissions extended far beyond ballyhoo. Almost any time industry officials were to give testimony, H&K prepared their remarks. In 1948, for example, agents prepared statements for industry leaders to give before the boards and publicized those statements through news releases and a booklet. H&K considered "a major activity" its time spent "answering requests for data and other information from the staff" of the congressional board, via General Echols or the four AIA members of the Industry Advisory Board of the committee. The agency assisted in preparations for the release of both commission reports and drafted a letter of transmittal to accompany the release of the Air Coordinating Committee's policy statement to the press.[25]

Hill and Knowlton also worked directly with members of Congress to promote AIA policies. In 1948, with Congress considering Air Force appropriations, Bert Goss wrote to Senator Styles Bridges, the Republican chair of the Appropriations Committee who had introduced a bill for funding exceeding the president's request. Goss requested from Bridges a statement for publication in *Planes*. "We realize you are currently engaged in an election campaign and that you may find it extremely difficult to get enough time to prepare the article," Goss wrote. "In view of this situation," the editor "has prepared a rough draft of the type of piece we had in mind." As further incentive, Goss offered "wide-spread publicity and promotion" for the article, as well as several hundred copies of the issue for distribution in New Hampshire, Bridges's home state. He enclosed back issues of *Planes* to "show the type of feature articles other congressional leaders have sponsored in the past." Bridges, an air power champion, complied with Goss's plan.[26]

Hill and Knowlton's work in the political arena did help the industry gain support in Congress, as evidenced by the 1948 appropriations battle. Secretary Symington's proposed seventy-group minimum for the Air Force had been approved by both commissions, so when President Truman and Secretary of Defense James Forrestal recommended a much smaller allocation, such advocates as *Aviation Week* considered it a "betrayal." The magazine ran a three-week long editorial campaign against decision makers in the administration for "stupidly closing their eyes to the lessons of World War II." Forrestal offered a compromise of sixty-six groups, which involved taking about 300 B-29s out of storage—a "mothball fleet." In the end Congress surprised no one by appropriating the larger amount. However, political support did not translate immediately into help for the industry, as Truman ordered his appointees not to spend the additional funds.[27]

Because favorable commission recommendations and assistance to elected officials could not assure the AIA of continuing government commitment to a strong air program, Hill and Knowlton had to move beyond the political arena to seek public support. AIA leaders had long understood the need to sell air power to the public. During the war they had approached then Speaker of the House Sam Rayburn for assistance. Rayburn assured them that they had a good program, but added that Congress responded to what "folks back home think." This advice provided the impetus for the campaign to convince the public that the United States required air power—and that the people should be willing to pay for it.[28] Because public support was paramount, Hill and Knowlton planned a program to take the industry's story "to the grass roots by word of mouth, by the printed word, and by radio." It would reach "taxpayers and voters, . . . editors and writers, educators, leaders of powerful national group organizations and many other molders of public opinion." According to the plan developed by the agency, the program would show

A. The need for the enactment of national air policy . . . ,
B. The vital role that must be performed by the Air Services currently, pending the development and perfection of the "push button era,"
C. The need for and the requirements for industrial preparedness planning,
D. The nature and cost of needed research and development . . . ,
E. The . . . accomplishments of aerial research and aircraft production in the war.[29]

One of the least expensive ways to reach the public is through the news media, so Hill and Knowlton turned to the media arena.

H&K's Campaign for Media Support

Much as they tried to set the political agenda, Hill and Knowlton executives also wanted to set the media agenda. As Bernard Cohen noted in his 1963 study of the press and foreign policy, the press "may not be successful much of the time in telling people what to think, but it is stunningly successful in telling its readers what to think *about*." Mass communication scholars Maxwell McCombs and Donald Shaw followed up on Cohen's observation by studying voters in Chapel Hill, North Carolina, finding that the news

John Hill, left, with Douglas PR executive A. M. "Rocky" Rochlen and another guest at the Aviation Writers Association annual meeting. The AWA figured prominently in H&K's "Air Power" campaign. (Courtesy of the State Historical Society of Wisconsin)

media exerted a considerable influence on voters' judgments of what they as a group believed were the major issues of the 1968 presidential campaign. In short, the authors found a strong correlation between news media content and voters' perceptions of key issues. If H&K could put air power on the media agenda, public interest in the issue would presumably increase as well.[30]

The AIA began its effort to reach interested journalists by working with the Aviation Writers Association (AWA). Because substantial interest in airplanes and flight already existed, many journalists specialized in aviation, and in 1938 they had formed this association of reporters and editors, public relations representatives (including H&K executives), and other writers associated with aviation. The writers' group was closely aligned with the AIA. In fact, its headquarters address was the same as the AIA's—which was the same office where Bert Goss worked. AIA and AWA coordinated the dinner that introduced the Finletter report to the press, and AIA member companies sponsored a cocktail party and dinner for the writers' annual convention. These writers were aviation loyalists. Some of them had helped to revise Congress's policy report to make it more concise and readable.[31]

The agency used numerous other methods to improve press and radio coverage of air power. H&K took to task those who made errors or misrepresented the aircraft industry. Doris Fleeson of the *Washington Star* received a three-page critique of her column, "The Air Force Lobby," with corrections or comments on five specific statements Bert Goss found questionable. The agency scheduled a series of luncheons so that AIA officials could meet with people in the news business. H&K claimed that this kind of approach resulted in numerous network programs and syndicated articles "graphically describing the industry's plight and the need for air policy legislation." Executives offered assistance gathering information and provided statistics to reporters. They also frequently ghost-wrote letters of appreciation from AIA chief Echols to journalists whose articles they liked.[32] H&K agents tried to magnify the demand for news on air power. When in 1947 Senator Owen Brewster gave an air power speech at the American Legion's aeronautics conference, H&K staff members became concerned that journalists in Indianapolis (the Legion's headquarters) might overlook the story. If the local wire service stringers failed to pick it up, and if New York papers did not ask for it, then Brewster's speech would effectively die. "As a result," public relations executive Sam Tyndall reported to H&K management, "the only method to get local bureaus to file stories was to create a demand for the story in cities outside Indianapolis." Agency staffers then managed to get sympathetic editors in Hartford, Connecticut, Paterson, New Jersey, and Seattle, Washington, and at the United Press in Detroit to ask wire service general desks for more information on Brewster's speech. The wires complied by asking their Indianapolis bureaus for full details on the story. Soon the story went across the wires' trunk lines to major cities, and newspapers and radio stations everywhere had access to the report. As a result, many papers carried the story. In New York alone, it appeared in the *Journal American, World Telegram, Times, Herald Tribune, Daily News,* and *Sun.* Radio coverage included two network broadcasts from New York and a spot on that day's *AP Radio* hourly newscasts.[33]

Hill and Knowlton thus used numerous tactics to work through the news media to inform taxpayers about the need for a strong air component to the military, and journalists did cover the campaign and the issue. Local media devoted 4,878 column inches to one portion of the air power program from March to June 1947. Most stories average twelve to fifteen inches, meaning that several hundred air power stories had appeared in papers around the nation. H&K's publicity of the Finletter report also helped to capture journalists' attention. The air policy report ranked fifth in importance on the editorial page and sixth on the front page of the nation's newspapers during the week of the report's release in January 1948. Not only did the media cover the report, but, according to Hill and Knowlton, they "wholeheartedly" supported the commission's findings. However, in allocating its budget of $300,000, the agency was more interested in specific subgroups than in the general public. AIA needed people who were so strongly committed to air power that they would actively encourage government action on the issue.[34]

H&K Energizes Interested Public Organizations

Discourse in the public arena is perhaps the most difficult to analyze, as there is no single "public agenda" or any organized arena where discourse takes place. Instead, there are many interested groups and individuals who hold meetings, write letters, give speeches, issue news releases, and call for action. Quite often, "public opinion" is taken as synonymous with the public agenda, but public opinion is also a troublesome concept. When most people refer to public opinion, they mean the results of polls, but this is a circular definition (a poll measures opinion, and opinion is the result of a poll). Moreover, opinion polling is not a suitable measure of discourse in the public arena, because polls are snapshot pictures of aggregated individual opinions at a given moment, while discourse is a process taking place over time. Opinion formation should thus be viewed, as communication scholar Vincent Price argues, as a social activity. When people in a collective lack consensus about a given circumstance, they adapt by communicating to reach a consensus. Thus, in addition to measures of public opinion, other ways of studying public discourse include reviews of actions by private organizations or institutions, public expression of opinion or debate by civic groups, individual opinions expressed in the other arenas, letters to issue advocates, and the behavior of citizens or consumers.[35]

People with direct connections to the aircraft industry composed the first group of public advocates H&K tapped for support. Employees of AIA member companies, subcontractors and their workers, and company directors could "take the story in person to groups who would not otherwise receive it." Goss made a list of important industrialists and financiers the program should reach, including National Association of Manufacturers leaders Charles Hook and Howard Pew, bankers such as Junius S. Morgan, and business leaders such as Laurance Rockefeller. Industry employees, especially those at supervisory levels and those located outside cities with aircraft plants, were encouraged "to write to editors on the air power situation." But it was crucial to identify the program with more than just self-interested insiders.[36]

Hill and Knowlton therefore looked outward for support, and it cultivated farm and union groups, women's clubs, and religious organizations. H&K gave special consideration to civic groups. The U.S. Chamber of Commerce made a public statement on air power and defense spending in May 1947, and the Veterans of Foreign Wars (VFW) took an even more active role, passing resolutions, issuing news releases, and calling for "the most powerful air force in the world." H&K even considered ten- to eighteen-year-olds, noting they would "be voting at the time when there is the greatest pressure for air disarmament." Executives asked the Air Power League, a nonprofit educational group, to develop a program targeted at children's interests, such as model plane building and scouting.[37]

H&K could reach such groups in several ways, including AIA publications. About 40,000 opinion leaders—college professors, state legislators, libraries, ministers, and business leaders—received *Planes*, the bimonthly magazine produced by the agency. An additional 10,000 copies were sent to print and radio journalists, along with a special clipsheet for media use. Another widely disseminated AIA publication was the *Aircraft Yearbook*, an annual volume of statistics and reports on the industry and its products. Staff members spent time with subcontractors, supplying materials for house organs, a booklet, and *Planes* to parts manufacturers and others interested in aviation. Finally, in cooperation with other aviation associations, the AIA offered writing fellowships and sponsored the publication of books on air power.[38]

The association could also reach members of private organizations through their own meetings and publications. The AIA's traveling speaker, Harvey Stowers, spent most of his time with civic clubs giving speeches prepared by H&K on the dire need for a strong air defense. The agency furnished mailings for VFW posts and provided suggestions for articles in the VFW's national monthly magazine. H&K also maintained regular contact with the U.S. Chamber of Commerce, and it planned meetings between AIA officials and influential business leaders.[39]

The most important conduit between the AIA and the public was the American Legion, which entered into full partnership in the "Air Power Is Peace Power" campaign in 1947. Although the Legion favored universal military training, which H&K officials felt would be unnecessary if the nation had a strong air program, the groups decided to proceed with a joint program. The idea, *Aviation Week* explained, "was that the Legion, one of the largest organized citizens' bodies, could carry the message of the hazards of a crippled air fleet to the grass roots in the hope it would filter up to Congress."[40]

The program to inform and enlist the 800,000 Legion members' active support took place at national, regional, state, and community levels during 1947 and 1948, virtually all with H&K's assistance. Nationally, Legion leaders made statements and called for legislative action, and the *Legionnaire* and *American Legion Magazine* frequently carried articles on air power. The program included as well a radio series, *A Report to the People on the Race for Air Power*, carried over more than 650 stations. H&K promoted the radio series by preparing a brochure and stories to be distributed to local newspapers. The agency also developed a comprehensive publicity handbook containing suggested speeches, editorials, news and feature stories, an agenda for an air power meeting, and drafts of messages to members of Congress. Executives sent to the Legion thousands of copies of *Planes* and 25,000 copies of a thirty-two-page selection from the *Congressional Record* for distribution to the air forces, Legion posts, and editors on the Legion's mailing list. H&K secured featured speakers for the Legion's regional air power conferences and offered assistance at state conventions with an air power theme or speakers.[41]

One last group offered vital assistance for the AIA: the member companies' biggest customer, the U.S. military. That the AIA had selected AAF General Oliver Echols as its president reflected a commitment to maintaining close ties to the military. The Department of the Air Force established a Directorate of Public Relations in September 1947, which had a staff of 110 by 1949. Bert Goss regularly met with AAF and Air Force officers, including those employed in public relations. Goss and another H&K executive, John Mapes, made speeches on public relations before the Army Information School on AAF public relations.[42]

The AIA also held annual conferences in Williamsburg for military, government, and industry officials. Closed, confidential, and off-the-record, the meetings provided a forum for discussing mutual problems and formulating potential solutions. According to Hill and Knowlton records, the second conference, held in 1947, included participation by sixty government and military officials from the Army Ground Forces, Army Air Forces, Navy, Bureau of Aeronautics, Civil Aeronautics Administration, Civil Aeronautics Board, Air Transport Association, and Department of Commerce, plus aircraft manufacturers.[43]

This close relationship enabled Hill and Knowlton to provide its expertise to improve military public relations. In 1947, for example, Bert Goss previewed an AAF film on air power. He disliked the film, finding it too lengthy, and vowed to "keep after the AAF boys" to make deletions. Hill and Knowlton executives prepared a draft of remarks for Symington's review prior to his appearance before the Finletter commission. Goss also conferred with Colonel C. J. Brown, head of the Army Air Force Office of Public Relations, about the overall organization and planning of the air power campaign.[44]

The flurry of activity by civic organizations and by private individuals who voluntarily spent their time promoting air power suggests a considerable level of popular support for the industry's cause. Opinion polls also reflected public support. The first postwar Gallup survey on the subject, taken in February 1949, found that 70 percent of the sample favored increasing the Air Force budget. More than a third of the people surveyed were in favor of a higher budget even if it meant higher taxes. President Truman received few letters on his air policies, but these generally favored strong aerial arm. One disabled veteran of the naval air forces wrote to Truman accusing the president of "gross negligence & betrayal of the trust of the nation." Another writer supported Symington in the seventy-group fight, telling Truman to "Leave your sec'y for air alone—this USA is with him."[45]

Coordinating the Campaign: Creating a Voice for an Industry

With so many groups taking part in the air power campaign, there existed a pressing need for coordination from the top. When Goss met with Colonel Brown, in addition to discussing campaign objectives and "final determination as to who should do what," they also talked about "who will coordinate or supervise the activities of all the various groups that will be affected or that may possibly participate." Whether or not so planned, Goss as the account supervisor took on the role of coordinator. One of H&K's most time-consuming roles consisted of serving as an information clearinghouse, providing assistance to journalists, government bodies, civic groups, the military, and individuals. This alignment of interested parties represented H&K's most important contribution to the air power campaign.[46]

Hill and Knowlton's first priority was keeping its client informed on all aspects of aviation issues, ranging from legislation to new technology. For this reason the Washington office frequently sent to all AIA members lists of upcoming events, meetings, and speeches of interest. The *Weekly Washington Bulletin* contained brief stories on legislative action, industry activities, and even annotated listings of press, radio, and book-length coverage of relevant issues. The agency also sent out regular "P.R. Memos" to AIA member companies. These topical reports might include discussion of a bill pending in Congress or a forthcoming article in *Aviation Week*—anything that manufacturers would find useful.[47]

Hill and Knowlton executives wanted to encourage industry interaction with legislators and aviation organizations, so they created a *Washington Information Directory*, published annually. This booklet included the names and addresses of every contact a manufacturer might need, ranging from the Senate Armed Services and House Post Office and Civil Service committee chairs to Civil Aeronautics Board members. A booklet on the two policy commissions, with background information on the history and major questions before the boards, supplemented the 1947 directory. H&K executives also planned the annual Williamsburg meetings for industry, government, and military officials.[48]

Goss and his staff worked to establish AIA as the definitive source of industry statistics and information for government agencies, the media, and the military. Executives compiled material for both the Finletter and the congressional commissions. "A great number of special studies have been prepared and supplied to these Boards on request," H&K reported. It even coordinated industry testimony before the various policy boards. The news media sought material from Hill and Knowlton, both directly and from *Planes*, which journalists had permission to quote freely. Military officials also requested materials from H&K, as when the Air Force requested a special run of the advance press proofs of Senator Bridges's *Planes* article ghosted by H&K writers, "so that one copy could be given to every delegate to the recent American Legion convention."[49]

Sometimes H&K even served as a conduit for information not originating at AIA. The agency sent a copy of the VFW booklet *Downpayment on Survival in the Air Age* to a military official in 1949, and it facilitated the purchase by other organizations of copies of the summary to the Finletter report. It printed a booklet of *Editorials on the Crisis in Air Power* to send to other editors. This booklet contained pieces from respected papers such as the *New York Times* and the *Washington Post*. H&K also excerpted a copy of a letter from the commander of the VFW to President Truman, made copies in patriotic red and blue ink, and suggested that the VFW send them to all local posts to hang as posters or send to legislators. The agency also sent the letter to the Air Force Association, urging its use as either a mailer to members or a full-page promotion in the *Air Force Magazine*. Executives made frequent use of reprints of speeches and articles presented by other organizations, many of which had been prepared by or with the assistance of H&K itself.[50]

Air Power Is Peace Power:
Effects of a National Opinion Campaign

With increased political, media, and public support, AIA began to achieve its goals. Procurement started to increase by the end of the decade, fueled in great part by military spending relating to the Korean "police action." Industrywide production, employment, and sales figures all began an upward climb by 1950. The AIA estimated sales for 1950 at 6,520 planes, with about 3,000 going to the military; by 1955, it estimated sales at 13,153 airplanes, with about 8,400 for the military. Net sales of twelve major airframe companies jumped from a low of $519 million in 1946 to over $1.38 billion in 1950 and more than $5.18 billion in 1955. Profits rose out of the red to $62.6 million in the black in 1950, according to the AIA.[51]

Along with a more secure financial position, the AIA had also taken steps toward achieving other long-term goals. Appropriations to the National Advisory Committee for Aeronautics (the predecessor of the National Aeronautics and Space Administration), together with Project RAND, an experimental Air Force–Douglas Aircraft partnership, and other projects fulfilled the industry's desire for "continuation of Government-Science-Industry partnership." RAND later became an independent think tank, but such federally funded research and development projects gave the industry hope that similar activities would continue. The AIA's main desire had been a long-term air policy, and although the Finletter and congressional commissions could not guarantee long-term funding for procurement or research, they did seem to offer a public commitment to air power. On the whole, as compared with that in 1943, the environment for aircraft manufacturing was much improved by 1950.[52] However, the improved status of aircraft manufacturing did not derive from the public relations campaign alone. The program had, after all, essentially failed immediately after the war. Although procurement remained higher than it had previously been in peacetime, it was hardly enough to ensure a prosperous industry, and H&K called 1947 "a year in which manufacturing companies again hit bottom."[53]

Numerous factors in addition to the campaign can explain increasing support for air power during the late 1940s. The romance of the airplane provided one incentive for confidence in air power. Not only fiction but also true tales of such romantic figures as the Wright brothers, Amelia Earhart, and Eddie Rickenbacker fed what one historian has called the "extraordinary affection millions of American men, women and children felt for the flying machine during the half century after its invention." So great was interest in aviation that, according to Hill and Knowlton, one company produced and marketed *Air Age News*, a six-day-a-week fifteen-minute transcribed radio program about aviation, which was broadcast over 315 radio stations throughout the United States, Alaska, Hawaii, Puerto Rico, and Panama.[54]

A small but growing number of citizens had begun to experience flight firsthand. In 1941 nineteen companies operated domestic airlines, with 370 aircraft flying over 45,000 miles annually. By 1950 the nation boasted thirty-eight operators flying 960 airplanes about 77,000 miles annually. Air travel, expressed as a fraction of railroad passenger travel, climbed from just over five in 1941 to thirty-three in 1950. These increases suggest growing trust in civilian air travel, which may well have translated into support for military air power.[55]

Then, too, large segments of the population already held an interest in national defense issues. During a one-month period in 1947, the AIA's traveling speaker filled twenty dates, most before Rotary Clubs, and this demand suggests that people were interested in defense and wanted to learn about air power. Although few air power supporters mentioned the Japanese aerial attack on Pearl Harbor, frequent references to the "lessons of World War II" bespoke a level of determination not to be caught short a second time, especially not in the atomic age. The atomic bomb unquestionably altered people's opinions about the airplane.[56]

The industry's own record during and after the war also encouraged support for air power. Its wartime performance, building some 300,000 planes, 800,000 engines, and 700,000 propellers, had impressed many Americans. The Berlin Airlift was just as remarkable. Beginning in the summer of 1948, the Soviet Union had blockaded Berlin by stopping all ground traffic from the West. Determined not to give up the German city so easily, the United States and British air forces flew over the blockade through closely guarded air corridors, taking off or landing a plane every ninety seconds for several months, in order to bring in tons of food, coal, and raw materials for Berlin's factories. The industry's record was not H&K's doing, of course, and it is difficult to imagine that people would not have known about these heroics without the agency's widespread publicity.[57]

In fact, such exploits as the Berlin Airlift may even have contributed to an "oversell" of air power. Many military and manufacturing experts argued that air power could bring world peace. "[I]f we can develop air power to its maximum potential, commensurate with technological possibilities of our day," wrote manufacturer and former Army Air Corps Major Alexander De Seversky, "we can create a force that will guarantee peace for the foreseeable future." Not everyone uncritically accepted the proposition that strategic air bombing had been the decisive weapon of the war. Defense Secretary Forrestal, for one, challenged the notion. Morale bombing especially had been a disappointment, at least prior to Hiroshima.[58]

Congressional support for air power probably had more to do with finding an alternative to President Truman's proposed universal military training than to blind faith in the airplane. As Senator Robert Taft wrote, "It seems to me so obvious that the air is more important than universal military training." A cheaper alternative than a large standing army, air power seemed a good choice to budget-minded Republicans like Taft. Although universal military training remained popular with the American public, for members of Congress it was "anathema." By April 1948 even Secretary Forrestal gave it little chance if Congress appropriated the extra funding for air power. The military training bill that finally passed provided for only a voluntary program.[59]

Most important to the success of the crusade for air power was the threat posed by "Communist aggression." The years of the air power campaign were fraught with international tension. Against the backdrop of the Marshall Plan, the Berlin blockade, and Communist activities in Yugoslavia, Czechoslovakia, and Greece, the AIA relentlessly promoted air power as the best hope for peace. The Air Force launched its seventy-group campaign, and the Finletter commission emphasized the likelihood that other countries would develop nuclear power. Gallup polls revealed that Americans increasingly said that they believed the Soviet Union wanted to "build herself up to be the ruling power." An employee of an AIA-member company, Piasecki Helicopter, mused, "with all due respect to AIA's effective PR work, we must not overlook the fact that the Russians are at least in part responsible for public and Congressional support of our expanded air power program."[60]

H&K consciously tried to avoid using the Russian threat as part of a scare campaign. Bert Goss twice reprimanded the AIA's speaker, Harvey Stowers, for including comments on "the Russian situation" in his speeches. Goss reminded him that "it is absolutely imperative that we do not get involved in any question of war mongering, and it is absolutely vital that we do not try to become an authority or a source of information about foreign developments." The last thing H&K sought was a "merchants of death" reputation that plagued other defense-oriented companies, so the speaker should refuse to make "any statements about Russia or any other country that can't be pinned down to someone else." H&K sometimes promoted aggressive statements by others, such as Senator Brewster's assertion that the country could not "afford to remain the world's third ranking air power." But, Goss told Stowers, even when quoting others, "use the least inflammatory material." Even so, the undercurrent of international events profoundly shaped the debate.[61]

By 1950 the AIA had begun to achieve its goals, but the air power campaign was successful only when other groups became interested—and these groups got involved only when events seemed to demand it. In the end, H&K's work was significant primarily because it linked advocates together. Journalists, government officials, and civic groups received information and materials they used to inform other people about an issue they considered important. Hill and Knowlton did not create their interest in air power. But by publicizing pro–air power statements from numerous sources, the agency fashioned a climate favorable to air power. This climate offered some measure of protection against taxpayers' complaints to members of Congress about increased Air Force appropriations.

By placing the debate about air power into the forefront of public discussion, Hill and Knowlton's activities indirectly provided occasions for opposing viewpoints to be aired. Serious review of policy options appeared in the news media, as in an article in *Fortune*, which noted that even with a strong air power program, "peace is not guaranteed." The various policy review boards made extensive use of industry and military sources, but they conducted exhaustive studies, with the Finletter commission alone hearing more than 150 witnesses in over 200 meetings. National defense had clearly become an important issue to significant numbers of people. In his famous warning against the dangers of the military-industrial complex, President Eisenhower also noted that "we can no longer risk emergency improvisation of national defense." Eisenhower went on to say that "we have been compelled in the U.S. to create a permanent armaments industry of vast proportions." [62]

Americans may have overreacted, or may have been too trusting in Air Force estimates of requirements. But the "inescapable fact" still remains, as John Lewis Gaddis points out, that the Soviet Union alarmed a good portion of the rest of the world, too. One of the few citizens who wrote to Truman regarding air power begged him not to sign the seventy-group bill, because "millions of loyal Americans like me" are "terrified to the core at the thought of what such an armament will mean to the future—and even present—policy of our country." Most others appeared to be convinced that the steps were necessary, however distasteful. The advent of the Korean conflict in June 1950 seemed to prove them right. [63]

Hill and Knowlton continued to work for the AIA for many years, but the hardest part of its work was done. "In the 1944–47 era and previously," H&K explained in 1951, "the major task of the industry's public relations was to win and retain public support for air power. Air power's role is now generally accepted." Once citizens and government officials agreed to and established a policy of peacetime armament, the aircraft manufacturers' position was more secure. H&K had not fooled or forced anyone to accept a military-industrial complex. But the agency's coordination of industry, military, and civilian support for air power, together with domestic politics, citizens' beliefs about airplanes and atomic bombs, and international events, created a climate where such a partnership seemed not only acceptable but necessary. [64]

By the time Hill and Knowlton accepted the aircraft account, its policies and approach to public relations had been fully developed. The air power campaign typified on a number of levels Hill and Knowlton's work for trade associations from the 1940s to the 1960s. The program that the executives designed for the aircraft makers followed a pattern that would be reprised and redefined over several decades for other corporate and association accounts. First, it shows the agency's role in the struggle to negotiate a balance between government assistance and protection when its clients wanted it and regulation or interference when they did not—free enterprise with an asterisk. It also demonstrates how the agency used grass-roots lobbying campaigns to cultivate favorable public opinion, which could in turn be used as a lever against its clients' opposition, in this case the government, in other cases organized labor or other business concerns. Third, the close relationship that H&K developed with the AIA was typical in that the lines between the staffs of the client and the agency blurred sometimes to the point of being indistinguishable. This allowed the PR agents tremendous sway over the policy and practices of its clients, which in turn enabled the agency to help an industry create and amplify one unified voice that made clear and consistent demands in all three arenas of public discourse. Finally, the campaign is typical in its effects, which were complex and indirect but still significant. With its impressive work for the aircraft manufacturers, H&K was rapidly becoming a force to be reckoned with, but, as Chapter 3 shows, its own steel client was the last to know it.

CHAPTER THREE

Client as Consumer

Selling Hill and Knowlton

After World War II, Hill and Knowlton's program for the steel industry, already perhaps the largest public relations account in the nation, swelled to even greater dimensions. H&K's expanded program included a community relations service, which provided materials to help local plants of the member companies conduct their own public relations activities; a campaign on capacity, to demonstrate that the industry was spending millions on expansion to satisfy the intense demand for steel; a drive to try to meet that demand by collecting scrap; and an institutional advertising campaign to educate the public on the economics of steel. Like much of the postwar business community, the steel industry made a major commitment to public relations, especially for campaigns that marketed the free-enterprise system. The steel program far exceeded anything Hill and Knowlton had previously conducted.

Consequently, the New York executives were shocked when a field agent, Harry Botsford, delivered a slap in the face. His February 1947 report indicated that at least three corporation presidents were full of criticism of the agency and the American Iron and Steel Institute. H&K's advertising program "stinks," the head of one company said. "It's a waste of money." "My company has probably contributed $250,000 to the Institute's public relations program," added another, "and I can't see where we have ever benefited any." All three agreed the "radio programs during last year's strike were terrible." Among many other comments, one complained, "The Institute people don't get out here often enough to see us. They seem to live in an ivory tower." As counsel to the AISI, Hill and Knowlton influenced steel industry policy over the long years of their association, but the internal crisis precipitated by Botsford's memo demonstrates the relationship could be reciprocal.[1]

H&K's response to the steel emergency indicates that the client was as important a consumer as journalists, elected officials, or any other recipient of the agency's public relations materials. "Advertising agencies," the historian Roland Marchand writes, "had to produce advertisements that pleased the client or lose the account." The PR agency faced much the same pressure. To curry the client's favor, H&K chose to intensify the AISI community program, even though the firm's executives believed that the best strategy for the steel industry was to target national opinion leaders. Mass communication research during the 1940s and 1950s suggested that individuals whose opinions others held in high regard led public opinion and therefore composed the most important audience of media messages. Information collected by the agency seemed to indicate that strategy was indeed effective for the steel industry. Yet when the company presidents complained, H&K acceded to their demands and focused more energy on the section of the program many of the clients preferred.[2]

The agency later asserted that the community relations program contributed to the creation of a climate of opinion favorable to steel and therefore intolerant toward President Truman's seizure of the mils in 1952. That claim will be explored in Chapter 5. More important here is the lesson learned by Hill and Knowlton: not only must the agency sell the public on its client, it must also sell its client on the agency. This meant that the public relations program was shaped as much by clients' desires as by any agency recommendation.

Business and Public Relations
in Postwar America

For American business the postwar years meant previously unimaginable production. Steel companies continued to produce at wartime levels, making more than 88 million tons of raw steel in 1948, as compared with a high of just over 89 million tons in 1944; by 1951 the companies would surpass the billion ton mark. Profits surpassed any the steel companies had seen since the 1920s, and in the dozen or so years following World War II, prices increased 141 percent, with a rate of return on equity after taxes averaging over 10 percent. Therefore, when the AISI placed profits at about 6 percent, many Americans were skeptical; when steel shortages kept Americans from making long-deferred purchases of automobiles and other goods, some charged the industry with keeping production low so prices would remain high; and when prices did rise, some accused the industry of trying to break the government's stabilization program and of monopoly pricing. Despite such problems, steel, and most other U.S. industries, flourished.[3]

Itself a business, public relations likewise thrived. According to the National Industrial Conference Board, "an attitude of complete acceptance of industry's responsibility for developing and maintaining good public relations" prevailed by March 1945, even though in a survey taken only six years earlier, "a large proportion of comments were summarized in the phrase 'we have no public relations program.'" Another survey similarly found "a great surge of interest" in PR in 1946, with nine of every ten companies increasing their expenditures. This growing interest continued throughout the immediate postwar era. Among AISI members, for instance, just fourteen companies had public relations departments in 1948, but by 1952 thirty did, with the number of in-house practitioners jumping from 246 to 387.[4]

Public relations boomed in great part because postwar prosperity in no way relieved the pressure U.S. business leaders placed on themselves to sell America to Americans. Executives in the National Industrial Conference Board survey mentioned dealing with labor as their biggest concern. However, they also listed "indicating the company's contribution to the general welfare, building confidence in the company's product, and promoting a belief in the free enterprise system." The latter, begun in the 1930s, had never stopped being a priority. During the war public relations practitioners wanted to make certain industry got proper credit for its war sacrifice and effort, because it seemed to them that labor got all the attention and praise.[5]

Public relations executives were among the most strident voices that demanded a rollback of the advance of labor and government into territory that business leaders claimed for themselves. The problem, one public relations man explained, was that "we find many Americans not only unconscious of the foundations of the American system but even believing certain things which are definitely untrue and accepting certain principles which are definitely un-American." *Printers' Ink* had begun to urge sponsorship of private enterprise campaigns during the war, explaining that "Free Enterprise Now Faces Crisis and Opportunity" and encouraging business leaders to "Begin Selling 'Free Enterprise' in the Kindergarten" and to "Tell the Public Why America's Future Depends upon Free Enterprise!" "Remain silent and die," a *Public Relations Journal* article exclaimed.[6]

PR executives often touted institutional advertising as one of the best methods of reaching important publics with the free-enterprise message. The historian Robert Griffith's study of the Advertising Council reveals the lengths to which American business leaders went after the war to sell America through institutional advertising. Advertising, Griffith writes, would secure public action through persuasion rather than through force of law. "Mistrustful of the untutored responses of ordinary citizens, the council feared that Americans did not truly understand the economic system," and therefore could be misled by propaganda attacks from unions or European socialists. For one of its biggest campaigns, the "American Economic System," the council raised unprecedented amounts of money—$100,000 each from General Electric and General Foods, with substantial additional amounts from such companies as IBM, Eastman Kodak, Procter and Gamble, and Republic Steel. Individual companies like Alcoa also participated, with that company's PR department dedicating itself in 1947 "to the promotion of the principles of the American system as it seemed to find exemplification in our own company," producing four-color advertisements for the *Saturday Evening Post* with the "underlying theme" of the "American economic formula, the heritage of a free people."[7]

This crusade was somewhat disingenuous, but many practitioners were sincere in their concern. Many agencies had their own institutional advertising services, Hill and Knowlton included. For some, the free-enterprise campaign may have merely helped to drum up business. But for others, it was a question of saving the United States from socialism. The field's top practitioners, notably John Hill and T. J. Ross, viewed government war planning as "the entering wedge for socialists," considering centralization "the great threat for the future." But they were not alone, because many business leaders joined the PR agents in encouraging participation in the campaign to sell America.[8]

A massive wave of strikes immediately following the war, which included a steel walkout, only exacerbated fears that uninformed Americans could turn to socialism. After Japan surrendered, the dam broke on all the frustrations labor felt during the war years. The major unions had promised not to strike during the war, and, on those occasions when workers did rebel, the Truman administration had intervened regularly on the side of business, drafting strikers and putting injunctions on union leaders. To many managers, the steel strike, which involved more workers than any other walkout in the industry before or since, seemed a throwback to the turmoil of the 1930s. In fact 1946 became the most strike-torn year in history. This apparent militancy troubled business and political leaders, but the climate had changed. Employers did not hire strikebreakers or request assistance from state militias; instead, they responded with public relations, legal and economic pressures, and such political measures as the Labor-Management Relations Act of 1947. The Taft-Hartley Act, as it is more commonly called, restricted unions by limiting their right to strike, brought back the injunction, and strengthened management's position on the National Labor Relations Board. It also forced union members to a sign an affidavit denouncing communism.[9]

If the Taft-Hartley Act calmed AISI members, the nationalization of steel in Great Britain warned them not to become complacent. Britain's Labour Party, pledged to nationalization of steel since 1946, made it law in 1949, although the implementation was delayed and a move toward denationalization took place by late 1952. Business leaders followed the story closely. *U.S. News and World Report,* for instance, published a telephone interview with its London editor on "What Socialized Steel Means."[10]

Executives in the United States perceived increasing interest in nationalization in part because pricing policies led some critics to call for antitrust action against steel. The industry's basing point price system, called "Pittsburgh Plus," had been used to regulate competition in the industry for decades. Companies determined the cost of steel by adding a base price for the product, usually set by U.S. Steel and its subsidiaries, to the cost of freight from Pittsburgh, regardless of the actual location of the manufacturing plant. The price of steel would therefore be the same whether it was sent by railroad across the country or by truck across the street. A Federal Trade Commission investigation convinced U.S. Steel's Judge Gary to agree to abolish the system in 1924, but the industry turned to a multiple basing point system, which was the same thing except that it calculated prices based on many cities rather than just Pittsburgh. The AISI's attorneys, according to Bert Goss, were in the 1940s "very nervous about saying anything with regard to prices or competition." However, Goss argued, "if they have their way and nothing is done in the way of popular education in competition, the industry may wake up with a public utility status imposed on it."[11]

Educating Americans
on Steel Economics

According to H&K, this and other problems faced by the institute could be solved by educating the American public. The United States was certainly not perfect, business leaders thought, but it was a success, and, the historian Howell Harris explains, "it only needed to be defended against government meddling and the criticisms of the ignorant or the hostile." AISI's public relations programs of the late 1940s reflected the trend toward more extensive programs that emphasized informing Americans about free enterprise. "So successful have been the assaults on capitalism and private enterprise in other countries," an H&K report warned, "that today the United States is almost the only major nation where communism or some form of socialism is not a dominant force." People sought to undermine free society by winning public acquiescence, the report said, and industry's only defender "has been industry itself," adding, "Today many industries of national importance are engaged in improving their relations with the public through information programs designed to explain the industry's problems and to point out its significant achievements." The steel industry would have to contribute its part to halt the advance of socialism in the free world.[12]

The agency planned an aggressive campaign to teach people about steel's economic position, usually incorporating an antigovernment, antilabor message. The program was as extensive as that for the aircraft industry—indeed, even more sizable and costlier—and it was highly praised by the business community. In 1946 the institute invested about $500,000 on newspaper advertising alone, "designed to explain to the public the basic economics of the industry." The campaign also included articles in *Steelways*, the AISI's trade magazine that began publication with a circulation of 30,000 in 1945, and *Steel Facts*, which were published on alternating months. According to H&K executive Merrick Jackson, by 1950 the eight-page *Steel Facts* had a circulation of 175,000, and it helped to generate over 12,000 letters and 2,500 telephone calls for more information on iron and steel. From 1947 to 1950 the AISI issued seven lengthy background memoranda on capacity, profits, technology, expansion, and scrap. News releases, a film, a comic book for distribution in schools, a radio program, three brochures, speeches by company executives, and preparation of congressional testimony rounded out the program.[13]

H&K materials from the 1946 strike likewise reflected the agency's economic education campaign. The AISI did not conduct negotiations or direct dealings with the union. Instead, the institute's PR program concentrated on fixing blame on the steelworkers. The agency assumed that strikers and their supporters had been confused or misled by un-American propaganda, but misunderstandings could be corrected. Steel could not meet current demand, the executives argued, and therefore it spent a great deal of money to expand. That meant profits were not actually high, so the industry could not afford wage increases. When workers walked out, production slowed, which in turn increased demand even more. Thus, shortages could be blamed on labor.[14]

Two brochures are illustrative of the general strategy and the tenor of H&K materials during the immediate postwar years, especially regarding steel's attitude toward labor. "Steel—Pacemaker for Peacetime" described U.S. capacity as the "world's greatest!" with production at "a peacetime record!" Graphs and charts showed wages were high, profits and dividends low as the industry poured capital into expansion. Another brochure explained that "Steel Spends a Billion Dollars" to increase capacity for consumers, more than the industry had earned in profits since the end of the war. Both blamed shortages on labor strikes and other "abnormal conditions" and insisted that the industry would soon catch up with demand.[15]

The agency targeted several groups for special attention, beginning with farmers. A series of ads, such as "Tilling with a Hundred Teams of Steel," listed reasons that they should support the industry. "More Headaches for the Farmer" sympathized with those citizens who had once again been "asked to break all food production records" when their tools had taken such a terrific beating during the war that "they can't be tied together much longer with rusty fence wire." The steelworkers' walkout had "hit at the heart of food production," because the pickets had cut the farmers' supply of steel.[16]

Members of Congress constituted another important group. In June 1945 the industry had, for the first time, established representation in Washington. H&K made contacts with government officials and reporters, formed relationships with representatives of other industries and trade associations, and furnished information to AISI members through a newsletter, *Washington Backgrounds*. The agency avoided direct lobbying, at the AISI directors' request, but it did establish a toehold for the industry in the nation's capital.[17]

More generally, H&K's AISI program targeted opinion leaders. "I don't think John Hill was a real scholar of public opinion theory," PR executive Harold Burson explained, but mass communication studies did have an important impact on the agency's approach to the practice of public relations. Most influential was Paul F. Lazarsfeld's research program at Columbia University, which focused on mass communication effects and which led scholars to concentrate on the role of opinion leaders, who dominated the public opinion process. Different people led opinion on different issues, but "personal persuasion was the strongest influence among all influences that made people change their minds," according to the Columbia scholars. Their study, *The People's Choice*, examined voters' decision making, but Lazarsfeld believed the results "have a meaning for the changing of minds in commercial advertising campaigns as well as in a political campaign." As *Printers' Ink* headlined his 1945 article, "Who Influences Whom—It's the Same for Politics and Advertising."[18]

Hill and Knowlton executives agreed with communication scholars that certain groups of people were influential with others on public issues, including those surrounding the steel industry. The target groups the agency identified are revealed in the mailing list for *Steelways*, the industry's magazine: 70,000 print and radio correspondents and commentators, members of Congress, libraries, business leaders, clergy in steel towns, college professors, and institute members received the bimonthly magazine in 1949. The agents assumed that these people would, through personal discussion with others, lead opinion on steel-related issues.[19]

Steelways appears to have accomplished its mission in leading or at least solidifying opinion leaders' respect for and belief in steel executives and their work. Articles focused on expansion, labor difficulties, users of steel, improvements in production, and other issues. The periodical gained a loyal following, a good record of reprints in publications for the general public, and, for a trade journal, a significantly high readership. Hill and Knowlton commissioned a study of *Steelways* readers in March 1948, and the results were impressive. Over 40 percent of respondents agreed, "I would pay for Steelways if it were for sale." Records also showed 84 percent of its readers felt that "the publication has given them a better understanding of the industry," 63 percent of the contents of each issue was read, and almost 80 percent read one or more of the features in every issue. In 1949 at least 7,500 publications and 1,000 radio stations used one or more feature from each issue of *Steelways*, according to its editor.[20]

Despite the success of *Steelways*, not all AISI members agreed with the national opinion leaders strategy. They wanted greater emphasis on public relations activities in their own communities. The economist John Kenneth Galbraith asserted that the growth of public relations indicated that business achievement alone was no longer enough and that business leaders increasingly believed their position in the community was slipping. This feeling may have fueled complaints such as one made by a disgruntled AISI member who grumbled, "The trouble with all of the publicity that has been used in the past, is that it has been solely gunned at people in the upper brackets of intelligence and has failed to make any impression whatsoever on 'grass roots' people." H&K's strategy was apparent to the steel manufacturers, but at least some institute members thought it ineffective.[21]

Hill and Knowlton did not target all of its materials at opinion leaders. The agency had begun a community relations program in late 1946, providing materials and information with the expectation that company PR executives would make extensive use of them on the local level. But these materials were not tailored to the individual community, and companies or plants that lacked public relations departments or counsel could not or did not take advantage of H&K's materials. One company president told H&K's Harry Botsford that communities "are not interested in industry figures as to wages, etc." Instead, he said, "what they want is specific data relating to their own area." Another added, "National advertising will not help to make any community program function easier or better," and a third protested that executives in New York could not "expect to know what steel people, especially workers and community residents, are thinking."[22]

Had Hill and Knowlton conducted more thorough evaluation of its programs, the executives might have been aware that its materials and strategies were not penetrating at the local level. An analysis of Hill and Knowlton's work during the 1946 steel strike, for example, indicated that AISI materials had little impact on the strike or its resolution at a small plant in Madison, Wisconsin. Public relations practitioners today are urged to use surveys, focus groups, and other measures of audience knowledge, attitudes, and behavior to judge the effectiveness of their programs. But evaluation was not common in the early decades of formal public relations, and H&K's limited evaluation efforts such as its *Steelways* survey were, if not pioneering, certainly unusual among public relations agencies during the 1940s.[23]

The lack of formal evaluation mechanisms meant that H&K executives were blindsided by the negative feedback from AISI member companies. The institute's public relations committee, chaired by Inland Steel's Edward L. Ryerson from 1944 to 1954, had approved H&K's national strategy. But the AISI included dozens of small companies whose leaders did not believe their needs had been given adequate attention. The agency had just separated from its Cleveland parent and had to consider every client vital, but more than any other the steel account had made the agency and could just as easily break it. A community-based project that gave personal attention to every AISI member company might secure H&K's position as the institute's counsel, even as it attacked what Hill called the "national problem of winning more friends for the steel industry."[24]

The Steel Industry's Community Relations Program

Community relations programs did not originate at Hill and Knowlton. Practitioners working in plants, smaller companies, or subsidiaries, such as U.S. Steel's regional and local PR executives, pioneered many of the techniques later used by H&K and other agencies. Community relations programs constructed an image of business as a good neighbor, according to the historian Elizabeth Fones-Wolf; they were not an alternative to free enterprise campaigns but a supplement. Jim Irwin, one of the original Wisemen whom Hill once considered taking on as a partner, had developed a system of community relations he called "the Dayton plan," developed for General Motors during the 1930s. His program, eventually applied to such industrial heavyweights as General Electric, Shell, Standard Oil of New Jersey, Monsanto, and E. I. duPont de Nemours, included four steps:

1. to find out what the public was thinking and saying about industry,
2. to separate the true from the false in uncomplimentary statements,
3. when statements concerned truth about conditions that should be changed, to establish different company policies or modify existing policies to eliminate the objections, and
4. to convey to the public, in every possible way, factual and complete information to replace the wrong and incomplete information that was unfavorably influencing public opinion.

Thus, a company would conduct polls in plant communities and use the results to help locate weak areas and plan activities to win community support. Irwin recommended plant tours, employee newspapers, speakers, family days, local publicity, advertising, and other measures to improve a company's relations with plant communities.[25]

Whether or not John Hill or his executives familiarized themselves with Irwin's plan, Hill and Knowlton in essence carried it out, helping local PR directors reach the public, and developing a "public relations audit" to AISI member companies. With its emphasis on finding out what plant neighbors wanted and on analyzing employee needs, the plan was worthy of emulation. In fact, it was perhaps the one way, other than opinion surveys, that H&K encouraged AISI member companies to listen rather than to speak. Within a month after Hill and the other executives received Harry Botsford's memorandum on company criticisms of the agency, they took steps to appease their discontented clients. First, the AISI sponsored regional meetings on community relations, such as one in Chicago attended by institute president Walter S. Tower, John Hill, *Steelways* editor Merrick Jackson, and two other H&K executives. Hill's speech drove home the successes of the national public relations campaign. "Certainly there has been a marked abatement in the past six months of criticism of the industry for such unfounded charges as refusal to expand," he told company officials. "No small part of the credit for this change in public attitude can be traced to the advertising and publicity procedures followed so intensively" by the institute and individual companies. Other H&K executives reviewed AISI community relations services and explained what field agents could do to help. Finally, they opened the floor for questions and comments—much of which turned out to be criticism, at least at the Chicago meeting, and reiteration of remarks Harry Botsford had heard in February.[26]

A round of plant visits for "Community Relations Meetings" constituted the next step. H&K's George Rose arranged the trips so that five field agents moved from region to region without having been to every plant in the area, but writing letters to let members know they had not been forgotten. "None of the plants will feel neglected," John Purcell explained, "and there will be activity in all the areas." Purcell went to Pennsylvania for a visit with Midvale Steel, where a Mr. Nalle, a new executive at Midvale, wanted to start an employee newsletter and had begun to consider holding an open house. Purcell reported, "we offered the services of Hill and Knowlton on both projects," and "I will keep in touch with Mr. Nalle." After the meetings, the PR agents informed the appropriate H&K department, such as publicity or radio, about which plants had requested a particular type of assistance, and that department would then send, for example, information on tactics for placing *Steelways* stories in local papers or a list of radio platters available from the institute.[27]

These visits demonstrated the need for H&K assistance if the community program were to make any significant headway on improving steel's relationship with the public. One vice-president told Purcell his Pennsylvania company was not interested in participation because the company was not "well liked," entirely missing the point of a CR program. Management resistance was another stumbling block. The same executive said, "it will not be easy to change the thinking of management," which had a "firm policy against a plant publication" and opposed other tenets of CR. Hill and Knowlton's Russell Crenshaw plotted ways to help the general manager and industrial relations manager for a New York company sell the program to top management. "They want us to send them material such as all of our booklets," Crenshaw reported, "so that they can use them on" their employer. Although the program eventually became quite popular, agency executives first had a significant sales job to overcome company resistance.[28]

Next, H&K distributed "Elements of a Steel Company's Community Relations Program," a chart with nine areas of CR activity. These were employee communication, booklet distribution, civic activity, community publicity and program planning, open-house programs, radio-television-film, annual reports, school programs, and institutional advertising. The agency prepared a "how-to-do-it" booklet for each of the nine areas, offering suggestions on using institute services or materials and on preparing them locally. For example, the employee communication component included meetings, direct mail, posters, plant magazines, and *The Editor's Assistant*, a newsletter for editors that included editorial and feature material prepared by H&K. The television program consisted mainly of offering steel films for play at the local station's convenience, a plan that was quite effective because, the historian James Baughman explains, "most channels aired just about any film footage they could find" in the late 1940s. Suggestions for the school program included use of booklets and films, tours, lectures, scholarships, provision of material to libraries, and more. Assistance from H&K's experts complemented the supply of materials.[29]

H&K then installed field agents in steelmaking centers Cleveland, Pittsburgh, and Chicago, facilitating better access to experienced public relations counsel for companies located far from New York City, both geographically and in terms of public relations sophistication. The agency explained it would help "the individual companies in handling the phases of community relations activities" and in developing "programs and special events for each of them." By the mid-1950s, field representatives were expected to call on each steel company at least four times a year.[30]

The public relations audit, introduced in 1950, completed H&K's community relations program for the steel industry. The agency explained the audit's purposes:

A. To determine the extent and effectiveness of a company's public and community relations.
B. To suggest methods for improvement.
C. To recommend for management's consideration an immediate and a long term public relations course of action for that company.

The audit provided a thorough examination of every aspect of a company's relations with its publics. An audit team visited each site and conducted hundreds of confidential interviews with everyone from local union leaders to journalists and cab drivers to employees' family members, covering such topics as safety, supervision, job security, working conditions, company publications, and sources of information about the corporation. The auditors also reviewed all printed materials, such as annual reports and employee publications, and assessed site policies and conditions—all at no fee.[31]

The CR program did not displace the AISI's national campaign. Newspaper advertising composed a major part of the institute's plan to reach the general public. In the year following 1 May 1947, H&K produced fourteen ads for the industry, with themes that reflected on both problems and accomplishments of the industry. Six presented information on company expansion programs, four stressed the low profit rate of the industry, three demonstrated that steel prices had risen less than prices generally, and one highlighted the industry's technological progress. Publication of *Steelways* and *Steel Facts* continued, as did the farm program, the speakers' bureau, and the publication of booklets, background memoranda, and *The Editor's Assistant*. As the authority on industry statistics, the AISI maintained an important role by providing data to the news media and government officials. The CR program amounted to an addition to the overall public relations mix of the steel industry.[32]

Although the AISI public relations program changed during 1947, it continued to involve broad dissemination of steel's opinions rather than facilitation of two-way communication between the industry and its publics. "As a change of pace from the usual technique of thanking itself for its benefits to the community, it may be well for a corporation to thank the public for its patronage," one PR critic said in 1946. H&K paid no heed to such advice, insisting that "large segments of the population remained uninformed about the industry or misinformed." "The purpose of the expanded program," a year-end report explained, "is to inform and enlighten the public regarding the steel industry," with national and local programs that complemented each other. "The country-wide program carries the story of steel's advancement to the public generally. In local communities, the individual company tells the story to its own employees and to the communities in which both company and employees live and work." Thus, the new CR materials focused on providing the industry's point of view, changing only in reference to the groups targeted.[33]

The First-Person Effect

Once established, H&K's expanded postwar program was quite popular with many of AISI's member corporations. The field representatives, John Hill reported, "found a sincere desire on the part of member companies to build up good relations in their respective communities." The agents made nearly 300 personal calls on member companies within the first year of the program. By July 1948 twenty-eight steel companies had received help on open-house programs and thirty-three others were in the planning stages, fifteen sponsored the educational radio series on local stations, thirty-five improved or started new employee newsletters, twelve asked for assistance with their annual reports, forty-six had made wider use of institute materials, and twenty-four increased their circulation of *Steelways*.[34]

Member companies also liked the public relations audit. Hill and Knowlton's new program involved a major commitment from the companies. A

February 1951 audit of Crucible Steel included trips to each of the corpora-tion's sites, including New York and Pennsylvania mills, a coal mine, river-boat operations, and four branch offices. Over 1,500 personnel were inter-viewed. Auditors had access to every employee and had the support of management, which had to request the service and then provide employees with the time to participate in the sometimes extensive procedure. The PR executives who analyzed Crucible's Park Works communication system, for example, found that job security concerned workers most, that safety prob-lems existed, and that ineffective communication processes meant that most workers got their information from the union. Despite the commitment the audits entailed, many companies participated in the program—ten in the first year, with about twenty others expressing interest.[35]

More important than its popularity is whether CR had any effect on the publics targeted in the local communities. *Steelways* editor Merrick Jackson reported that of the first eight companies to conduct an audit, six had "acted favorably on one or more of the recommendations," but the agency appar-ently took no steps to measure the effectiveness of the new or improved em-ployee newsletters, annual reports, open houses, or other communication tactics. In a fourth-year review of the program, executives compared the number of companies undertaking various categories of activities, such as speeches or publications, not changes in attitude or behavior of plant-town residents. If Crucible took steps to improve the safety of the Park Works bil-let yard, described in H&K's report as a "death trap," then certainly some good came of the program, and undoubtedly employees felt better about the company than they had before. However, because it did not conduct evalua-tion, the agency had no way of judging the effectiveness of the program.[36]

In contrast, H&K carefully examined the influence another aspect of the AISI program, *Steelways*. In 1949, the magazine won a top award from the International Council of Industrial Editors, and, more importantly, a 1955 Starch survey of readers, cited earlier, showed remarkable success for a trade journal. The agency kept close track of feature stories that appeared as re-prints in general interest magazines, meaning the stories reached readers of such publications as *Reader's Digest*, *Science Digest*, and even State Depart-ment publications, in addition to its regular mailing list. Furthermore, up-ward of seventy universities and colleges used the magazine in courses ranging from industrial arts to engineering. According to editor Jackson, an average of twenty-two requests to reprint material came for each issue. None of this means that readers had been convinced by what the agency had written, but the fact that almost two-thirds of *Steelways* readers in the Starch survey had filed the last issue for reference speaks volumes. At least some of the opinion leaders targeted by the agency had found something in the journal's columns worth saving.[37]

Thus, available evidence suggested that opinion leaders, whom H&K believed the most important recipients of industry materials, were influenced by the national program; about the community program there is no evidence. Because CR was well liked by company heads, the institute continued to fund it, even though there was apparently no concrete proof of its effectiveness. Why would steelmakers favor a program without any evidence that it worked?

It is likely that a "first-person effect" governed institute behavior regarding the community relations program. The third-person effect, described by W. Phillips Davison, suggests that people at times base their decisions on the assumption that a media message will have an effect on other people, even if there is no evidence to support the assumption. According to Davison, "this hypothesis predicts that people will tend to overestimate the influence that mass communications have on the attitudes and behavior of others." "I don't believe it," a person might say upon seeing an advertisement, "but I'm sure others will." In this case the managers themselves believed the messages were effective and thus assumed others would be affected in the same way: "I believe it, so others will, too." H&K did not have to justify CR's budget, as it did certain other parts of the public relations program, like national advertising or the trade magazine, to AISI members. Perhaps CR *was* effective. Certainly H&K executives thought it was a useful supplement to the overall program. But the agency had to balance what it considered the best strategy, targeting opinion leaders, with the strategy desired by the client regardless of its effectiveness. "Oftentimes, the question of effectiveness is sheer irrelevance," public relations critic Irwin Ross wrote in 1959; "what is important is not what the PR practitioner does for the client, but what the client *thinks* he does."[38]

By 1949 the CR program had begun to pay dividends to industry public relations. H&K field representatives held nearly 500 meetings with company members, assisting with 1,700 speeches and visits by 73,000 people on plant tours and 313,000 at open houses. This assistance bred familiarity that proved useful during the 1949 labor negotiations, which focused primarily on insurance and other employee benefits. Several company PR directors, including John Ubinger of National Steel in Pittsburgh and Ned Bowerfind of Republic in Cleveland, helped with industrywide activities in addition to representing their own companies during the fact-finding hearings Truman had ordered, including sitting in on advisory group meetings with H&K executives, while U.S. Steel's John McDonald offered suggestions on a booklet, *Facts behind the Steel Strike*. In return, the field men explained the special strike program to member companies, offered assistance on developing materials (including writing letters to editors of newspapers that published unfavorable editorials), and provided the facilities of the Washington office to company officials who were testifying before the fact-finding board. Agents made numerous suggestions for local activities, ranging from letters to employees to radio appearances and community advertisements and meetings, and such member companies as Columbia Steel, Inland, and Bethlehem followed through on one or all of the suggestions. In addition to informing interested parties about each company's position, this emphasis on the local helped the industry with its lobbying efforts, because H&K's New York office insisted "it is desirable that each Congressman *not* be handed identical materials by each and all of the companies making calls." John Hill received numerous letters in praise of the field men, whose popularity only grew with time.[39]

The Client as Consumer

The CR program was not simply a result of an internal crisis. Institute directors by no means rubber-stamped every request made by the agency, and they would not have approved CR if its only purpose had been to improve H&K's hold on their account. Furthermore, the overall institute public relations program had just begun to expand. In June 1948, for example, Hill and Knowlton considered creating a special department for production of materials on steel for teachers, an idea it successfully pitched to institute directors. Eventually the program included hiring educators as full-time consultants (most notably Dr. Albert L. Ayers, who in 1953 joined the firm from a position as associate director of the Joint Council on Economic Education), holding conferences for teachers, and cooperating with textbook publishers, as well as providing classroom materials. This inventive program suggests that increasing commitment to public relations made by the institute might have resulted in greater community participation as well.[40]

However, the exact form that the program took, especially with its emphasis on field agent visits, was a direct result of the complaints made by a handful of unhappy steel managers. The agency retained its role in client policy making, not only of the AISI but at times even of its member companies. In 1950 executives called on various companies' board meetings, such as when John Mapes, Lee Sellers, and Gordon Growden visited Atlantic Steel in Atlanta. Nevertheless, the 1947 crisis reveals that the client played a reciprocal role in the policy making of the agency.[41]

Client considerations probably contributed to other aspects of the steel PR program, too. A major institute project during the late 1940s was the restoration of the first ironworks in North America, located in Saugus, Massachusetts. Hill and Knowlton wrote a history of the works, which had first begun production in 1643, and publicized the renovation and the opening of the site to the public. The project, undertaken primarily for educational purposes, carried an element of prestige for the manufacturers, who could now trace their roots as community and industrial leaders back three centuries. H&K executives may have learned to watch for opportunities like the discovery of the Saugus works to try to please the client even while contributing to the overall public relations objectives of the industry. In the same vein, the agency made it a point to consult more than the few top industrialists on the AISI public relations committee about its program. On at least one occasion field agents asked steel executives for their opinions on an advertisement on profits prepared by the agency. Most liked the ad and ordered reprints, but some did offer negative feedback, which the agency took seriously. Finally, Hill and Knowlton took steps to keep member company officials informed on the successes of agency efforts. After Admiral Ben Moreell of Jones and Laughlin testified before the Presidential Steel Board and the Senate Banking and Policy Committee in 1949, for instance, H&K sent several packets of press clippings to Moreell. Client opinions simply could not be ignored.[42]

Day in and day out, as other clients came and went, Hill and Knowlton continued to serve the steel account. For the most part, work for the institute was pedestrian—distribution of industry statistics, contact with journalists, production of *Steelways* and *Steel Facts*, preparation of speeches and booklets, and so forth. During the 1960s the agency took an increasing role in product promotion. Only during labor negotiations, which occurred every three years, did work on the steel account get truly exciting—and, given their predictability and the fact that the institute never directly handled collective bargaining, sometimes not even then. Fascinating or otherwise, H&K held its flagship account firmly in hand for about thirty years, perhaps in part because of the lesson it learned in 1947.

PART TWO

Influencing Discourse

CHAPTER FOUR

The Great Margarine Controversy

Public Relations and Politics

I n 1949 *Gourmet* magazine published a cartoon depicting a baseball player missing an easy catch, while a fan screamed, "Oleomargarine fingers!" A year later Jimmy Durante sat down to breakfast, telling Don Ameche, "Hand me two pieces of bread." Ameche responded, "There. Are you going to put on some oleomargarine?" to which Durante retorted, "Oleomargarine nothin'! I'm gonna use that new stuff, substitute just approved by the government—butter." Durante's radio audience roared with laughter.[1]

Margarine and its country cousin, butter, became national objects of derision because from 1948 to 1950 they sat at the center of controversy in the U.S. Congress in a battle that ranged from ridiculous to absurd. At issue: repeal of federal regulations that had governed the sale of oleo since 1886, especially the heavy tax and color restrictions that seriously inhibited the sale of yellow margarine. Among other oddities, members of Congress pronounced eulogies over "the old milk cow," brandished a plastic replica of a Guernsey on the House floor, and threatened to move a calf, a cow, and a farmer's daughter into the House office building. As with the aviation account, the client's goals seemed to contradict Hill's antiregulation philosophy, but agents argued that the margarine monopoly constituted an unfair threat to butter producers, thus violating the spirit of fair competition that free enterprise entailed. Perhaps the opportunity to employ many of the arguments that had so often been used against the steel industry was irresistible. Whatever their reasons, even the sometimes stodgy Hill and Knowlton executives joined in the butter-versus-oleo antics, resorting to such tactics as hiring detectives to investigate "butterlegging" in Indianapolis and trying to organize a cow parade.[2]

These unusual tactics notwithstanding, H&K did affect the outcome of the oleo debate. It did so not by influencing discourse in Congress, although executives did assist elected officials by providing information to be used in their speeches, or by changing public opinion. Instead, H&K influenced most its own client by urging the butter lobby to alter its policy to a compromise position that in turn changed legislators' goals. Zeroing in on the color ban, which was politically more acceptable than taxation, Hill and Knowlton changed the debate about oleo and butter and therefore, indirectly, affected political action.

Congress and Hill and Knowlton
Take Up the Oleo Controversy

Hill and Knowlton's political experience with the aircraft manufacturers made it a good choice for the embattled dairy industry. The agency had grown significantly since its founding. Its clients included the National Fertilizer Association, National Retail Dry Goods Association, American Shipbuilders Council, Soap and Glycerine Producers, and Hewitt-Robins. The Washington office made the agency particularly attractive to the butter client, which, comprising three groups, the American Butter Institute, National Cooperative Milk Producers Federation, and National Creameries Association, together represented virtually all dairy farmers and about a quarter of the total population of American farmers.[3]

In the spring of 1948, flush from the victory of the favorable Finletter and congressional board recommendations, Hill and Knowlton rapidly discovered that guns were much easier to promote than butter. Oleo had been invented in 1869 by a French chemist, but, because it looked, felt, and tasted awful, it had been tagged the "poor man's butter." By the late 1940s that image was changing. New formulas and production processes made oleo increasingly palatable, even as its price remained substantially lower than butter's, and poverty during the Great Depression and butter shortages during World War II had forced many to sample the improved product. Standard brands pure enough to gain consumer confidence appeared, Parkay in 1937 and Blue Bonnet in 1943. Commonly believed more natural and healthy, butter lost another advantage when margarine manufacturers began to fortify their product with Vitamin A, and a scientific study demonstrated that margarine consumption did not harm children's growth. These factors combined with shortages of butter and its high cost after the war to give the oleo manufacturers tremendous momentum.[4]

Dissension among farmers also caused problems for the dairy interests. Margarine manufacturers began to use domestic oils exclusively, in part to gain the support of cottonseed oil and soybean farmers in the South and Midwest, and the American Soybean Association officially backed the National Association of Margarine Manufacturers' (NAMM) drive for repeal in 1946. Some of the largest butter makers, notably meatpacking companies, also produced margarine and refused to support butter. A 1948 Gallup survey indicated that 39 percent of farmers in the sample favored repeal of oleo taxes. Even dairy farmers shared a sense of defeatism. As early as November 1947 the head of the Butter Institute charged many processors with having resigned themselves to the loss of butter's place in the industry, and the Milk Industry Foundation hesitated to join the fight on behalf of butter. "The prevailing attitude of the press toward the butter case is so antagonistic," the foundation's director of information explained, that other farmers feared participation "would merely draw the wrath of the press down on themselves."[5]

Journalists and citizens alike demonstrated support for repeal of the tax and color ban. Stirred to action by Selvage and Lee, the margarine manufacturers' public relations counsel, national magazines such as *Better Homes and Gardens, Business Week, Harper's, Newsweek, Reader's Digest,* and *Time* all published pro-oleo articles. *Life* reported that housewives could save $6 million and 88 million "woman hours" a year in the kitchen if they could buy margarine that had already been colored yellow. (Consumers had to add coloring to white margarine by stirring it in greasy mixing bowls before molding and refrigerating it, or purchase special squeeze bags which, when mishandled, burst—"all over the kitchen," according to one dairyman.) Dairy farmers accused local newspapers likewise with favoring oleo over butter, and NBC's H. V. Kaltenborn suggested that his listeners write to their representatives in support of oleo, adding, "I urge my wife to buy margarine because I don't like this unfair discrimination." Opinion polls showed that the majority of the public favored the repeal, and groups like the Consumer's Union demanded an end to the regulations. If consumers voted with their dollars, then even in Wisconsin margarine enjoyed high approval ratings.[6]

Confronted with such strong opposition among the media and public, Hill and Knowlton could only hope that political advocates would save butter. Yet by the time the dairy groups retained the agency, political lines had been drawn. Members of the GOP-controlled Congress introduced upward of fifteen bills calling for repeal in 1948, and a coalition of urban and southern representatives, mostly Democrats, lined up for oleo, while those from the agricultural states of the Midwest and many cornbelt Republicans favored protection of butter. Intense interest on both sides made for a labyrinthine passage of the one oleo bill that survived the House.

Representative Mendel Rivers, Democrat of South Carolina, refused to allow his repeal effort to founder in the election-year politics of March 1948. Rivers persuaded his colleagues to sign a petition to discharge the bill, which had stalled in the House Agriculture Committee. The necessary number of signatures was accumulated on 1 April—something the dairy interests had assumed could never happen because legislators usually eschewed petition in the interest of getting along. The tenor of the debate in the House typified the oleo fight in general. "The American baby was threatened with loss of milk, and eulogies were solemnly pronounced on 'the old milk cow and what she means to America,'" the *Nation* reported. Despite H&K's hurried attempts to gather support for the dairy position, the House passed the Rivers bill, 260 to 106. Rivers claimed that it marked the first step in the emancipation of housewives from their mixing bowls.[7]

The 1948 Emergency Campaign

H&K executives lacked enough time to develop a campaign to influence the House vote, but, under the supervision of John G. Mapes in New York, they put together a temporary program for the rapid enlistment of political support to delay a vote in the Senate, where Finance Committee hearings on the bill would begin in May. Hill and Knowlton assumed that mobilization of the dairy industry would demonstrate the "immense political importance" of farmers. For $6,000 a month the agency would work to gain the support of allied groups including the feed and supply industries; campaign to reach editorial writers and columnists; release a national press statement in Washington; sponsor a series of radio talks by sympathetic legislators; publish a booklet on the importance of the tax for dairy industry survival; and conduct a market survey of "margarine deceptions." H&K counseled dairy leaders on ways to get others involved and prepared numerous written materials, including a "how-to" manual for local organizers. This explained how to call a meeting; provided speech material, form resolutions for groups to approve, and model press releases; and described how to write letters to congressional representatives and get local press coverage for meetings. *"This is an election year,"* Charles Ellsworth reminded other staff members. If the vote could be postponed, he said, a "Butter Is Better" campaign might turn things around. "Meanwhile, the idea is to hang onto that yellow color."[8]

Hill and Knowlton's emergency plan emphasized several themes, first and foremost the importance of butter to the dairy industry as a whole. Fluid milk prices would go up, the public should be warned, if farmers could not rely on using surplus milk to make butter. Because cows produce more milk during the summer than in other seasons, there must be either a surplus in summer or a deficit the rest of the year, and butter was the "balance wheel" of the industry. The reason for preventing margarine manufacturers from coloring their product yellow was to stop margarine fraud, not to inhibit sales. Last, the farmers themselves were a selling point. They were depicted as the typical American farm family fighting the evil Wall Street monopolists who controlled the margarine industry.[9]

With the campaign underway, H&K realized almost immediately that the drive for farmer participation would require significantly more energy from the agency than the "Air Power Is Peace Power" campaign had. John Hill wrote to the heads of the three dairy groups only a few weeks after the campaign started, saying, "it appears unlikely that the program as now conceived will produce as much help from the grass roots as we should all like to see." He proposed sending more H&K agents into the field, paying all expenses to bring dairy farm wives or members of ladies' auxiliaries to Washington, and intensifying efforts to get local cooperatives and creameries to run a series of advertisements the agency had prepared. In November the firm hired a full-time representative to take the butter story personally to editors of small newspapers across the nation.[10]

Because the grass-roots campaign reaped little reward, the farmers had to depend on dairy-state senators to kill the oleo measure. They did their best. Michigan's Arthur Vandenberg, the president pro tempore, referred the bill to the Agriculture Committee, where it was sure to languish. But the Senate overruled him and sent the bill to the Committee on Finance. Perhaps one result of H&K's temporary campaign, which had urged participation by state and regional leaders, farm and club women, gourmet chefs, and "three or four average dirt farmers," was that Finance received more than 100 requests from butter producers and processors to appear at the hearings. After just two days of hearings, the committee reported out favorably on the Rivers bill, with an amendment requiring proper labeling and display in restaurants. But dairy lawmakers were not willing to admit defeat.[11]

Dairy-state representatives used every available strategy to stop the bill from reaching the Senate floor. Republicans tried a party appeal to convince leaders in the Senate to postpone consideration of the issue. Wisconsin Representative Reid F. Murray, for instance, pointed out to members of the Senate Policy Committee that his state had "the largest solid Republican delegation in the Congress." Dairy senators emphasized that more important issues—an antilynching bill, housing, and federal aid to education—also shared the docket, and that, in an election year, the senators would not want to alienate voters. They threatened a filibuster, for which Hill and Knowlton began to prepare speech material, and in fact Wisconsin's Alexander Wiley, although caught unprepared, issued oleo's death blow by talking through the entire period allotted for discussion of the repeal on one of the final days of the Senate's session.[12]

When the Senate failed to vote on the repeal issue, Hill and Knowlton claimed victory, saying, "the odds against gaining any success for the cause of butter in that emergency appeared slight indeed" in April. "However, the tactics recommended and subsequently carried out were, along with the legislative logjam, successful in ending the emergency, at least temporarily." The dairy organizations had evaded the immediate crisis by a whisker, or, more accurately, by the length of Wiley's impromptu filibuster.[13]

Regrouping: H&K
Urges a Policy Change

Farmers and PR agents alike recognized the victory as "no more than a breathing spell," so the executives moved quickly to develop a long-range plan. They outlined three basic objectives for the dairy industry: retaining regulation of oleo, regaining goodwill for the butter and dairy industry lost during the battle, and generating support for long-term measures. But, in a statement to the dairy farm leaders, H&K insisted that the industry needed a firm policy on oleo before a program could succeed. "A measure prohibiting the use of artificial color in any table spread, enforced by Food and Drug Administration and not by taxes, may be the most supportable position to take," the report concluded.[14]

As early as April 1948 Hill and Knowlton executives had urged the butter lobby to change its policy from a defensive to a more proactive stance, which they could accomplish by focusing on the potential for fraudulent sale of margarine as butter. "If we analyze the dilemma that faced us when oleomargarine producers insisted on their rights, it became necessary for us to defend our position if we were to get anything less than outright repeal of taxes and the free privilege of absolute imitation," an H&K staff member wrote in a memorandum. "It would seem to me that our strategy at this point should be to try to win our equal rights and let the oleomargarine people define how far it goes." Put another way, the butter lobby should agree to the repeal of the oleo tax, but should also insist that those who wanted butter should be assured they were getting it, not the cheap imitation. Then, when the margarine tax was repealed, dairy groups could claim victory, because they would have both urged repeal and gained safeguards against fraud.[15]

Emphasis on margarine fraud in restaurants and stores was a good strategy. It had been a real problem during the early part of the twentieth century, indeed had been one of the reasons for establishing the color ban in the first place. Most people preferred their table spread colored yellow, but an H&K survey found that more than half the sample believed some restaurants would serve yellow margarine while claiming it was butter, and two-thirds wished to be told which it was. Finally, surveys of restaurants did find significant fraud, up to one-third serving margarine when the customer asked specifically for butter. H&K blamed even families, who were wont to ask one another to "pass the butter" when the dish on the table contained margarine.[16]

But H&K's emphasis on butterlegging, "the passing off of colored oleo as butter, at butter prices," in grocery stores was misleading, as their own investigation made clear. In November 1948 H&K hired Pinkerton detectives to go to stores and ask for butter, which the clerk wrapped and handed to the detective, who then took it to a chemist for analysis. A week-long survey in Indianapolis turned up not one case of margarine fraud. Instead, it found three cases where the butter contained some combination of rodent hair and excreta, insect larva and viscera, and cinder. That undoubtedly contributed to the decision not to make the survey public.[17]

Dairy leaders initially resisted bringing up the issue of color, and only when the seriousness of the situation finally sank in did they adopt Hill and Knowlton's recommended course of action. In September 1948 Charles Holman, butter's chief lobbyist, believed oleo had enough votes to put over the repealer if it came to the Senate floor, and a change in policy would require dairy senators to allow the bill through, at which point, he predicted, oleo senators would remove any protection for butter. Bert Goss, finding Holman's estimate "sound," recommended that the agency "had better go along," at least during the first round of the battle in Congress. However, all signs pointed toward another showdown in 1949, and it became increasingly clear that butter would have to offer some compromise or lose altogether. When local organizations heard about the new "no tax, no color" proposal, finally advanced by H&K's three-group dairy client on 27 October 1948, they quickly endorsed it, as did editors of dairy publications.[18]

If the new policy proved popular with many farm organizations, margarine manufacturers were less pleased. Paul Truitt, head of the NAMM, called it "entirely unacceptable," because it provided "no relief to the house-wives," and sought only "to confuse the issue." He called butter's stake on the color yellow "ridiculous," but added, "we are glad to have the represen-tatives of the butter interests publicly admit they have been wrong about margarine." Although oleo makers suggested no company should control a color, the new strategy caught them literally red-handed, because Unilever, the world's largest margarine manufacturer, had just won a court case ap-propriating red for its soap, Lifebuoy.[19]

The NAMM's reaction put butter on the offensive for the first time. But-ter had made a major concession, but margarine insisted on imitating its competitor, a fact exploited by the dairy industry in ads and a background memorandum. Nevertheless, disinterested observers pushed for "no mar-garine compromise," and even some in the dairy industry agreed with the margarine manufacturers. "Why bother about whether the oleo boys color their stuff yellow?" the American Butter and Cheese Review asked. "We are convinced that the butter—and dairy—industries are fighting a losing battle on their present course." Another dairy journal added that the oleo situation "continues to be handled about as poorly from a P.R. standpoint as it is possible to handle an issue."[20]

Despite some criticism, Hill and Knowlton detected a softening in oppo-sition to butter following the policy change. However, the agency still faced an uphill climb. "Some newspapers and other oleo fellow travelers," Hoard's Dairyman reported with a straight face, "have either innocently or inten-tionally misinterpreted the new dairy stand." Even Elsie the Cow was too busy to hold a press conference in opposition of oleo, as H&K requested.[21]

The 1949 Campaign

More encouraging for dairy interests was that Hill and Knowlton's ambi-tious long-term program was in full swing by 1949. It encompassed state organizational work, including print and radio advertising, editorial confer-ences between local farm leaders and journalists, national publicity, a speak-ers program, and a straw poll of politicians' views; preparation of such lit-erature as a booklet on economics and background memoranda on fraud, butter costs, and prices; and an educators' program, which would explain butter's position as the "balance wheel" that used up surplus during the summer. The agency also continued to impress upon members of Congress the importance of dairy's position. Goss suggested to Charles Holman that to dramatize the potential for fraud, the industry should consider introducing a bill that would permit the sale and restaurant use of horsemeat under conditions identical to those permitted oleo under the House bill—coloring, preservatives, and flavoring all allowed. Holman rejected the idea, but H&K did use a display at the 1949 House Agriculture Committee hearings that compared butter and oleo, real milk and filled milk, beef and horsemeat under a banner that read, "Which twin is the phoney?"[22]

Dairy-state lawmakers renewed their battle with vigor when the oleo bill came up again in 1949. The House Agriculture Committee reported out H.R. 2023, which repealed the tax but only for intrastate commerce, essentially ruling out colored margarine. At that point Representative William R. Poage, Democrat of Texas, offered a straight repeal amendment that contained none of the protections the farmers demanded. Poage's repeal bill survived the House, but in comparison to the 1948 Rivers bill it passed by a narrower margin, and debate on the House floor had been furious. It seems likely, as H&K contended, that the new policy offered a middle ground for some members of Congress—just not enough to defeat the bill altogether.[23]

Once again the possibility of removing the "domestic tariff," as a Finance Committee witness termed it, hinged on the Senate. To counter the Poage bill sent up by the House, dairy-state senators offered the Gillette-Wiley amendment, which removed taxes on all white oleo and on yellow margarine produced and sold intrastate. H&K promoted it in advertisements, booklets, and news releases, claiming that the provisions would protect consumer, farmer, and oleo maker alike. They also prepared statements and collected information for use at the Finance hearings.[24]

Senate Finance hearings quickly took on the air of farce. "At most of the sessions," one of the PR executives reported, "only a lone senator was in attendance." The hearings were hardly worth attending. Testifying before the panel, Representative Reid Murray of Wisconsin informed committee chair Walter F. George that Murray's wife considered George one of her "favorite senators," and Senator Edward J. Thye of Minnesota kept his colleagues spellbound with tales of the various types of butter churns his family had used over the years.[25]

Hill and Knowlton added to the theatrical air of the hearings with new revelations regarding the Unilever monopoly and, Perry Mason–like, by identifying oleo's star witness as an impostor. The monopoly argument, so often leveled against H&K's clients rather than on their behalf, was compelling. In 1949 the top four manufacturers of oleo produced about half the nation's supply. Unilever, featured in a 1947–48 *Fortune* series that freely accused the conglomerate of monopolistic practices, produced 40 percent of the world's margarine. In comparing the Big Four with 2.5 million dairy farmers, H&K was not being entirely fair. Butter was made in factories and cooperatives, not on the farm, and had been since the mid-nineteenth century. Still, Glen Householder of the Purebred Dairy Cattle Association caused a mild sensation when he introduced a cable from London revealing that John Jelke Co., a Unilever margarine subsidiary, had plans to expand to all forty-eight states, after Jelke's representative had tried to downplay the company's size and significance.[26]

H&K's other coup came when it investigated Merritt W. Nash, who claimed to be a dairy farmer from Fall City, Washington, and who told the committee that dairy farmers found the butter legislation embarrassing. "So glib, so transparently a phony" was this witness that H&K asked Charles Holman to contact an associate in Seattle, who found that Nash was not a typical farmer but had a degree in advertising and managed a luxury ranch owned by the Stetson hat company. Holman's colleague telephoned the wire services in Seattle with the information that Nash did not speak for Washington farmers and telegraphed the Senate committee to the same effect, much to the chagrin of oleo interests.[27]

Still, the margarine lobby had lined up impressive endorsements, including the American Federation of Labor, American Home Economics Association, National Association of Consumers, and the National Association of Retail Grocers. Representatives of these and other organizations appeared or sent messages to the Senate Finance Committee to urge repeal of the tax and color restrictions. Not unexpectedly, the committee supported repeal without the Gillette-Wiley amendment, and butter once again faced a vote in the Senate. Dairy leaders hoped that the grass-roots campaign had stirred more interest in protection of the industry.[28]

The Grass Roots

Wisconsin

Wisconsin, a state where half of the farm income was derived from milk and the stiffest state antimargarine law was on the books, seems the most likely place that H&K's campaign would have succeeded. Dairy groups like the Wisconsin Creameries Association (WCA) had notable control over state policy. The WCA's political effectiveness later led a political scientist to include it on a list of organizations that had "exerted significant influence on regulations" within the state. An affiliate of the National Creameries Association, the WCA consisted of cooperative creameries, where farmers pooled their supply of cream and hired a manager to produce and sell the butter. However, a review of the activities of the WCA shows that H&K's campaign had only mixed results on the state and local level.[29]

Strange though it may seem, the local farm groups apparently had no understanding of the immense role H&K played in their campaign. The WCA newsletter never mentioned the agency or the existence of any outside counsel, but it did criticize oleo on more than one occasion for its campaign. When a NAMM-inspired editorial in an Illinois paper resulted in a flood of letters to an Illinois senator, WCA officers editorialized, "such 'inspired' mail being received by Senator Lucas is a direct result of this selfish, press agent program being promoted by the oleo association." Meanwhile, Hill and Knowlton planned similar activities for the dairy interests. The WCA's officers also thanked Russell Fifer, of the American Butter Institute, for the tip on the source of Lucas's mail—information that was probably unearthed by Hill and Knowlton. Along the same line, they mentioned that a fraud investigation was underway, but it seems doubtful that the farmers knew they had hired Pinkertons to go butter shopping in Indiana.[30]

Officials of the WCA did understand their own role in protecting butter, but Wisconsin's campaign was not nearly as extensive as H&K executives had intended. The group's secretary-treasurer published an article demanding tax repeal with color protection, but in a journal directed toward an audience of other dairy farmers. The WCA newsletter regularly urged members to write to their representatives in Congress and commented on radio and press coverage of the issue, but H&K's packet of speeches, editorials, and articles resulted in apparently limited use. The WCA's officers sent members a copy of a Dairy Industry Committee pamphlet, which they recommended be added to the speaker's kit, and mentioned that they had copies of a speech, "Butter vs. Imitations," available on request.[31]

The WCA did reprint in full the H&K background memorandum on the new butter policy for its membership, but for these association members it was an old idea. At the WCA's annual meeting the dairy farmers had passed a resolution on 29 September calling for the repeal of taxes if the color ban held—a month before H&K released the "new" policy in Washington—and some cooperatives had advocated that position months earlier. Association president R. M. Steinhauer concluded that the majority of creamery owners and operators felt the same way, but only the WCA supported a bill to repeal oleo taxes in Wisconsin's legislature in 1949.[32]

Although not as extensive as it could have been, the campaign did have its successes. Local groups passed resolutions in support of the farmers, all of which were passed on to the state's senior senator. Alexander Wiley dutifully read many such resolutions before the Senate or placed them in the *Congressional Record.* One, from a farmers' organization in Barron County, where Wiley owned a farm, specifically backed the National Milk Producers Federation's demand for a ban on the sale of yellow oleo. Similarly, the

Wisconsin Guernsey Breeders' Association resolution praised the dairy industry for its stand on repeal of taxes, which it contrasted with "the oleo monopoly" and its "unfair trade practice of consumer deception by coloring their product in imitation of butter." Another allied organization pledged a dollar per member to help fight the oleo repeal. Editorials likewise provided ammunition for Wiley. Articles from the leading dairy publication, *Hoard's Dairyman*, published in Wisconsin, as well as from small-town papers, insisted that only butter should be yellow. The state also produced many witnesses for the congressional committees investigating the oleo issue.[33]

But the WCA also had difficulties, beginning with money. Association leaders had to beg for financial contributions that they had promised to the national organization, so its newsletter, more than anything else, asked for money—more even than it requested members to write to their congressional representatives. In early February association leaders reported that most of the creameries had failed to pay their levies of twenty cents per thousand pounds of butterfat handled by each plant. By April they had collected $8,500 of their original goal of $10,000–20,000. Finally, in December, the officers asked creameries to pay a dollar for each of its patrons, which by the following month had evolved into a checkoff system, where the creamery simply deducted the contribution from farmers' checks.[34]

Worse, some Wisconsin groups came out in favor of yellow oleo. The Wisconsin division of the American Association of University Women went on the record in support of tax repeal because oleo was nutritious and the taxes discriminatory. The Wisconsin Retail Food Dealers Association, based in Milwaukee, favored repeal both in the state and nationally, because of the amount of money its members could save on licensing fees, and a state group called the "Wisconsin Committee for the Repeal of Discriminatory Legislation against Margarine" began a petition drive in 1949, probably as part of the margarine campaign.[35]

Perhaps most startling of all, several Wisconsin newspapers editorialized in favor of tax repeal. "Butter will continue to be in demand to the millions who want it and can afford it," an editorial in the *Milwaukee Journal* argued. "And the dairy industry has other outlets for any loss occasioned by a decrease in the sale of butter." The *Green Bay Press-Gazette* agitated against any tax that protected one state's industry over another's, whether oleo, oil, or sulfur. The *Wisconsin State Journal* in Madison advised the farmers to spend their money promoting the qualities of butter rather than securing government restrictions on margarine. Perhaps the dairy interests took solace in a letter to the editor from Paul Orme, of the WCA, who responded that butter had been yellow for 3,000 years and that the yellow on cabs was protected by law.[36]

Thus, far from securing a deluge of support for the butter makers, H&K's grass-roots campaign had not marshaled unified support even in America's Dairyland. Wisconsin's oleo law did remain on the books until 1967, and even then restrictions included a tax and a ban on serving oleo in schools and restaurants, although patrons of the latter could request it. But H&K's campaign had not been particularly effective.[37]

Rhode Island

Given all the encouragement for letter writing by farm advocates to their lawmakers, a review of congressional mail is another way to measure the success of the campaign. Both dairy groups and publications urged members to write to their representatives in Congress. *Hoard's Dairyman*, the most widely read and respected of dairy publications, conducted a letter-writing crusade that included publication of a list of all senators' names and suggestions on what dairy farmers should include in their letters. One editorial advised farmers to use the telegraph or telephone to impress representatives with their extreme interest. Groups like the WCA also promoted letter writing.[38]

An analysis of one senator's mail shows that the letter-writing campaign provoked inconsequential grass-roots activity. Rhode Island had a small dairy industry but no margarine-making plants. Its senior senator, Democrat J. Howard McGrath, favored repeal, although not particularly strongly. Although studies of congressional mail have found that people most often write to those legislators with whom they agree, dairy farmers might have selected McGrath as one who could be swayed by their political power. In reality, Rhode Island residents showed little interest in the issue. During 1948, McGrath received only twenty-six letters about butter and oleo, and of those just one, from the Providence Sales Committee of the New England Milk Producers Association, opposed repeal.[39]

The volume of McGrath's mail regarding oleo taxation increased after the dairy organizations changed their policy on taxation, but the vast majority of writers still asked McGrath to vote in favor of oleo. Of fifty-two messages received in 1949, seventeen protested an excise tax for beauty and barber shops that had been attached to the oleo measure, compared with three endorsing butter: the Milk and Ice Cream Drivers and Dairy Employees Union; W. D. Knox, an editor at *Hoard's Dairyman*; and Hill and Knowlton's clients. H&K's circular, which included a letter, a background memorandum, and a pamphlet explaining the new dairy policy, was blatant. "The dairy farmer's vote is politically sensitive; Dairy farmers always vote to protect their interests," a headline reminded the senator. It also implied that all mail supporting repeal was tainted by the slippery fingers of margarine manufacturers. The remaining letters all opposed butter. In fact, one butter and cheese company wrote to encourage McGrath to vote for "any legislation that will free oleomargarine from its present restrictions," because, the writer said, the danger of fraud was "small." Two other writers favored repeal simply because they were tired of the butter lobby.[40]

Congress: Discourse on Butter among National Advocates

Lack of constituent pressure despite the grass-roots work meant H&K had to work directly with members of Congress to attempt to influence the political debate. A review of two separate debates in Congress, one in each house, shows the extent to which the agency was able to shape discussion, especially the frames used to explain the situation. The first debate took place in April 1948 when the House took up the issue of discharge of the Rivers bill from the Agriculture Committee, the second previous to the Senate vote in January 1950.

In urging discharge of the bill from the House Agriculture Committee, about a dozen representatives spoke, invoking numerous frames to explain why the tax and color ban should be repealed. The frames most frequently mentioned by the representatives suggested that the tax was discriminatory, a legal frame, and that tax must be repealed because that was what the public wanted, a political frame.[41] Others favored economic frames, arguing that oleo prices would remain low,[42] that even if butter production slowed it would make more whole milk available for consumption,[43] and that given butter shortages and the high cost of living, the tax hurt more Americans than it helped.[44] Two representatives argued from a health frame, noting that margarine was just as nutritious as butter.[45] Finally, five members of Congress took issue with the "protection against fraud" frame, noting that butter makers, like their counterparts in margarine manufacture, also added yellow coloring to their product,[46] and that butter already had protection by federal statute.[47]

An analysis of the Senate discussion, which came at the end of the controversy, indicates that modification in the debate had occurred in the intervening months, with new emphasis on the fraud frame H&K had promoted. The exchange was dominated by Guy Gillette, Democrat of Iowa, for butter, and for oleo, James William Fulbright, Democrat of Arkansas. Gillette began by conceding many of oleo's points. Margarine, he admitted, was "palatable," "wholesome," "nutritious," cost less, and its makers had "a right to sell their product in an untrammeled way in the market place." All of that, he said, went unquestioned. "Then why do they not go ahead and sell it?" he asked. The Gillette-Wiley bill offered that opportunity, but oleo makers, he asserted, wanted to color their product yellow "to usurp the good will and market butter has built up over scores and scores of years."[48]

Oleo advocates, however, repeatedly dismissed the fraud frame. Fulbright told his colleagues that "provisions were included in an effort to satisfy the complaint—which I think was not altogether genuine—that there might be some deception in the local sales, in a restaurant." He noted that some butter makers added yellow coloring "in an attempt to deceive the people and to make them believe that the butter was produced in the summer time when it is naturally yellow," and that butter was the "only product which by special act of Congress is expressly exempted from having the statement made that it is artificially colored." Fulbright also recommended that the dairy farmers should "spend on ascertaining how to can fluid milk half the money they spend on attempting to maintain the present legislation." Then, surplus milk could be used whenever demand increased.[49]

The exchange ended with Gillette's speech, which shows obvious signs of assistance from Hill and Knowlton because it repeated the main points and evidence the agency had advanced throughout the controversy. The senator quoted butter and margarine consumption figures, discussed the oleo giant, Unilever, and its monopoly on red soap, and cited the restaurant survey H&K had authorized for the butter lobby. He concluded by reiterating oleo's good qualities—"the palatability, the cheapness, the wholesomeness, the nutrition of oleomargarine"—and the desire of dairy farmers that the discriminatory taxes be repealed. But the main issue, he said, was "protection or destruction of the outlet for small butter-manufacturing plants."[50]

The debate had changed, but only because butter advocates had conceded so many points: "the palatability, the cheapness, the wholesomeness" of margarine. Hill and Knowlton had influenced political discourse by urging butter's advocates to focus on one issue, color, which forced the opposition to respond. Unfortunately for the farmers, oleo's advocates convincingly rejected that frame.

Repeal with Regulation of Oleo

Oleo senators scored a comparatively easy victory when the issue finally came to a vote in January 1950. Despite Alexander Wiley's adroit manipulation of the system, the only restriction on oleo originating in Wisconsin was the work of that state's junior senator, Republican Joseph R. McCarthy, whose amendment directed the Federal Trade Commission to police oleo advertising. Two other amendments set sanitary standards and required a triangular shape for all oleo, although the latter was dropped in conference. After investigation of various aspects of the issue, the Treasury and Agriculture Departments, Federal Trade Commission, Food and Drug Administration, and Bureau of the Budget all recommended repeal, and President Truman signed the bill into law in March.[51]

The dairy industry did not collapse. Although some butter makers reported losses, the immediate effect was not displacement of butter but overall increase in fat consumption, with both oleo and butter sales increasing. That trend had been apparent as early as July 1948, when a survey by the *Cleveland Press* indicated 70 percent of the families participating in a panel study were buying margarine, and in fact were buying 78 percent more margarine than only six months previously. Margarine production rose from over 614 million pounds in 1945 to 937 million in 1950, while butter producers made about 1.7 billion pounds of butter in 1945 and just over 1.6 billion in 1950. After 1950 butter production slowly decreased while margarine steadily increased. However, the margarine tax did not protect butter, because if denied oleo, some people would turn to other substitutes— lard or oils for cooking, peanut or apple butter for spreads—because of butter's prohibitive price. Most people preferred butter: a Navy test showed 83 percent of sailors preferred butter, compared with only about 3 percent who chose oleo. But many Americans could not find or afford it.[52]

Despite the lack of detrimental effects after the law's passage, the issue for many farmers had been a serious one. When WCA members reported "yellow margarine might be able in ten years to so undermine the butter market as to make it practically impossible to use and market" the butterfat then produced, they were wrong. But they had been genuinely fearful. One survey of Wisconsin farm families showed two-thirds of the sample believed repeal of the oleo tax would lower the price of butterfat, and dairy advocates frequently warned of impending depression. They did not know when, but, like many business forecasters, they believed it would happen.[53]

But not all farmers had been so pessimistic. Many of those encountered by H&K's field representative expressed little concern about imitation products. "They say they will go into the oleo business themselves if they have to," the agent reported, "and match other substitute dairy products as they appear." Others, notably the *American Butter and Cheese Review*, showed a will to fight it out in the market, declaring, "The heck with oleo; let's sell butter on its proven merits!" Finally, as the *Farm Journal* tried to remind its readers, the cheese industry provided another tremendous market for their milk. In fact, its editors suspected the reason for the increasing consumption of margarine was that farmers were putting more surplus milk into cheese. Cheese production slowly increased from 1.12 billion pounds in 1945 to 1.19 billion in 1950, and it continued to rise steadily, possibly contributing to a shortage of butter and therefore demand for substitutes.[54]

H&K and Political Discourse

Although Hill and Knowlton convinced the dairy farmers to focus on a frame that was more politically acceptable, this tactic did not salvage dairy's case—although it did apparently draw the vote closer in the House. Margarine advocates responded by denouncing the fraud frame and by offering sound arguments for other ways of looking at the problem. Representative Thomas Abernathy, Democrat of Mississippi, asserted that butter's demands for a ban on colored oleo, "are simply pleas not to be forced to compete fairly and squarely with the products from the other American farms." And, during the closing days of the controversy, Senator Fulbright trivialized the consumer protection frame by insisting that fraud was not the real issue. Fulbright spent considerable time showing "repeal of the antimargarine laws" would not "injure the dairy industry, much less destroy it." Speaker after speaker found the threat of butter fraud negligible. In the words of one Maryland representative, "evidence on scores of pages of committee testimony refutes this tale" of butter fraud, continuing, "practically all margarine is sold fully packaged and labeled" at the grocery counter, not in restaurants where fraud apparently occurred most often.[55]

Once people had made up their minds, changing their opinions about what constituted the problem proved virtually impossible. Both the media and public—with the exception of some of those connected with the dairy industry—appeared convinced that the problem was the butter lobby's grip on Congress, not oleo fraud, and members of Congress voted with constituent opinion. As a Wisconsin representative told his House colleagues in 1949, "I do not suppose that anything that may be said in this argument will influence a single vote."[56]

H&K had only minute effects on any political group except indirectly through influence on butter's own advocates. The agency's grass-roots campaign put virtually no pressure on senators like McGrath who opposed the tax and color ban. In dealings with probutter members of Congress, executives supplied information for use in speeches and floor debate, but this provided only support—not persuasion. The most effective action taken by H&K executives was their insistence on the new policy that offered some members of Congress a measure of escape. Ohio Republican Robert A. Taft, for one, had expressed early his approval of repeal, but added, "I certainly want to give a complete protection against fraud." However, political maneuvering, especially in conference, weakened even that small victory.[57]

Although the butter lobby did not emerge from the margarine controversy with the outcome it would have preferred, Hill and Knowlton had provided two important services to its client. Representative Herman C. Andreson, the Republican from Minnesota who had threatened to bring a calf, cow, and farmer's daughter into the House office building, termed the new law "a complete victory" for the "oleo trust." But Hill and Knowlton characterized the vote as win for butter (and, not coincidentally, for the agency), because the law made concessions to dairy farmers to protect consumers, specifically the sanitation and advertising regulations. That was true, but executives acknowledged also that "oleomargarine interests and their editorial adherents will proclaim their victory." However, the minor restrictions on oleo may have been the lesser of the services the public relations agency provided.[58]

Given that several Wisconsin organizations and dairy publications urged tax repeal before H&K convinced top dairy officials to do the same, it seems likely the leaders had lost touch with their own organizations. Perhaps because of the 1947 steel situation, when H&K executives realized that not all AISI member companies were happy with the program that the largest companies had approved, Hill and Knowlton agents were particularly sensitive to the importance of contact with all client members, not just organization leaders. This understanding helped the agency to realign member needs with organization activities. One field agent reported some dissatisfaction with the Washington office of the Milk Producers Federation, leading Charles Ellsworth to suggest in December 1949 that the agency plan a questionnaire for members once the Senate vote had taken place. "We don't really know, from our end, whether we are doing a job for our client or not," he wrote. Despite this plan and a vow to continue the battle in state legislatures, the dairy organizations and the agency soon parted ways, most likely due to lack of funds.[59]

Although Hill and Knowlton had secured only a moral victory, the butter controversy had been beneficial to the agency. It had given executives greater experience in the political arena, and the change in dairy policy illuminates the impact of H&K's role as counsel. By influencing policy, agency employees affected, albeit in small ways, federal regulation of another industry. More significantly, John Hill had almost nothing to do with the account. Hill had continued to rise in influence in the public relations community, serving, for example, on the editorial board of the trade publication *Public Relations News*, and the agency had grown to the point that he did not even meet the heads of the three dairy groups until the program was well underway. The policy making role had been undertaken by the agency's second tier, Goss and Mapes, meaning that participation in the client's policy making had been fully institutionalized within the agency. Altogether, the butter controversy prepared the public relations agents for one of the firm's watershed moments: the steel strike of 1952.[60]

CHAPTER FIVE

The Mills Are Seized

Public Relations and Public Discourse

The 1952 steel labor negotiations gave Hill and Knowlton an opportunity to demonstrate that its long-term program for the American Iron and Steel Institute had improved public understanding of the industry and its problems. The threat of a work stoppage during the Korean War led President Harry S. Truman to order a government takeover of the mills in April, and the agency, in addition to its regular work for the institute, created an emergency task force to assist the "Companies in the Steel Wage Case" during the crisis. Would its job be made easier by almost two decades of public relations programming?

The most important goal of all the participants in the dispute—industry, administration, and union—was to try to control the issue by framing it in a manner that interpreted the situation in ways that favored their own organizations, and to disseminate those frames as widely as possible. Public relations materials offering frames for understanding the conflict appeared on every side. H&K produced booklets, speeches, and over 100 news releases in just a few months. The federal government divided over the issue. Truman's advisers and members of Congress could not agree about what the problem was and how it should be solved, but they all talked about it in the media and in legislative sessions. The steel union favored government intervention as long as it helped the union win its demands, and the CIO used news releases, brochures, and speeches just as the industry did. And many other organizations and individuals contributed to the public discourse surrounding the issue, including judges, journalists, and representatives of other industries and unions.

A comparison of the frames offered by these groups and the comments that private individuals made in letters to the principal advocates reveals that despite a massive campaign, Hill and Knowlton had little effect on the resolution of the problem. The campaign did influence discourse among members of the public by adding to the information and opinions that were available for consideration. But influencing discourse did not mean it changed public opinion or led more people to call for the remedies that the industry prescribed. One historian has argued, "the steel crisis developed as it had because the nation never understood the issues in the controversy." However, the real battle was neither for public opinion nor between union and industry, but between Harry Truman and Benjamin Fairless, head of U.S. Steel, and big steel held its ground until Fairless won.[1]

The campaign did have important indirect effects. In echoing important voices, the agency reinforced the beliefs of the steel executives and people who thought like they did. This fortified their determination to hold out for what they believed was right. At the same time the campaign provided a justification for steel executives' behavior. By creating the appearance of public support, the agency helped the executives rationalize their position: they were fighting not for money or power but in the national interest and with the support of the public.

The Crisis: The Steel Strike of 1952

At the base of the steel problem was the Korean War, which had begun in June 1950 and intensified when Chinese Communists intervened on behalf of North Korea in November. After a meeting of the union's Wage Policy Committee in November 1951, the steelworkers sought a "22-point program" including a wage increase and benefits that would close the gap between the steelworkers and other CIO unions, such as miners and autoworkers. The big steel corporations countered that they could not raise wages without also boosting prices. The Korean conflict eliminated the possibility of a direct settlement, because government stabilization agencies had to approve both wage and price policies.[2]

Federal agencies quickly entered the fray. The Office of Price Stabilization, attempting to control prices and therefore inflation, concluded that the companies could absorb as much as a forty-cent per hour wage increase without a corresponding price increase. However, industry negotiators disagreed and refused to pay the higher wages. At the end of December both sides agreed to accept certification of the dispute to the Wage Stabilization Board (WSB), and after an emergency convention of the steelworkers, the strike was postponed for forty-five days. On 20 March the board released its recommendations, which the public and labor members endorsed and the industry members violently opposed. The total cost of the package was about twenty-six cents an hour; the fairness of the recommendations to the industry was questioned by many, both inside and outside the industry. Noting that the WSB had not granted all of its demands, the union still voted to resume negotiations, complying with the board's recommendations. But the industry rejected the report out of hand. The steel companies and the union had submitted their demands "to the umpire named by the government," one journalist asserted, "but when the decision came down, and the companies did not like it, they shouted, 'Kill the umpire.'"[3]

The industry's actions are best explained by the fact that the primary fight was not between union and industry but industry and government. Despite union members' worries, the business leaders had accepted collective bargaining. Privately, they even admitted the legitimacy of some of the steelworkers' demands. But the steel companies were not willing to concede anything to the government. They saw the strike as an opportunity to break the government's role in setting prices, as an article by Inland Steel's Clarence Randall made clear. "We resent price controls," he wrote in the *Atlantic Monthly.* "We say that price controls are not required because the operation of natural laws, supply and demand, will themselves adjust prices. The thing we dislike about it is that those natural laws are suspended by government." Harold Enarson, one of Truman's advisers, well understood the industry's position. "Even as the industry and the union made their respective cases on wages to the Wage Stabilization Board," Enarson recalled, "the industry began its persistent campaign to storm the citadels of price stabilization. It felt that the government would talk tough, as in 1946, but when the chips were down would prefer labor peace to disastrous strike."[4]

Even more than price control, the industry hoped to break what Hill called "the unholy alliance between labor and the administration." One steel magnate branded the WSB's union shop recommendation not only "unfair" but "illegal." In all three postwar steel strikes the federal government had become a principal party, and the industry leaders had had enough. "It was quite an unnecessary strike," U.S. Steel's Irving Olds reflected a month after it had ended, "which became a reality primarily because of bungling and the playing of politics at Washington." But the prime force pushing for government intervention had been the industry, forcing a confrontation.[5]

With a strike imminent President Truman felt compelled to act. He ordered seizure papers drawn up as a threat, but when the industry called his bluff by repudiating the WSB recommendations, he ordered Secretary of Commerce Charles Sawyer to seize the mills and operate them on behalf of the government. The move quickly landed the administration in the courts opposite the millowners, but throughout weeks of hearings and appeals the seizure was maintained. On 2 June the Supreme Court ruled Truman's action unconstitutional, 560,000 workers quit the mills, and a fifty-four day strike ensued. On 26 July the parties reached an agreement, ending the labor-management-government battle.[6]

Frames before Government
Seizure of the Mills

The many players in the steel crisis defined the problem of the steel negotiations in different ways. A variety of frames appeared in the press, speeches on Capitol Hill, and in union, industry, and government materials. Each group assumed that people would use these frames to interpret the meaning of the steel dispute in a way that favored their own positions.

The Steel Union

The United Steelworkers of America (USWA), under the leadership of Philip Murray, faced an uphill climb in trying to convince the public that they deserved a raise. Organized labor has to a certain extent always been portrayed unsympathetically or inaccurately in the American news and entertainment media. The union also had to deal with internal problems. Recovering from a 1951 illness, Murray found himself battling David J. McDonald, the union's secretary-treasurer, for control of the union. Furthermore, although Murray was known as someone who got along with people, the bad image of other labor leaders added to the USWA's difficulties. When World War II ended, John L. Lewis, the former CIO leader who had called strikes even during the war, was arguably the most hated public figure in the United States, with polls showing that 87 percent of Americans had an unfavorable opinion of him. By contrast another labor leader remembered Murray as "friendly and conciliatory" and "very likable," and even conservatives like radio commentator H. V. Kaltenborn and U.S. Steel's Roger Blough found Murray "sober," "intelligent," and "sincere." On the other hand some business leaders may have found Murray's responsible brand of labor militancy more threatening than Lewis's, for it presented a respectable challenge to management control of working conditions. The strike wave and the inflation that accompanied the end of the war also contributed to public dissatisfaction with unions, and the passage of the Taft-Hartley Act in 1947 reflected increasing intolerance for labor power.[7]

The union reportedly spent at least $1 million on public information during the wage dispute. Over the years labor generally had become increasingly interested in public relations, and the steelworkers had created a Publicity and Education Department to keep members and the public informed. This department utilized the radio, press, television, pamphlets, recordings, and its own publication, *Steel Labor*, to reach its publics. Copies of one pamphlet were mailed to ministers, public officials, teachers, editors, and libraries, with a total of 85,000 sent to opinion leaders. *Steel Labor* went to the homes of all USWA members and had a circulation of over a million.[8]

As a member of the CIO the union also had solid financial and moral support of a much larger organization. Because Philip Murray was head of both the USWA and the CIO, at times the two were indistinguishable. The CIO's publicity department regularly promoted the steelworkers' side in the negotiations, especially in its *CIO News*. It also sponsored radio programs on three networks and, with its Political Action Committee, produced thirteen quarter-hour films for television, which sometimes touched on such relevant issues as the Taft-Hartley Act.[9]

Prior to the seizure the union concentrated on four frames. Most important was the industry's unwillingness to conduct good-faith negotiations. "It takes two parties to make a bargain," Murray said in December 1951. "The Steelworkers Union cannot sign a contract alone." Second was the union shop. In union shop factories, the USWA explained, management could hire anyone, and workers could seek employment wherever they chose, but upon employment all workers had to join the union. The labor frame for understanding the union shop was that it was neither illegal nor unusual and offered genuine security. Such corporations as General Motors, Ford, Firestone, Goodyear, and even steel companies like Crucible and Kaiser had signed contracts that provided for the union shop. Furthermore, U.S. Steel and most other major steel producers had signed union-shop contracts with other unions, such as coal, railroad, and steamship workers' groups.[10]

The union also explained repeatedly why union members needed a wage increase despite the inflationary threat that some said it posed. Steelworkers like everyone else had been hard hit by inflation and wanted it controlled. The union had sought a strong Defense Production Act to keep prices low, but steel manufacturers and others had fought against it, and now the workers had no choice but to ask for higher wages to survive the rising cost of living. Finally, Murray insisted that the recommendations were not inflationary because the steel industry could afford wage increases without raising prices. A CIO news release said that the wage increase would cost the companies an additional $2.10 per ton, by the union's calculations, "a far cry from the $12 a ton the companies are asking," and companies could easily pay the lower cost because profits were at near record highs.[11]

Thus, the union said that it sought a well-deserved and necessary pay increase and other adjustments. The USWA had in the national interest followed all laws and government requests regarding collective bargaining. Although the workers' representatives had negotiated in good faith, they could not reach an agreement with an industry that refused to bargain even though it could afford to pay.

The Steel Industry

The manufacturers turned to public relations, as they had during labor disputes in 1937, 1943, 1946, and 1949. By that time Hill and Knowlton had ten major clients and as many as 150 employees in nine cities. Steel still dominated its attention, however, with at least a dozen full-time staff on the account. But during the steel crisis that number multiplied many times. After the case had been sent to the Wage Stabilization Board in January 1952, Hill and Knowlton organized a second steel account, the "Companies in the Steel Wage Case." This group of sixty-two corporations included sixteen which were not AISI members. The agency established headquarters in a Washington, D.C., hotel, where at least four members of the staff would be available at all times during the WSB hearings.[12]

The union was not the only group to face internal dissension. Amid the steel crisis, Hill had a confrontation with John Mapes, who had once been the firm's largest stockholder other than Hill. Mapes had left H&K in 1950 to open Group Attitudes Development Corporation, a research and counseling firm, with the proceeds he earned from the sale of his H&K stock. Mapes took with him Jane Stewart, Hill's office manager, and Gordon A. Growden, who worked on steel's community relations program. Their defection was uneventful, although a colleague suggested to Hill that "parting from Mapes must seem like Lee without Jackson to you." But Jim Rowan, who ran the AISI speaker's bureau, tried to solicit part of the steel account away from H&K to Group Attitudes in May 1952. When Inland's Edward Ryerson informed Hill of Rowan's actions, Hill fired Rowan and wrote to Mapes, "I have been saddened and hurt beyond words," adding, "it seems to me that if you had wanted to approach the steel industry you would have done so in a clean cut straightforward way." The internal crisis did not seem to affect agency performance.[13]

A statement of the steel companies released by Hill and Knowlton on 4 April 1952 reveals the direct contrast between the union frames and the fundamental frame used by the industry before the government takeover. The problem was that greedy workers were asking for a raise that the industry and the nation could ill afford. The steelworkers were among the highest paid industrial workers in the nation, so a cost of living increase was not necessary, they said. Profits were down because the industry was making sacrifices for the defense effort. Moreover, in the spirit of the law enacted by Congress to prevent inflation, the companies said that there should be no increase in wages or prices. But if wages were increased, prices would have to be, too. The agency used elaborate statistics to prove the industry's case. "A steel wage increase would plunge the country into another major inflationary spiral," an agency executive wrote in an internal memorandum. Therefore, "in all public statements it is important to stress the threat to the national economy and the general welfare involved in the union demands—to show how the average citizen would be hit by higher living costs and taxes." The selfishness of the union in not accepting a generous sixteen-cents-per-hour increase, offered in the eleventh hour of negotiations, would undermine the economy and the security of the nation.[14]

The Federal Government

Harry Truman had the distinction of being one of the most unpopular presidents in American history during the steel negotiations. A Gallup poll found that only 23 percent of the respondents in a December 1951 survey approved of the way Truman was handling his job, compared with nearly 60 percent who disapproved. That month would prove to be the low point in his ratings, but the stagnating war in Korea and charges of bribery and corruption in his administration had taken a toll.[15]

During the initial negotiations people expected the administration to act impartially, but from the start Truman was inclined to distrust steel managers and sympathize with the union. Truman's experiences in the Senate and with the strikes in 1946 and 1949, as well as management's opposition to his reelection in 1948, had strained his relationship with business. Meanwhile, organized labor had been one of his most stalwart political allies. The Council of Economic Advisors, along with the stabilization agencies, counseled the president to stand firm, insisting that the industry could absorb wage increases, whereas a price increase would "ring the bell for another round of inflation."[16]

Truman's public statements about the steel problem focused always on the national interest. In a letter to Murray, in which the president asked the union to postpone its strike while the WSB examined the situation, Truman wrote, "the Nation simply cannot afford a stoppage in steel production, even a stoppage of limited duration." Losses in production "would have an immediate and crippling effect on mobilization schedules." This reflected genuine concern on the part of administration and military officials. Truman aide John R. Steelman recalled that the seizure was "made in absolutely good faith and with great reluctance" because "the Defense Department just screamed so loudly and so emotionally" that the country had to have steel.[17]

Still another factor in the debate was the 82nd Congress. The lame-duck president's unpopularity among the general public was easily matched by that in Congress. Although Truman's party controlled both houses, the 1950 elections had strengthened the ranks of the president's critics in both parties. Members of Congress offered other frames that citizens could consider, the most important of which was an attempt to discredit the WSB. In March, Congress voted to investigate the WSB, a move that seemed to suggest that the board's recommendations were out of line.[18]

The News Media

The union, the government, and the industry were not the only advocates generating frames of interpretation for public consumption. The news media also tried to explain the situation. Before the takeover, many of the media frames overlapped with those expressed by the industry. The most conservative of the newsmagazines, *U.S. News and World Report*, said that other unions were "likely to try for pay raises that match, percentage-wise, the increase proposed by the Board in steel." A week later the same magazine focused on steel profits. An article analyzing U.S. Steel's numbers concluded, "the big loser in any drastic cut in profits will not be the companies or stockholders, but the U.S. Treasury."[19]

However, not all journalists agreed with the industry. Liberal opinion-leading periodicals sided with the union. Harry Conn, who wrote for *New Republic*, said the steelworkers were entitled to a wage increase, and the *Nation* defended the union shop, arguing, "the majority that want a union shop should not be forced to work side by side with others who take all the benefits the union wins but refuse to bear their share of the union's expenses or help decide its policies." H. V. Kaltenborn of NBC ignored both the industry and the union to blame the Truman administration. "Both unions and steel producers remember," he said in December 1951, "that the administration has always allowed wage increases and then always allowed price increases." The problem was the government. "While the government pretends to control both wages and prices, normal collective bargaining cannot function," Kaltenborn said. "Whichever side expects to wangle concessions from a vote-hungry administration compels federal intervention."[20]

Framing after the Government
Seizure of the Mills

Although none of the frames used during the negotiations disappeared, the situation changed after the seizure. New frames were added regarding the greater role of the Truman administration, and old frames became less important or changed in significance. Truman's actions affected the ways many people interpreted the situation.

President Truman's Frames

Truman spoke to the nation over eight television and radio networks on 8 April, telling the nation of his decision and his reasons for taking the mills. "Our national security and our chances for peace depend on our defense production," he said, and "our defense production depends on steel." Indeed, not only losses in the Korean War, but also "the possibility of hostile attack, grows much greater" with a strike. He argued it was a national emergency and that in normal times the dispute might not have arisen. Truman said he had not invoked the Taft-Hartley Act because it would not remedy the situation, given that the strike had been delayed for so long by the union. A settlement, not another delay, was needed.[21]

The president also challenged the industry's frames. "When you look at the facts, instead of the propaganda," he said, "it is perfectly plain that the Wage Board's recommendations in the steel case do provide a fair and reasonable basis for reaching a settlement." He said that steel profits were $2.5 billion a year at $19.50 a ton, and that profits would increase by $3 more per ton due to the Capehart amendment to the price control law, an increase the industry had neither solicited nor expected. That increase would allow the industry to boost wages for the workers to a level the union found acceptable. Certainly the corporations would not need still another price increase to bear the costs of the wage increase, and "if we knuckled under to the steel industry, the lid would be off. Prices would start jumping up all around us — not just prices of things using steel, but prices of many other things we buy, including milk and groceries and meat."[22]

Not surprisingly, members of the Truman administration supported his interpretation of events. Labor Secretary Maurice J. Tobin, for example, spoke at the USWA convention to show his support for the union. Because the union had accepted the WSB's recommendations, even though they were deficient from the union's point of view, Tobin said, the industry should be expected to do the same—compromise in the public interest. Even Commerce Secretary Sawyer, who publicly admitted he did not want the job of running the mills, said the country was in a perilous situation, and steel production was essential to the national welfare. And Office of Price Stabilization head Ellis Arnall continued to insist that the steel industry was entitled to no price increase except under the Capehart amendment.[23]

After the case had gone to the courts, however, the administration attempted to downplay the issue, a job made more difficult by the vocal response of the industry. Staff members tried to avoid comment on the issue for two reasons: to allow the courts to decide the case on its merits, and to avoid making commitments that might in turn make negotiations more difficult. "In view of the intemperate and dishonest attacks on the President in this and similar propaganda by the steel companies," White House counsel Charles Murphy told Sawyer in a note accompanying a copy of an H&K brochure, "I must say that it is very difficult to counsel a policy of restraint."[24]

Steel Industry Frames

Although presidential takeovers were by no means new, industry response was one of shock. For John Hill, the act was unprecedented, stunning, "historic." Eleven years later he devoted an entire chapter of his autobiography—"The Mills Are Seized!"—to the incident. Temporary operation of industry property had occurred seventy-one times in American history, under Presidents Lincoln, Wilson, Franklin Roosevelt, and Truman. Steel company railroads had been seized and operated by the Army only one year prior to Truman's 1952 order. However, the seizure was different in that the Korean situation was not technically a war, and the action had been taken against the industry rather than to put down a labor uprising.[25]

Truman's takeover invigorated the staff at Hill and Knowlton. A team of more than fifty worked on the campaign, borrowing PR people from the AISI account and from each of the major steel companies, even hiring specialists as needed. They prepared material for presentation before legislative committees, spoke to editors and writers, held press conferences, "engaged in virtually all kinds of public relations activity and employed every known communications tool," according to Hill.[26]

Hill and Knowlton claimed that

thirty-nine booklets, editorial reprints and other matter were distributed to the tune of six million copies; six advertisements appeared in more than two hundred daily newspapers with a combined circulation of some thirty million; the steel companies' case was broadcast in eight TV speeches and four network radio programs; forty other speeches and radio appearances were secured in the Pittsburgh, Chicago, Washington and New York areas. More than a hundred news releases and statements were issued.

The "Companies in the Steel Wage Case" spent over $1.6 million by September 1952.[27]

The normal AISI program, with its budget of $1,770,00 still considered the largest PR account in the nation, was maintained, as were individual company public relations programs. This work also bore upon the strike. For example, a May 1952 *Steelways* article by H&K executive Richard Cheney discussed "Some Facts about Profits," and *Steel Facts* followed the plunge in output that accompanied the strike, commenting on the millions of tons of production lost to strikes since the end of the war. U.S. Steel had a huge public relations section as well as solid support from its advertising agency, Batten Barton Durstine and Osborne. U.S. Steel executives made eight speeches during the crisis, with distribution of 803,990 copies of those talks, and ads included "The Facts about the Steel Wage Offer," which insisted that the company's June 1952 proposal should produce a satisfactory settlement.[28]

Perhaps the most conspicuous part of the H&K's emergency program was its institutional advertising campaign. The series included a compilation of newspaper editorial comment; "A Threat to American Freedom," which emphasized "it is your fight"; a report on "Why the Talks in the Steel Wage Dispute Are Stalled," which explained prices, the union shop, and the government's usurpation of power; and "News That Could Not Be Suppressed," which quoted a dissatisfied member of the WSB. The ads were mentioned in *Commonweal* and in the *Nation*, although derisively, suggesting the campaign was highly visible. (The former said the companies ran full-page advertisements "almost daily," while the latter complained "they spent millions of dollars on full-page advertisements trying to convince the public that the union and the President were in cahoots against democracy.")[29]

With the seizure of the mills, the most important frame for the industry became the constitutionality of Truman's actions, and "socialism" and "totalitarianism" became the battle cries of those opposing the seizure. Complained Republic Steel's president, "the Government now makes more decisions about your and my business than you or I do." Inland's Clarence Randall, the industry's leading spokesperson during the crisis, released a statement the day of the seizure, saying "it is unbelievable that this should happen in a free America. . . . That is government by decree and not by law, and it is precisely the sort of thing we fought three wars to resist in other lands." This oblique reference to the boys in Korea was made more forcefully in Randall's televised speech the following day.[30]

H&K became very explicit on the charge of socialism. A background memorandum released on 14 April asked, "Are we to push steel into socialism through the back door?" The agency asserted "government policy has been moving toward this climax for some twenty years." A wage increase without a price increase would cut steel tax payments (steel companies paid over $1 billion in taxes in 1951), which the Treasury would have to make up either by printing more money—inflation—or by taxing everyone else more. This raid of the public money was socialism.[31]

Socialism preoccupied nearly all American business leaders, but steel executives had special cause for worry. A study of business journals published from September 1951 to February 1952 found that government activity labeled "welfare socialism" was one of the top editorial concerns, and that business journalists regarded communism "as the logical and probably inevitable outgrowth of socialism." Although British voters had returned the Conservatives, pledged to denationalize steel, to office in the autumn of 1951, American steel executives still keenly felt the threat of nationalization. Truman had suggested that the U.S. government enter the steelmaking business if the steel industry would not reinvest to expand capacity. In 1949 almost one in five of the respondents of one survey believed the government should do so. For these reasons, not only AISI but most of the steel companies' public relations campaigns sought to "counter socialistic demands for business-crippling legislation," as one steel company explained, "and to promote public understanding of the importance of private enterprise to the general welfare of the United States."[32]

By focusing on the legality of Truman's actions and on socialism, the industry effectively obscured the real obstacle to resolution of the crisis, prices. "Rather than providing a new context for collective bargaining," the historian Maeva Marcus contended, "the seizure became the subject of a great constitutional debate." In the attempt to direct the country's attention to the industry's price demands, the administration had inadvertently given the industry an illustration of the danger of socialism that it had for twenty years claimed was imminent. For the next weeks, the union was almost forgotten.[33]

Although socialism dominated, the profit, inflation, and wage frames continued to figure in the steelmakers' strategy. Randall challenged the president's statement that the industry made $19.50 a ton in profit, noting he "neglected to say that he takes at least two thirds of that away in taxes," a point Truman later conceded. Moreover, the corporations needed profits to invest in more mills and equipment. "Most of their cash resources are now going into new plants at the government's urging," Hill and Knowlton explained. This was an important point for steel to make, given the postwar shortage that some had blamed on steel's unwillingness to expand. Agency figures showed that hourly earnings rose by about $0.77, as compared with $0.655 for all manufacturing industries after the war. Steelworkers' wages had increased faster than the cost of living, and employee benefits appeared generous. The agency emphasized that "the best interests of the nation would be served by no wage increase, and no price increase, in steel making at this time," making the workers seem both greedy and un-American. Hill and Knowlton also became more forceful in its claims about inflation. "Today," the agency said, "many unions are waiting on the outcome of today's steel situation, to see what *they* can get." Other unions had contracts coming up for review, and if steel wages went up, the pattern would spread.[34]

Finally, the steelmakers expressed their disgust with the union shop clause of the WSB recommendations. Management had long resisted the union shop. Even in writing NIRA codes, industrialists, especially members of NAM, insisted that the open shop be retained. During the seizure the union shop frame also touched on communism. "There are thousands of workmen in the steel industry who, for reasons of their own, have refused to join the union," H&K said. "As free Americans, they regard this as their right." The shop clause recommended by the WSB would give the union leaders the right to force discharge of a worker who refused to pay dues, which H&K called "an outright attack on every man's freedom of choice," "little different from forcing an American to belong to a particular party, or a given church, before he can eat. That is a Russian concept of a man's future."[35]

Steel Union Frames

After the seizure the USWA became an almost inconsequential player in the drama, even though it tried to focus attention on the industry's poor negotiating record. The union supported Truman's actions, stating that "the President, recognizing the justice of the Steelworkers case, was determined not to permit the industry's attempt to blackmail the Government to succeed." In other words, the problem was not the union. It had accepted the WSB's recommendations and, as the CIO said, "it is not our job . . . to bargain with the steel industry over prices," but prices were the biggest obstacle to a solution. More importantly, the seizure had made the union less relevant. Murray reminded a Senate committee, "do not let the industry's cries of anguish distract you from one fact. At this moment, despite the seizure, the Steelworkers of America are still receiving 1950 wages and paying 1952 prices." [36]

Union leaders, like Truman, continued to emphasize the industry's wealth. They argued that the companies were trying to gain from the Korean conflict at the expense of their employees by raising prices unnecessarily. "The record of the 1950–1951 upward price movement proves conclusively that higher wages *followed* after prices had skyrocketed," USWA officers reported. "They came only as workers, through their unions, fought to protect their living standards." [37]

The union also recognized the steelmakers' fundamental conflict with the government, but individual members continued to concentrate on the industry's unwillingness to negotiate with labor. "The steel industry is on a strike against collective bargaining," a union resolution said. "The steel industry is on strike against the Government's price regulations which apply to all other industries. What the steel industry wants in effect is a special Government license to gouge the consuming public." Yet one union convention delegate told his colleagues, "this industry has never accepted this Union, and the only way they are going to accept it is when we make them accept it." Said another, "If Randall is looking for a fight, he is going to get a damned good one." [38]

Much of the union's reaction to the events consisted of rebuttal of the industry's public relations campaign. Some members accused H&K's advertising campaign of displaying "union-busting attitudes," calling the ads "expensive and vitriolic." Murray repeatedly charged the industry with using taxpayers' money to subsidize the campaign, because advertising was a deductible business expense. Labor also dismissed the industry's complaints about the seizure as "nothing but a lot of hooey," pointing out that steel executives had never come out against seizure before, when it had been used to stop labor. And, they defended the union shop clause of the WSB recommendations. "Your union is striking for union shop and I'm not ashamed of it," Philip Murray told a group of steelworkers. "I think that everybody that receives any benefit from this labor organization ought to pay his way." [39]

Of particular concern to the CIO was the charge of socialism, which came dangerously close to equating unionism with leftist extremism—an image it desperately wanted to shed. Having expelled its Communist members, the union did its best to combat the charge during the strike, placing articles in newspapers and magazines, arranging radio and television appearances by CIO leaders, filling requests for speakers, issuing news releases, and publishing stories in the *CIO News*. Murray reiterated the union's anti-

Communist position, saying that the steelworkers had demonstrated their loyalty to the country.[40]

The union was more proactive in its insistence on compromise. "We are seeking acceptance from the industry of the compromise recommendations of the Wage Stabilization Board," Philip Murray told the news media. "It should be clear to all that the industry is not disposed to make a settlement with the union" in the "spirit of fairness and equity" that the union had displayed throughout the negotiations.[41]

Frames in the Media Arena

The news media overwhelmingly favored steel's position against the president. Publishers generally disapproved of Truman, and the takeover provided them with an opportunity to editorialize against him. *Tide*, an advertising and public relations journal, reported that "top dailies across the land angrily editorialized against the government's seizure of the steel mills." Hill and Knowlton's review of 800 articles found only about two dozen that were unfavorable toward the industry, and its collection of editorial comment from the days immediately following the seizure showed support ran strong. Conservative papers like the *Cleveland Plain Dealer*, the *Chicago Tribune*, and the *Detroit Free Press* mentioned socialism, totalitarianism, and demagoguery as characteristic of Truman's actions. The *St. Louis Globe-Democrat* went so far as to say that "Adolf Hitler in his wildest days never topped President Truman's hysterical denunciation of the steel industry." The *New York Times*, while more moderate, also criticized the president, arguing that his actions were "not consistent with American principles."[42]

H&K enjoyed successful placement of steel industry materials, particularly with small newspapers and radio stations. Public relations executive Roy Battersby reported to Hill that of fifteen papers in ten states, eleven had used an article prepared by H&K called "What the Steel Seizure Means." Two, *the Waveland (Indiana) Independent* and the *Okabena (Minnesota) Press*, reprinted the article without editing it in any way, meaning the industry's frames were repeated verbatim. Only two objected to the content of the release. Of twenty-eight radio stations in twenty-one states, twenty-two used a report called "How the Steel Wage Controversy Affects You." Four other stations said they found the report interesting or useful, leaving only two that rejected it out of hand. But even national media made extensive use of agency materials. The conservative *U.S. News and World Report* wrote almost directly from H&K materials to the effect that "in the six years since World War II, U.S. business has invested more than 100 billion dollars in new plant and equipment."[43]

Journalists also introduced new frames not mentioned by the industry in criticizing the president. *Congressional Digest* believed the seizure had value "if it brings into sharp focus the present alignment of the traditional American balance-of-power system of government," which had been "badly unbalanced through the gradual but steady increase of Executive power in recent decades—and a corresponding decrease of legislative power." *Life* also found the president's action distasteful. "All he can possibly have gained by handling the strike threat in this reckless way," the magazine opined, "is a phony campaign issue." One labor publication alleged that U.S. Steel and other large corporations used cost-padding techniques to disguise their real profits.[44]

Some in the news media did criticize the industry. Liberal magazines like *New Republic* asserted that the president "would have been delinquent in his duty had he failed to seize the steel mills." The magazine responded to the industry's constitutionality frame by arguing the Taft-Hartley Act would not have solved the problem and that it was not the sole means of handling disputes. It also demonstrated that the forty-nine largest steel companies could give their workers a thirty-five cent hourly raise without a price increase, a figure it derived by applying government guidelines to AISI statistics. Even *U.S. News and World Report* commented on the salaries management took home. When reporters asked Randall how much he made, he told them $105,000, explaining he had not taken a pay increase since May 1950, and had not taken a raise later that year when the union won a 10 percent raise for steelworkers.[45]

Frames in the Political Arena

The most significant event occurring in the political arena was Senator Robert A. Taft's statement that he believed Truman's actions provided grounds for impeachment. The Ohio Republican's suggestion created an entirely new way to interpret the situation. One of the most important political advocates, the senator was sometimes called "the second most powerful man in the capital." As he understood it, the Taft-Hartley Act, which he had co-sponsored, was not intended to destroy unions but to restore equality in labor relations. As the Roosevelt-era Wagner Act had limited management, Taft-Hartley sought to define unfair union practices. Labor violently disagreed, but Taft's "middle road" was favored by many business executives, and by John Hill, who served on the public relations advisory committee for Taft's campaign for the Republican presidential nomination during and after the steel crisis. Ignoring the law was, in Taft's eyes, an impeachable offense, for Congress had clearly set out an equitable method for dealing with labor disputes.[46]

Other politicians reproved the industry. Senator Hubert Humphrey, Democrat of Minnesota, identified the industry's attitude toward government as the primary problem. "The issue," he said, was "whether or not the Government of the United States is willing to be bludgeoned into submission to the extortionate price and profit demands of the United States Steel companies." The best way to avoid government intervention, he advised steel managers, was to settle disputes before they got to the government. Tennessee Democrat Estes Kefauver, in contention for a presidential nomination, declared that steelworkers deserved a pay hike, which could be granted without a substantial increase in steel prices.[47]

Frames Expressed by Private Advocates in Mail

Letters sent to Truman, Murray, and H&K reveal that private citizens did listen to the arguments made, but having access to all of them meant that people could pick and choose among the many frames offered. Unfortunately, Hill did not save the letters people wrote to the steel companies in care of H&K, nor did the agency keep records about mail until after the steel seizure. However, letters written to Truman and Murray throughout the crisis are available for analysis.

Although letters are not indicative of public opinion, they are an excellent source of information on the frames used by private individuals in discourse about public issues. Mail does not mirror public opinion as it is measured in polls. In fact, the two sources may indicate that the exact opposite opinion is predominant. As Leila Sussman has argued, mail is usually one-sided. But political mail is nevertheless a rich source of information, revealing much about the writers and the recipients. In this case, because mail to more than one of the advocates is available, comparison of the frames used by people favoring the positions articulated by different actors is possible.[48] Mail is important, too, because of the way it is used by advocates, whether members of Congress or industry and union officials. A 1956 study found that members of Congress spent an enormous amount of time on their mail. And, because writers generally contact legislators who agree with their own opinions, political actors can almost always say that their mail is positive. This point is particularly important because a 1945 survey of legislators found that they ranked their mail first as a method of measuring public opinion.[49]

An analysis of letters sent to the "Companies in the Steel Wage Case" (in care of Hill and Knowlton, whose address was published at the bottom of each institutional advertisement) showed overwhelming support for the industry. The agency processed over 13,000 pieces of mail after the seizure, with more than 85 percent of all writers favoring the steel industry, staff member Leigh Smith reported to Hill. Some offered "friendly suggestions," which for the most part urged the industry "to adopt a 'tougher' attitude in fighting the union and government actions." The agency also received almost 60 letters from steelworkers or members of other unions, of which 42 were for the steel companies or against the union. A second report showed that Inland's Randall had received 269 letters and U.S. Steel's Fairless, 572.[50]

Some people who wrote to the steel companies sent copies to Murray. One such writer chastised the industry for not being tough enough, saying "we certainly hope you never surrender to the union dictators on the UNION CLOSED SHOP issue. The Socialism and dictatorship of the Washington, D.C. administration, and union dictatorship in these United States of America have pretty nearly taken the word 'united' out of our setup." Another commented on the irony of "the tragic contradiction of fighting battles in faraway lands to protect our economic and personal life against the ravages of despotism, of which the seizure of the Steel Mills is only a further minor example." The third criticized H&K, for being one-sided, and the industry, for its exorbitant profits and for having created "the ever higher standard of living" that in turn "demands and necessitates an ever increasing wage rate."[51]

The union did not keep records of the number of letters received or the arguments utilized by the writers. The union received nothing near the volume of mail that H&K or Truman did during April and May. Most letters were intended to encourage Murray, as in the case of one former steelworker who now owned stock in U.S. Steel and who just before the seizure wrote, "don't give up an inch." However, Murray received so many letters after the seizure that complete quantitative analysis was not conducted. Rather, files containing both pro- and antiunion messages were sampled to allow examination of the frames utilized by the writers. Thus, two of four files of letters written in April by individuals including steelworkers, totaling about 100 letters, were reviewed. This analysis yielded nine basic frames of interpretation.[52]

The vast majority of writers echoed frames first suggested by Murray and other union leaders in favor of the USWA position. Over forty asserted that the situation called for compromise, and that because the union had accepted the WSB recommendations, even though they did not meet all of the steelworkers' demands, the industry should, too. Almost forty writers argued that the companies were stalling, and although the union had waited patiently, the "barons" should not be allowed to run the country. Twenty added that the real problem was the cost of living, and that workers desperately needed a wage increase. Twelve supported the union shop demand, but only three suggested that industry figures on profits or prices were wrong and that the companies were trying to break the stabilization policy. Four individuals took umbrage with industry "propaganda," much as Murray had in many of his speeches. Finally, twenty-seven writers did not attempt to interpret the issue, instead writing to thank or encourage Murray in his efforts for the union, such as one Los Angeles writer who told Murray, "public opinion is definitely on the side of President Truman, the W.S.B., you and your people." Perhaps because the union was not a major player, but only another viewer of the drama between industry and government, few letters to Murray were negative toward the union during this period.[53]

Union members and others had apparently paid close attention to Murray and the CIO public relations program. The union's frame of fairness and compromise was the best received by the letter writers. Given the cold war context and the fear of inflation many Americans expressed, "compromise" embodied the spirit that seemed necessary to handle the nation's most pressing foreign and domestic problems. This is not to suggest that people interpreted events only through Murray's frames, but that certain frames resonated best with what people thought.

Unlike Murray, Truman played an increasingly important role in the crisis, resulting in a deluge of mail that was analyzed by White House aide Harold Enarson. His report from just one week after the seizure showed that the staff had examined over 1,600 pieces of mail. "So far they run about half and half," Enarson commented, although later reports indicated greater support for Truman. "The theme of most of the pro letters was that the President had exercised leadership, had laid out the facts, had stood up to the steel companies." Of those condemning the seizure, "almost every letter touches one of these points: that the President distorted the profit picture, that he deliberately ignored the union shop recommendation, that he evaded the Taft-Hartley Act, and that he acted as a partisan."[54]

A cursory examination of Truman's mail confirms Enarson's conclusions. Of the "pro-seizure" group, many writers congratulated the president for "fighting for the things the little fellow" stood for, calling him "brave" and "another Abe Lincoln." Many steelworkers insisted that wages were much lower than the companies made out, while another group focused as Truman had on national security and the war effort in Korea. Finally, many wrote in response to industry public relations efforts. One schoolteacher who heard Randall's radio broadcast wrote, "please ignore his inane 'remarks.' Keep on as you are going," she added, "and maybe we'll get some of these profiteering pigs down off their high horse."[55]

In the group opposing Truman's efforts, a large number insisted that the president's actions were dictatorial or socialistic. Even one steel union member wrote in protest. "If this trend continues, what is to prevent the seizure of our cars, our homes, and even our liberties by Big Government?" he asked. Others suggested that union leaders were dictatorial or condemned the WSB recommendations, including the union shop, as unfair. However, as Enarson noted, more writers disagreed with Truman's verbal attack on the industry than his decision not to use the Taft-Hartley law. "I bow my head in shame for you. To have the world see our 'national head' denounce the free enterprise system by attacking the steel industry as you have done," commented one writer, "must give the impression of sympathy for foreign ideologies."[56]

Resolution of the Steel Crisis

The Supreme Court handed down a decision on 2 June 1952 that surprised not only Truman but the steelmakers. The Court voted six to three in favor of the industry's case that the president did not hold the legal authority to seize the mills. Maeva Marcus, in her examination of the constitutional aspects of the seizure, observed that many of the justices' opinions warned of the danger of too much executive power. They apparently did not believe the government's assertions that the Korean conflict created an emergency so dire as to justify suspension of the industry's rights. However, the justices could not agree on what Truman should have done, and the decision did not command use of the Taft-Hartley, putting the president back in the uncertain position he had faced on 8 April.[57]

Truman chose to return the mills to management, and, not wanting to invoke Taft-Hartley with its eighty-day waiting period, he asked Congress for instructions. His "expressed feelings," an aide recalled, "were that Mr. Murray had given them 125 days at his personal request, he was not now going to turn around and hit him over the head with an 80-day club." The Senate responded with passage of the Byrd amendment to the Defense Production Act, which "requested" rather than directed the president to use Taft-Hartley, and some members of his staff made the same recommendation. He refused. "I have asked them twice to give me advice on how to meet this situation," Truman said of Congress, "and all the advice I get is that I have done wrong, and that I ought to be impeached." Five months after their strike deadline, the steelworkers still did not have a contract, and "in the absence of a wage agreement," a CIO news release explained, "our members have no alternative other than to cease work." The president ordered the secretary of defense to take measures to "make maximum use of the production capacity of that portion of the steel industry which is not affected by the current strike."[58]

Despite having postponed the strike numerous times, and having participated in every meeting called by government or the industry, the union's
image suffered when it walked out. Leaders knew the CIO would take a
beating. The union's Wage Policy Committee promised that workers would
produce "the essential military products necessary to carry on our fight
against the menace of Communist aggression," and it told the public and
American soldiers that workers supported "the nation's defense effort with
all their spirit." They were on strike "because, as self-respecting Americans,
we have been forced on strike by a profit-hungry industry which has refused to pay fair wages and grant fair working conditions to its employees."
Still, Murray's mail during July and August was often disapproving.[59]

Truman finally reached the point of intolerance for the entire situation in
late July. He called Murray and Fairless to the White House and ordered
them to negotiate an agreement. The settlement included provisions for a
retroactive wage increase, paid holidays and three weeks of vacation after
fifteen years' experience, and a modified union shop. In other words, neither the union nor the companies had gained anything from the strike, because the settlement was similar to the offers that had been made all along.
However, the administration had allowed a price increase greater than it had
said met the standards necessary for price control.[60]

The strike did not place the country in the dire position that Truman's advisers had prophesied, but it did hamper the defense effort. Whereas a record 105 million tons of raw steel had been produced in 1951, only 93 million
tons were produced during the strike year. Despite the Defense Department's warnings that "we could not stand even one day of strike," events
convinced some administration officials that the nation could have with-
stood a much longer work stoppage and led some Americans to believe that
Truman had purposely exaggerated the threat. However, by 3 July aircraft
deliveries had been affected, with shortages of landing gear, for instance.
Some military production lines were closed down—a mortar shell line, a
military truck line, Ford's bazooka rockets—and plans for production accel-
erations had to be abandoned altogether. When the strike ended, the industry quickly established new production records, producing nearly 112 million tons of raw steel in 1953, in an effort to make up for lost work.[61]

Influence of H&K's Campaign on Public Discourse

The review of mail to the principal advocates reveals that H&K did influence
public discourse by adding to the frames of interpretation possible for con-

sideration among those who were interested enough to follow the issue. However, it is not clear that the campaign effectively stimulated discussion among the general public. Hill and Knowlton authorized a study of its institutional ads, finding that just over half of the sample recognized one or more of the ads. Of these, 70 percent recalled at least one of the points made specifically in the ad, while only 36 percent agreed with the ideas expressed. The researchers noted a large percentage of "undecided" responses (56 percent in the agreement question) and suggested "the possibility of a reluctance on the part of some respondents who approved of the government action to commit themselves." And only one in five of those who remembered the ads spoke to anyone else about them—compared with 70 percent who reported they did not.[62]

All of these factors indicate that repetition of industry frames by the companies, journalists, and politicians did not necessarily mean that the general public saw, read, agreed with, or discussed the material. Inland Steel conducted a survey in mid-May and shared the preliminary results with Hill and Knowlton. "To reach the public," Inland's public relations manager recommended, "get in step with these things":

1. Companies want to keep steel flowing; essential to war and defense effort, and to economic welfare of nation. . . .
2. Seizure is undemocratic, the Russian, not the U.S. way . . . it takes us down the road of government control of all industry.
3. The Government has no right . . . [to] force acceptance of wage increases and the union shop; that is the dictator's way; we should solve disputes by agreement.

Indeed, these were important themes—socialism, profits and prices, and "our boys" in Korea—but the survey does not prove the campaign led people to hold those beliefs in the first place.[63]

The industry's most powerful frame, socialism, did seem to strike a chord with many in the public, as reflected in the letters, but screaming "socialism" was hardly a new idea. The same argument had been made in earlier steel disputes, and industry leaders continued to believe the threat of socialism was very real. Indeed the whole steel battle was bounded by what labor journalist Mary Heaton Vorse called the "emotional context" of the Korean conflict. Claims of socialism and communism would have been made without industry materials that emphasized that frame. The nation was well schooled by 1952 in recognizing communism in business and politics, and some people might have believed that government seizure of private property without due process was an indication that Truman was slowly leading the country down the path of the very scourge the United States was fighting in Korea. No one, not even in the most liberal periodicals, questioned the characterization of the United States as at peril from Communists. And even a year later, when their support for participation in the war in Korea had begun to flag, about two-thirds of the college-age men in one survey reported that the war's aims were either "tremendously important" or meant "quite a bit" to them. At most, then, industry claims may have reinforced fears about communism during the 1950s.[64]

H&K's Influence on Public Opinion and Social and Political Action

All the groups succeeded in disseminating their frames in the media, halls of Congress, and to the public, and all affected what at least some people said and thought about the issue by adding to the mix of possible frames of interpretation of the dispute. The question is, how did this influence the outcome of the steel controversy?

Public Opinion

"Never before, in time of controversy," AISI president Walter Tower claimed, "has steel stood so well in public opinion." Survey data suggest a muddier picture. An Inland Steel poll revealed a moderate position among the American public immediately after the takeover, showing "a slight majority approved seizure but on an emergency basis only and to prevent a strike." And, "the public does not buy the strictly legal arguments that it is a violation of the Constitution and not authorized by law," with only one-third saying that the president exceeded his power, Inland's PR manager reported. However, a Gallup poll conducted in late May showed 43 percent disapproved of the seizure, while only 35 percent approved of it. Perhaps the campaign did have some influence on individuals' responses. More likely, individuals had been influenced by federal court decisions that repudiated Truman's actions. Regardless of the survey results, agents at H&K concluded on 24 April that "public opinion continues to run overwhelmingly on the side of the steel companies in the present controversy."[65]

According to Hill, public support "reflected more than the immediate reaction of national opinion to a full and forceful presentation of the facts. It also reflected the effectiveness of a decade or more of public relations work on the part of the steel industry in keeping the public informed of the industry's achievements, purposes, and aims." Steel executives agreed. "The success of the short-range campaign we conducted during the 1952 steel strike was only possible because it was consistent with an established program that had been going for a long time," institute PR committee chairman Ryerson said in September 1952.[66]

But AISI surveys from 1943, 1946, and 1955 show that the steel industry had not changed many public perceptions in the postwar era. An increasing number, from 6 percent in 1943 to 19 in 1955, listed the steel industry as having the best working conditions, but the number who believed that steel was the most dangerous employer remained steady at about 35 percent. Moreover, sometimes changes in the numbers had more to do with external events than the industry's public relations program. Respondents listing steel as having the most labor troubles dropped from 47 percent in 1946 to 34 percent in 1955, but the strike in 1946 had been the largest in history, and the 1955 percentage actually represented a return to the 1943 level of 33 percent. One area showed strong improvement, public perception of steelworker wages, with 17 percent naming steel as the paying the highest hourly wages in 1943, and 32 percent in 1955. But this change probably had more to do with the union and with the wage increases workers received after strikes than with industry PR.[67]

Perceived changes in public opinion could have been caused by several factors beyond the AISI program. Attitudes toward business overall had changed considerably since the 1930s. Radio commentator Eric Sevareid pointed out that, "owing to years of prosperity, and to the prodigious contribution of American industry in the war," by 1950 "a politician can't attack business as such and get away with it," although big business was still "considered fair game." Truman's unpopularity was another factor. The war effort was bogging down, people had grown impatient with economic controls, and McCarthyism had shaken trust in a federal government already rocked by corruption charges that resulted in the resignation of the attorney general. Truman's personal popularity was at its lowest before the seizure, and although it actually gained a few percentage points during the seizure, it is likely that some would have opposed anything the president did. All of these elements contributed to opinion about the industry in 1952.[68]

The campaign also seemed to help mobilize opinion *against* the industry. Both Truman and Murray received letters from people annoyed or enraged by steel advertisements, speeches, and brochures. Editorials also criticized the campaign. H&K's work may have had a net effect of zero—mobilizing some, antagonizing others, who then called for action against the industry. Put simply, individual responses to the campaign varied.

Even if the campaign did change perceptions of the industry, the meaning of "public opinion" for the resolution of the steel case is ambiguous. "Although we are all of us within history," wrote C. Wright Mills, "we do not possess equal power to make history," for some people have greater means of power and influence than others. Industry leaders and people like them, who held policy-making positions with the power to take action on their beliefs, overwhelmingly supported steel, and they would have supported any industry in steel's position, regardless of the facts and opinions H&K presented. All of the groups fighting for public opinion did so to a large extent only to try to demonstrate the existence of support for what they were going to do or what they wanted the other actors to do. While many apparently did believe, as John Hill insisted, that public opinion was the ultimate arbiter, they sought only to change opinion, not to listen to it. An H&K memorandum from the 1949 steel negotiations suggested that "the companies will find it difficult to resist presidential pressure unless in the meantime they have succeeded in more strongly consolidating and fortifying their position with the public." This use of public opinion as a lever continued in the 1952 negotiations, when Hill wrote that the companies' "best chance" of gaining union approval of their latest offer was "through pressure of public opinion upon the leaders of the Union."[69]

Political Action

Advocates in the political arena generally disapproved of Truman's actions and at times used information provided by Hill and Knowlton to support that position. The Senate approved the Ferguson bill to deny Truman the funds to pay for government operation of the mills, 44 votes to 31. One member of Congress submitted a story from the *Chicago Tribune* (given to him by the public relations agency) into the *Congressional Record*. The Department of Commerce's Office of Business Economics prepared a report on steel profits using statistics generated by the AISI. Similarly, the National Association of Manufacturers and the U.S. Chamber of Commerce denounced Truman and asked Congress for legislation that would prevent government seizures of industry, halt government changes in terms or conditions of labor during the period of seizure, and prohibit the WSB from handling labor disputes until price and wage controls ended.[70]

However, not all political actors opposed Truman. Senator Wayne Morse, maverick Republican from Oregon, supported Truman when he insisted that the president did have inherent powers under the Constitution in defending the nation's security and safety. Twenty-nine Democratic and two Republican senators voted against the Ferguson bill, and, although the public relations agents may have given some politicians ammunition, publicly expressed opinions among government officials ranged the spectrum.[71]

Furthermore, some members of Congress disliked the industry's program. Senator Hubert Humphrey for one told the steelworkers that the industry's actions had been offensive to him. "They have been propagandizing the American public, they have been misleading the American public, and they have even been misleading some of the members of Congress," Humphrey said of the industry's leaders. "I say that the steel magnates of this country are guilty of gross distortion of the truth, and I say that they are guilty of character assassination of the members of the Wage Stabilization Board and of the President of the United States."[72]

None of this indicates that the industry's campaign persuaded anyone to call for or take any political action that they would not have done otherwise. Conservative senators were hardly likely to oppose the steel industry, no matter what its public relations agents said. Likewise, the NAM would have called for political action in support of any industry in steel's unenviable position that spring. The campaign also had little or no influence on one of its primary targets, Truman himself. One presidential adviser later said that Truman did not depend "very much on newspapers any more than he relied on the polls in terms of decision making," a contention that opinion poll results would support. Truman aides also agreed that political letters had negligible effect on administration decision making, but they did pay attention to mail. The only obvious effect of Enarson's report on mail was that his identification of numerous letters reflecting "bewilderment and concern" led officials to select one letter for a public response that allowed the president to clarify his position. H&K's influence on public discourse did not affect political action.[73]

Influence on Labor

This is not to suggest that the campaign had no important effects; certainly it influenced labor. Steelworkers were often unimpressed by company public relations efforts, exemplified by those at Fairbanks Morse who "renamed the company's pamphlet service the 'trash rack' and thanked the firm for providing more fodder for the union paper to refute." However, the industry's greatest success came at the expense of the union. Both the news media and the public generally seemed to believe the source of the problem was not prices but wages, perhaps in part because Hill and Knowlton called the group it represented "Companies in the Steel Wage Case." Some in the news media preferred to see the issue as one of prices. In March 1952 the *Nation* pointed out "the issue now is prices." *New Republic* likewise asserted in July "for months now everyone has known that the major issue in the strike has been the price of steel." However, the burden of not having reached an agreement lay at the feet of the union seeking wage increases in many media references, and one poll indicated that almost 90 percent of the sample believed the steel dispute was "all about wages," while only 31 percent mentioned prices as an important issue.[74]

Influence on the Industry and the Agency

The campaign also affected the steel executives who sponsored it by creating a flood of positive mail in addition to the favorable political and media environment. The letters provided a rationale for continuing its unpopular position of refusing to settle. "Strong public opinion," Clarence Randall said in July, "is pressing the companies not to yield further to union demands in the steel strike." His evidence was that "all day, every day, by mail, by telegram and by telephone calls, Inland is being urged to stand fast and not sign a contract that will prevent a non-union man from working." He then quoted from many of the communications the company had received. Thus, the industrialists could argue they were taking a specific action because the public demanded it, despite the fact that the actions had preceded the supportive letters.[75]

The campaign and the letters that resulted from it also bolstered the executives' own spirits and reinforced their determination by creating the appearance of public support. As the industry's chief spokesperson, Randall took much public harassment. His speech was comprised of "rantings and untruthful allegations," according to the USWA. One union member who worked for Inland, Randall's company, threatened a walkout: "we are ready to shut the Inland Steel plant down and let it rot, let it stay out until hell freezes over," he said, "and let Clarence B. Randall and his flunkies stay in there and try to protect their precious machinery." The United Auto Workers' Walter Reuther claimed that "if they ever put him on the operating table and open him up they will find a cash register where his heart ought to be and they will find a calculating machine where his conscience ought to be." Against such criticism, seeing his own views voiced by others must have been comforting. Moreover, while Truman routinely received thousands of pieces of mail, the inundation of public support for Big Steel was almost entirely new. The executives did care about their mail. After a much less important speech during the 1949 labor negotiations, Randall had written to John Hill to let him know that "I am simply submerged in mail. For two weeks now I have been hard at it every day with two secretaries trying to keep abreast of it." Such support was rare. For many years, steel had been, in Hill and Knowlton's words, "the whipping boy." Now it was the hero.[76]

The public relations program also benefited Hill and Knowlton, which received accolades from many of mass communication's elites. Hill told one steel executive that the program had "attracted a good deal of attention in public relations and advertising circles," noting that trade publications like

Tide and *Advertising Age* were "devoting quite a good deal of editorial space to discussion of the work." Not all public relations practitioners agreed with the manner in which H&K handled the crisis. "The ads don't show any milk of human kindness or finesse," one said, and another added, "taking full-page ads to shout at Truman was bad." However, the agency received unsolicited compliments from some, giving executives the idea of sending a questionnaire to other mass communication leaders for their opinions on the steel case. This informal survey resulted in a stack of letters commending the agency for its institutional advertising. The publisher of the *Los Angeles Examiner* wrote that the program "was an outstanding example of public relations," which left the public "much better acquainted with this issue than any similar matter in recent years," while the editor of the *Wall Street Journal* said he thought "the steel industry was decidedly on the right track in taking its case directly to the public in the form of advertising statements." Public relations executive Robert Bliss found the program "superbly executed with good timing and in a direct, forthright manner." Such support may have encouraged H&K executives much like the mail fortified the steelmakers.[77]

An industry victory was especially vital to the agency. When Truman first took over the mills, some steel executives wanted to take the case to Carl Byoir and Associates, and John Hill rushed an emergency plea to AISI's public relations committee to keep the account together. "I am confident we can demonstrate Hill and Knowlton, Inc., is best equipped by long experience in steel industry and by familiarity with present case to do the overall job for the companies in this crisis," he telegraphed. "I feel that the industry is entitled to this demonstration in view of large investment in our organization over 18 years and to avoid the serious risk of having it appear that there is a cleavage in the industry." The agents were dismayed when rumors suggesting that Byoir was behind the steel campaign appeared in print, and they quickly placed an advertisement in the *Wall Street Journal* explaining what the agency had done for the steel industry after the seizure—an ad that caused some controversy in PR circles because of its self-promotional nature.[78]

In the end the greatest beneficiary of the campaign was not the steel industry but Hill and Knowlton. Catering to the highest echelons of industrial corporations and trade associations, the firm subsequently used the Steel Wage Case as a selling point for the its services. The crisis was prominently featured in Hill's book, which was sent to prospective clients, and in a mailing to presidents and directors of steel, aircraft, distillery, chemical, and petroleum corporations, all industries where the agency had developed strong connections. "Perhaps history will reveal the true motives of all sides—labor, management and government—in a struggle in which the only loser was the public," a contemporary wrote. Those motives may not be entirely apparent even today, but the only clear winner was the public relations firm Hill and Knowlton of New York.[79]

CHAPTER SIX

Smoke and Mirrors

Public Relations and the News Media

Alton Ochsner was a man on a mission. In May 1953 the surgeon wrote in the *Nation*, "my colleagues and I are convinced that the products of cigarette smoking are responsible for lung cancers." In September he made similar allegations at a Kansas City medical conference, and coverage of his remarks appeared in daily newspapers as well as *Time* and *Reader's Digest*. At the Greater New York Dental Meeting in December, Ochsner, a former president of the American Cancer Society, said the male population of the United States would be "decimated" if "cigarette smoking increases as it has in the past, unless some steps are taken to remove the cancer-producing factor in tobacco." After the meeting cigarette stocks dropped one to four points, although they rebounded within a few days.[1]

Ochsner's was not a one-man crusade. During the 1950s a growing body of medical research suggested that tobacco caused cancer, heart disease, and other ailments, research that scientists brought to the attention of the public through the mass media. Physicians in growing numbers agreed that smoking could be hazardous, so many added their voices to those of researchers and members of volunteer organizations in a chorus that warned the public to stop smoking. Ominously for the tobacco industry, during 1953 cigarette consumption began to drop, evidence that the public increasingly believed there existed a link between smoking and disease.

When it became clear that the health crusade had made headway with the public, the cigarette makers took to the airwaves and the print media with a message of their own. Together with Hill and Knowlton, the manufacturers created the Tobacco Industry Research Committee (TIRC) to promote the notion that the case against smoking has not been proved; *Business Week* would call H&K's work "one of PR's best finger-in-the-dike jobs" ever. Manufacturers also turned to advertising, particularly of filtered cigarettes, to respond to the health scare.[2]

Both the tobacco industry and health professionals relied on the news media to disseminate information and opinions about smoking. The battle boiled down to two basic frames, "smoking is hazardous," and "there is a scientific conflict about smoking." Health activists and cigarette manufacturers alike had a relatively easy time setting the media agenda. But in this battle for media coverage, the cigarette producers had a distinct advantage— the expertise of their advertising and public relations agents. The manufacturers could not displace medical news, but, by insisting that there existed two sides to the tobacco story, H&K convinced reporters to include both frames in their stories, thus providing the only reassurance some smokers needed.

Genesis of a Health Scare: Doctors' Criticism of Tobacco

Tobacco smoking has been condemned in Western culture since its introduction to Europe. Although some believed it had medicinal value, tobacco was denounced as early as 1601, when the British *Calendar of State Papers* reported that surgeons believed a patient died because of insatiable tobacco smoking. In the United States southerners introduced Union troops to cigarettes during the Civil War, and tobacco opponents, mostly from the Midwest and often temperance advocates, demanded regulation. By the turn of the century, when the American Tobacco Company began mass manufacture, demand existed, but so did an anticigarette crusade. Led by Lucy Page Gaston, the National Anti-Cigarette League in 1901 agitated for an end to the sale of cigarettes, and fourteen states banned or severely restricted their use, while others prohibited their sale to minors. Disenchantment with Prohibition later contributed to the repeal of antitobacco laws.[3]

During the early decades of the twentieth century, tobacco opponents began to build a medical case to support their suspicions. One of the first significant research projects, conducted by Herbert Lombard and Carl Doering in 1928, disproved several cancer theories. Cancer was not contagious, and neither housing conditions, height, nor weight was a significant predictor. The study did find two factors later considered important, heredity and tobacco use. In testing for lip, jaw, cheek, and tongue cancer, the doctors found pipe smoking the most important variable. Although they were not widely reported, such studies began to have an impact, as a small number of American physicians recommended that patients stop smoking or filter their cigarettes.[4]

The issue largely disappeared during World War II because of a lack of funding and because antitobaccoism seemed unpatriotic. Research that did appear was often characterized by wishful attempts to find ways people could continue to smoke. Two doctors published in the *Journal of the American Medical Association* a report on the findings of a German researcher whose survey of the literature indicated "without reservation" that tobacco was carcinogenic. The Americans were much more cautious. "Tobacco tar may be considered at least weakly carcinogenic," they concluded. Even more resolute advocates would have faced an uphill battle, because tobacco corporations got all the free promotion any industry could desire during the war: Winston Churchill's fat cigars and Franklin D. Roosevelt's jaunty cigarettes seemed ubiquitous. Roosevelt listed tobacco as an essential food, and popular brands were shipped overseas by the billion, leaving a shortage at home. Despite warnings of danger, then, the 1940s solidified tobacco's place in American culture.[5]

Soon after the war a renewed interest in research, funded by the increase of money given to universities and hospitals in the postwar science boom, helped doctors accumulate enough medical evidence to alarm tobacco manufacturers, smokers, and doctors. Major studies associating lung cancer with smoking appeared by Ernest Wynder and Evarts Graham in the *Journal of the American Medical Association* (1950); by Richard Doll and Bradford Hill in the *British Medical Journal* (1952); by Wynder and Graham with Adele Croninger in *Cancer Research* (1953); and by Alton Ochsner in 1952 and 1954. All the researchers were convinced smoking was more than merely "associated with" cancer. Indeed, Ochsner opened his 1954 book with the sentence, "Smoking causes cancer," a declaration industry defenders considered libelous.[6]

Because they covered such stories, popular magazines were instrumental in creating the health scare. *Reader's Digest*, the first strongly antitobacco American magazine, published articles questioning the safety of tobacco as early as the 1940s. A January 1950 article also criticized smoking. "Think over the many theoretical and actual kinds of damage which smoking causes," the article said. "Discount them all you want. Then look in vain for any evidence of any measurable *good* effect. Then speculate with incredulity as to why we go right on smoking." In June of that year a doctor wrote to the *Journal of the American Medical Association*, saying that the *Digest* article raised questions about nicotine, indicating some doctors were aware of criticisms appearing in the popular press. Additionally, one citizen wrote to President Truman about excessive use of liquor and tobacco, referring to the *Digest* information as cause for alarm. The researchers' claims in the news media had taken a toll on what people thought and said about smoking. A 1952 article, "Cancer by the Carton," attracted just as much attention.[7]

By 1953 other magazines had joined the *Digest* in covering the smoking story, but many continued to downplay reported risks. *Science Digest* and *Science News Letter* covered major studies but in brief with guarded conclusions. *Life* explained a 1953 report by Wynder and Graham, but the magazine felt compelled to add, "they do not necessarily mean everyone should promptly stop smoking, for this might create nervous ailments in smokers who would feel they had lost a comforting relaxation." Ironically, Graham died of lung cancer in 1957, and he had quit smoking, contrary to *Life's* interpretation, precisely because of his research findings. Positive news about tobacco was given good play, such as a two-page spread in *U.S. News and World Report*, when one researcher found that "Smoking Mice Live Normal Span." Most people did not want to believe their habit was dangerous, and articles in popular magazines reflected hope that smoking might be safe.[8]

Responses of radio commentators also varied when it came to cigarettes. H. V. Kaltenborn, whose interest leaned toward foreign policy rather than domestic problems, did not comment on the tobacco scare. Walter Winchell's broadcast on 29 November 1953 defended the industry, claiming that the tobacco companies had supported cancer research and noting that American Tobacco alone had contributed $250,000 to the Damon Runyon Cancer Fund in just one year. However, a month later, Winchell had grown more concerned. "The scientists may be unconvinced that the cigarette is guilty," he said, "but I am fully convinced that it is very far from innocent."[9]

Actually the Federal Trade Commission, not the health scare, brought most of the negative press to the tobacco industry before 1953. The commission frequently brought action against cigarette companies, often for misleading health claims, but it was handcuffed because it had to work on a case-by-case basis. For example, in 1950 the commission issued cease and desist orders against Camels for claiming that they aided digestion and relieved fatigue and against Old Golds for their "Not a Cough in a Carload" campaign. Both companies had changed campaigns by the time the orders

were issued. Camels had switched to a thirty-day mildness test which produced no evidence of throat irritation, and Old Golds proclaimed "A Treat
Instead of a Treatment." A warning against one company did not affect others, even for closely related phrases, and a change of wording in an ad might
mean the commission would have to bring an entirely new suit against the
company for making essentially the same claim. Finally, in an attempt to
regulate the tobacco industry more closely, in 1955 the commission created
guidelines restricting health claims and testimonial ads.[10]

Health Groups in the Media

Voluntary health organizations were fundamental to the disclosure of antismoking researchers' contentions. These groups were well positioned to
conduct campaigns about cigarettes, to reach a mass audience with information meant to persuade people to stop smoking. But such groups as the
American Cancer Society (ACS), and especially individual doctors, lacked
the organization, funding, and knowledge about public relations strategies
needed to argue convincingly about such a highly valued commodity. One
major obstacle to conducting an effective campaign against smoking was the
failure of the many concerned groups to work together. Organizations with
an interest in the smoking issue, in addition to the ACS, included the American Medical Association, the American Lung Association, and the American
Heart Association. Their research agendas overlapped, there was no coordinated release of information, no pooling of resources, no sense they should
do anything more than what they had always done. Correction of any one
of these omissions would have aided the antismoking cause.[11]

Although they overlooked many opportunities for a more effective antismoking campaign, the volunteer groups did keep the issue in the news. Reports on medical research made 1954 one of the worst years the tobacco industry faced. An article in the *New England Journal of Medicine* reported
that about 60 percent of Massachusetts doctors surveyed believed heavy
smoking led to lung cancer, and many of them had changed their smoking
habits. Another survey found that about 80 percent of doctors agreed that
heavy smoking "may have serious effects on body physiology," although
there was less agreement on the relationship between smoking and lung
cancer. An American Cancer Society study conducted by Hammond and
Horn and released in August asserted, "it can no longer be doubted that an
association exists between smoking habits and lung cancer death rates." If
that were not damning enough, Americans soon got word of a British study

of 40,564 doctors that indicated that although the number of deaths was small, the deaths due to lung cancer increased as the amount of tobacco smoked increased.[12]

The health groups habitually provided such information to the news media. The largest of the organizations, the ACS, believed an informed public would choose not to smoke, and therefore called not for tobacco prohibition or even regulation but for decisions by individual smokers. In other words, it believed that publicizing the risks associated with smoking would solve the problem. The ACS was the most active in making health claims against smoking in the news media, two times more than all other groups combined.[13]

An examination of the media relations of one of the ACS-associated doctors, Evarts A. Graham, reveals the uncertain relationship between medical researchers and the news media. Graham was a highly regarded physician who won such awards as the American Medical Association's Distinguished Service Medal, the ACS award for outstanding contribution, and the Lister Medal of England's Royal College of Surgeons. In 1933 he had performed the first successful surgery to remove an entire human lung. Graham understood that publicity was important to the ACS and to the antismoking cause. When society staff members requested information from the doctor for news releases, he always complied. In fact, he sometimes complained that the ACS had not done enough to promote various aspects of smoking research. He also praised other researchers when their work received wide media coverage. "I am very glad [Cuyler Hammond] has been given so much publicity in the press and in some of the popular magazines," he told ACS officials after Hammond and Horn's 1954 study hit the press. "The information is so important that it should reach everybody."[14]

As a nationally prominent physician, Graham had frequent personal contact with journalists. He received invitations to speak over the radio and appear on television and in films. He also spoke at meetings, which one state-level ACS official told him would assure press coverage, something that would be good for both fund raising and public education. Graham observed great interest among journalists regarding cigarettes. In a letter to an ACS official about a news brief he had written, he said, "I knew it was for the use of the newspapers," adding, "since they are always eager to get what information they can about the relation of cigarette smoking to cancer of the lung I emphasized that particularly."[15]

Yet Graham had no idea how to prepare information suitable for press use. Charles Cameron, the ACS medical and science director, requested that the doctor write a 500-word article on cancer. "These articles will be distributed through our press facilities throughout the nation, appearing in both large and small newspapers," Cameron explained. Graham's article would be part of a compendium on different types of cancer and would be used for educational and fund raising purposes. The director specified that the piece should "be couched in language understandable to the lay reader." Graham returned an article that included statements like, "One of these is the so-called epidermoid cancer with its variant, the undifferentiated carcinoma." Cameron was understandably dismayed, especially because other scientists sent similar offerings. He told Graham that the material was inappropriate, and a rewrite by the ACS press section left Graham's piece in an unrecognizable form: "The problem is early detection. There is a way. The 'silent shadow', as it is called, can show up on an x-ray long before the person is aware that something is wrong." Graham approved the revision.[16]

Other researchers displayed a similar lack of PR sophistication, which not only limited their effectiveness but actually hurt their cause. A Hill and Knowlton memorandum indicated that Alton Ochsner's performance in a newsreel "was so terrible that it would do us more good than harm." It was bad enough that a staff member arranged to buy a print, saying "this should come in handy in our files." More seriously, a 1957 *Reader's Digest* article analyzed tar filtration for the leading cigarettes and found Kent's "micronite" filter the most effective. With its reputation as an antitobacco magazine, *Reader's Digest* information seemed objective and reliable, particularly because it appeared to be an endorsement from eminent scientists Hammond and Horn. Kent introduced its "improved micronite filter," and Lorillard reported that sales of Kent increased 500 percent in two months. Similar claims had been advertised before, but, public relations consultant Chester Burger reported, "many of the public believed the editors of the *Reader's Digest* when they would not believe the manufacturer. The editors were an independent, respected source; the manufacturers had a self-interest."[17]

A lack of public relations expertise showed itself also in the problems caused by the health groups' inability to work together. Media stories generated by the health organizations focused almost exclusively on the possible connection between smoking and lung cancer, when impressive studies on links with other forms of cancer, heart disease, and other illness also existed. Lung cancer accounts for less than 15 percent of the deaths attributed to cigarettes, so an emphasis on lung cancer was detrimental to the overall effort to educate people. The most outspoken researchers—Alton Ochsner, Ernest Wynder and Evarts Graham, and Cuyler Hammond and Daniel Horn—all studied lung cancer, but a public relations agency like Hill and Knowlton would have helped the health groups create a more united front.

In sum, the health groups did affect media discussion about smoking.

They believed that research findings were important news and that it was their job to publicize those findings. Cigarettes became an issue that concerned people as stories about smoking appeared frequently enough to capture people's attention, enough even to convince some to smoke less or not at all. The ACS in particular was active at both the national and local levels, and it enlisted the assistance of the doctors it funded to promote the message about smoking. Although the society realized the importance of making its messages accessible to the general public, at times the doctors failed to do so. Meanwhile, groups that could have promoted other aspects of the smoking and health issue, like the American Heart Association, were less active in trying to reach the public through the news media. The scientific evidence against cigarettes was building, but the problems the health groups encountered left room for a strong tobacco industry response.

The Tobacco Industry and the Media

Public Relations

Widespread news coverage, the consumption slump, and the small drop in stock prices in late 1953 signaled to the manufacturers that the claims against smoking had been effective, and the industry took action. A group of manufacturers called together by Paul M. Hahn, president of American Tobacco, met in mid-December in New York City. Included were executives from R. J. Reynolds, Philip Morris, Benson & Hedges, United States Tobacco, and Brown and Williamson. On 15 December a delegation of four met with Bert Goss and other Hill and Knowlton executives at the Plaza Hotel, explaining that two important groups of tobacco growers and all the major manufacturers except Liggett and Myers had agreed to participate in a public relations program. They hired Hill and Knowlton to "serve as the operating agency of the companies, hiring all the staff and disbursing all funds." By 22 December the agency had developed a PR program, and on 4 January it announced the creation of the Tobacco Industry Research Committee through a newspaper advertisement headlined "A Frank Statement to Cigarette Smokers" and signed by fifteen cigarette manufacturers, tobacco warehousers, and growers' groups.[18]

Although most of its experience was in heavy industry, H&K was a good choice for the manufacturers. Such corporate accounts as Avco, California Texas Oil, Studebaker, and Procter and Gamble indicated that the agency was both prestigious and capable. Extensive trade association work had given it the experience to help the cigarette makers set up a program from scratch. The butter campaign and the steel account had given it the opportunity to build contacts in and gain understanding of the agricultural community, and Washington work for steel, butter, and aviation had sharpened political skills that would be put to use when the firm helped to create the Tobacco Institute in 1958.

H&K's relationship with two other industries embattled by health claims, liquor and chemicals, also gave it an edge. As *Tide* noted, "What's happening to the tobacco business today in the form of adverse publicity is old hat to the much-plagued, more maligned U.S. liquor business." In 1950 H&K had performed a four-month survey of the industry and its problems, made recommendations, and supervised a program for the Licensed Beverages Industries Tax Council, including an external newsletter, a review of advertising policy, the establishment of a women's division, and an expansion of personnel. The chemical industry's situation, particularly relating to the use of chemicals in food, was even more closely related.[19]

The Manufacturing Chemists' Association retained the agency in 1951 to combat the negative publicity the industry was receiving in connection to congressional hearings on chemicals in food. Bert Goss noted that "it would never be possible to prove that foods were safe, owing to the wide differences in human ability to absorb foods . . . and so on," making it "difficult to promise the public that chemicals used in foods will be safe." The agency's program sought to establish the association "as the authoritative source of information of industry-wide problems and policies," recommending that H&K should prepare a background memorandum and a booklet on the industry's position, develop suggestions for member company activities, enlist the support of interested groups such as nutritionists and educators, and develop a speakers' bureau. These activities primed the H&K staffers for what one called "the most challenging problem our organization has ever faced."[20]

Hill and Knowlton's view of the tobacco problem was very different than the doctors'. As one agency employee described it, "There is only one problem—confidence, and how to establish it; public assurance, and how to create it—in a perhaps long interim when scientific doubts must remain." The situation was more than "solely charges concerning the harmful effects of cigarettes," because such accusations could raise questions about the "integrity of the manufacturers producing cigarettes." It was not a health problem, but one of contradictory, possibly mistaken, scientific research and the consequences of that confusion for the industry.[21]

Hill and Knowlton thus stressed the view that there existed within the medical community a controversy about the evidence against tobacco. As John Hill wrote, "the public is in danger of being convinced that there is only one side. All the industry has a right to ask or expect now is for the public to understand that the case has not been proven and that there are 'two sides.'" A scientist affiliated with the TIRC argued that introducing evidence on the "opposite side" was dangerous because people would recognize "'two sides' to a question which most of us believe has many more than two facets involved." But, as Hill saw it, the way to bring about public understanding of the industry's side was "time and patience, and the inauguration of some important research projects." At least one of Hill's contemporaries thought the strategy was effective, because it insisted that public health was paramount, but, A. M. Rochlen added, it also "operates to raise a doubt in the minds of the general public that some of the sensational accusations and conclusions were justified."[22]

Therefore the agency recommended that tobacco manufacturers form a "Cigarette Research and Information Committee," which would sponsor both medical research and editorial and statistical research, all under the auspices of the public relations counsel. Executives considered independent scientific research essential, even though industry leaders had hoped to avoid this approach. The companies argued they had conducted considerably more research in their own laboratories and had sponsored more work at universities and hospitals than was generally known. Dissemination of information already gathered should solve the problem. But John Hill "emphatically warned the companies that they should probably expect to sponsor additional research," wrote H&K vice president Bert Goss, who had transferred to the New York office from the capital in 1951.[23]

Hill and Knowlton favored the research approach for several reasons. Only through research positive toward smoking could the industry demonstrate that a controversy existed. Additionally, by funding scientists indirectly through the committee, the companies could argue that researchers were independent, not controlled by the companies. The industry could also assert that it was not engaging in monopolistic practices. Manufacturers feared the Justice Department not only because the American Tobacco trust had been dissolved in 1911, but also because they had been investigated for price-fixing and other charges in 1939 and again in 1946. For this reason the industry had sponsored no joint ventures prior to formation of the TIRC. The *Raleigh News and Observer* reported in early January that the Justice Department had informed cigarette manufacturers that they could not act in concert to combat the medical claims, and even contributions to medical research would have to be made as individuals rather than a group. The TIRC provided a way around this predicament because it was an independent organization with its own research and public relations agendas. Finally, members of H&K's staff said they did not believe that smoking caused cancer, and research was the only way to disprove the scientists' accusations.[24]

The early history of the Tobacco Industry Research Committee and the Tobacco Institute is indivisible from the history of Hill and Knowlton. A 1960s Brown and Williamson information sheet on the agency said that the public relations counsel "is so intimately involved in the affairs of both" the TIRC and Tobacco Institute "that a proper separation of functions, as well as a strict definition of operations is virtually impossible" in a two-page document. The memo further explained that the TIRC's executive director, W. T. Hoyt, had been on H&K's payroll since the committee's founding, and Carl Thompson, a full-time H&K New York employee, was "apparently regarded as the principal contact or informational source" at the institute. Although the PR agents met regularly with the individual companies' counsel, in essence, the TIRC was Hill and Knowlton.[25]

Provided a 1954 budget of $1.2 million by the manufacturers, Hill and Knowlton helped the industry put together the committee's Scientific Advisory Board (SAB), selecting members who could support the idea that a medical controversy existed. Corporation research directors interviewed potential members of the SAB and a scientific director, choosing for that position Dr. Clarence Cook Little, former president of the University of Michigan and of the American Association for Cancer Research. Little had written in 1944 that although no definite evidence existed, "it would seem unwise to fill the lungs repeatedly with a suspension of fine particles of a tobacco product of which smoke consists," whether from tobacco or city air. His statements as director, however, insisted that the case had not been proved. The SAB consisted of men such as McKeen Cattel, professor and head of the pharmacology department at Cornell, and Leon Jacobson, professor at the University of Chicago and director of the Argonne Cancer Research Hospital. Another board member, Paul Kotin of the National Cancer Institute, said he believed cigarettes were partially guilty but sat on the board to see that the industry faced its responsibility. The conflict on the board contributed to the idea a medical controversy existed, even though growing numbers of doctors believed the opposite.[26]

By the time Little was appointed in June, the TIRC had already conducted significant public relations work. The account was supervised by Dick Darrow, who had come to Hill and Knowlton from Glenn L. Martin when John Mapes defected from the agency in 1950. In its first six months of existence, the committee issued eleven press releases, built a library of information on the scientific case for and against smoking, assisted at least two dozen reporters with stories and editorials, published several brochures, monitored press coverage, established personal contacts with doctors, medical organizations, and science writers, created mailing lists, attended or covered state, national, and international medical and scientific meetings, and began to work through its international offices to coordinate information gathering, particularly with the British industry. It had also begun development of a congressional information package to inform tobacco state representatives about the issue. In November the committee issued its first scientific research grants, totaling about $82,000.[27]

Hill and Knowlton considered different responses to the scientists who promoted the antismoking messages. "We must early decide our own attitude toward the findings of men like Wynder, Rhoads, Ochsner, et al.," the staff economic writer said:

We have a choice . . . of:
(a) Smearing and belittling them;
(b) Trying to overwhelm them with mass publication of the opposed viewpoints of other specialists;
(c) Debating them in the public arena; or
(d) We can determine to raise the issue far above them, so that they are hardly even mentioned; and then we can make our real case.[28]

H&K chose a combination of these approaches. Goss instructed the staff to remember that it did not wish to add fuel to fire by stirring more interest in the doctors' claims. The staff monitored medical journals and conferences, and although they did not actively try to counterattack by sending pro-tobacco doctors to medical meetings, executives gathered information and sent a compendium to doctors across the United States. The agents wanted to avoid direct debate with the scientists.[29]

Avoiding rather than seeking publicity, H&K's goal was to ensure that reporters consulted the agency before publishing articles on smoking. "Our sole interest," Goss wrote, "is in knowing what is being written and in getting our side of the story over if an article is scheduled for publication." To this end they provided background memoranda on the TIRC and on research positive to smoking, and they met with science writers and editors to explain there was more than one side to the smoking story. They also attended medical meetings with prepared statements in hand whenever negative news was expected. When editors printed or broadcast stories the public relations experts considered factually incorrect, they scheduled meetings to explain the industry's position. Hill and Knowlton reported to TIRC chairperson Timothy Hartnett that one negative radio program had been postponed after such a discussion. In another instance, Goss—a former *Newsweek* editor—met with a *Newsweek* journalist who "expressed appreciation for the call and said he would get in touch with us whenever he wrote anything on cigarettes in the future." The manufacturers' success in this endeavor caused one tobacco critic to remark, "like a tail of a kite, no story about the risk of smoking goes anywhere without a tobacco industry rebuttal trailing along behind."[30]

Hill and Knowlton emphasized several themes within the "case is not proved" frame, all based on credible claims that the medical community tried to counter. First, they forced the scientists to defend not only the results their studies had produced, but their methodologies. Animal experimentation might be useful, but who could be sure mouse skin was comparable with human lung tissue? And painting mice with tar was not the same as inhaling smoke into human lungs. Other data collected by anticigarette scientists could be dismissed as statistical hogwash, because correlation did not prove smoking caused cancer and because characteristics of the smoker might not have been accounted for in statistical studies. Nonsmokers might be more cautious, eat differently, go to the doctor more, or hold less risky jobs than smokers. Antismoking doctors admitted that they did not understand the mechanisms by which tobacco caused cancer, but they maintained that medicine should err on the side of caution, citing the example that doctors did not wait until they understood cholera before they closed contaminated public wells.[31]

The industry also asserted that the charges against cigarettes came from a handful of doctors who were either puritanical zealots or publicity hounds. E. A. Darr, head of R. J. Reynolds, exemplified this tactic when he said in 1953, "One of the best ways of getting publicity is for a doctor to make some startling claim relative to people's health regardless of whether such statement is based on fact or theory." Again, the tobacco industry had what seemed like a reasonable argument. Many of the early studies about smoking had been conducted by the same researchers: Wynder and Graham, Doll and Hill, Ochsner, and a few others. Wynder had studied with Graham, Hammond worked under Raymond Pearl, who had conducted an important antismoking study in the 1930s, and Ochsner taught Luther Terry, the surgeon general whose report in 1964 declared smoking hazardous. This is not surprising, given that students often adopt their mentors' research agendas. But these researchers did seek attention. Wynder acknowledged to Graham that "now that the problem has been brought to such a forefront of the public opinion, I think that more money will be given to this type of investigation from all the public cancer fund-raising agencies." Hammond and Horn sensationally announced the results of their American Cancer Society study before actually completing it, because, they said, their findings were shocking. Whatever their motives, such actions lent credence to the TIRC's accusations.[32]

The industry stressed too the amount of money it spent on research. The *Wall Street Journal's* coverage of a 1955 study that provided the "missing link" between smoking, tissue changes, and lung cancer concluded with Timothy Hartnett's statement that $90,000 in grants had been allotted for study on human lung tissue alone. This sounded like a great deal of money, but compared with profits and with the amount spent on public relations and advertising, medical research was a low priority. Tobacco critic Elizabeth Whelan points out that from the mid-1950s to the mid-1980s, tobacco companies spent about $100 million for research, less than one-tenth the industry's annual advertising budget. The TIRC could announce it had $500,000 budgeted for research in 1954, but in a budget of $1.2 million, public relations was deemed more important than science. Moreover, much of the research funded did not directly relate to smoking and health; one survey of TIRC grantees found that 80 percent of the scientists said none of their research looked at the health effects of smoking.[33]

As long as some nonsmokers got cancer and other lifelong smokers did not, the tobacco industry could point out smoking was not the sole cause of the disease. The "Frank Statement" advertisement drafted by H&K executives said there was no clear evidence that cigarette smoking was one of the causes of cancer. "Medical science," it asserted, "has no greater challenge than to track down the real causes of this disease." The manufacturers often blamed industrial pollution, car exhaust, and other factors. But Wynder and Cornfield had demonstrated in 1953 that rural versus city living did not affect the cancer rate of physicians, indicating that air pollution was not as great a cause as the industry insisted. Ochsner added that air pollution could not explain the different rates of cancer between men and women—nor could he understand why the tobacco industry was so willing to accept pollution studies based on the same methodologies as the cigarette research. Yet people unfamiliar with the complete body of medical evidence might have found the manufacturers' claim easy to believe.[34]

The industry's biggest problem in early 1954 was legitimacy. Hill and Knowlton executives realized that they needed credible health professionals to counter tobacco's medical opponents. The doctors on the Scientific Advisory Board had impressive credentials, with connections to top universities and hospitals across the United States, and the TIRC used its association with these doctors to assert that tobacco opponents lacked conclusive evidence against smoking. At least some people trusted TIRC officials. "Many will argue that an impartial investigation can hardly be expected from a body of experts paid by the tobacco industry," Waldemar Kaempffert, a science writer, wrote in the *New York Times.* "Dr. Little is an eminent geneticist, a type of scientist who has the courage to face facts and to state them." The TIRC's mere existence helped to promote the idea that the medical evidence was not yet convincing.[35]

Advertising

The tobacco industry did not depend solely on the program devised by Hill and Knowlton. Manufacturers also used advertising to defuse the health scare, particularly with the introduction of filtered cigarettes. Before the crisis, Viceroys were the only filter-tips on the market, but each leading corporation introduced at least one filtered brand in 1953 or 1954, and the six majors added eleven new brands in four years. In 1950 filtered cigarettes accounted for less than 1 percent of total American cigarette sales, but by 1955 the share was 19 percent. And there were other product innovations. "Scared smokers, like the trusting children who followed the Pied Piper of Hamelin, are turning to filter-tip cigarettes, to king-size cigarettes, to king-size filter-tip cigarettes, to 'denicotinized' cigarettes, to filter holders, for promised 'health protection,'" Alton Ochsner noted in 1954.[36]

Despite their popularity, filters could not eliminate risk. Good filters removed some of the harmful components of smoke, but they also removed flavor, so smokers who chose the most flavorful filtered cigarettes were selecting the ones with the least protection. "The manufacturer soon discovered that any filter would suffice as a symbol of safety," Senator Maurine Neuberger asserted. "The only reward for high filtration was low flavor and consequently low sales." People smoked more filtered cigarettes, which used less tobacco per cigarette, and some filtered brands used stronger tobacco to overcome the filter, making them more harmful than regular cigarettes. A congressional investigation later revealed that most filter-tips produced as much or more nicotine and tar as nonfiltered brands. Filters could remove some nicotine and tar, but no one understood which ingredients in cigarettes were harmful, making it impossible to know if the filters removed the right substances.[37]

Although filters were not entirely effective, misleading advertising apparently led some smokers to believe they offered protection. Herbert Tareyton cigarettes offered a "Selective Filter" of purified cellulose and activated charcoal which had "unusual powers of selectivity which hold back elements that can detract from the pleasure of smoking" without removing the "full-bodied flavor." Pall Malls, king-sized like Tareytons, claimed "fine tobacco is its own best filter," and popular actress Rosalind Russell told smokers, "L&M Filters Are Just What the Doctor Ordered!" Smokers were understandably confused by such claims, which were nearly unavoidable.

Tobacco companies spent about $38 million on television, newspaper, and magazine advertising in 1954 with a disproportionate amount on filters. For both frightened smokers and a worried industry, filters seemed like a good solution to the scare.[38]

But advertising was not merely a solution to the health scare; advertising excesses also helped to cause and perpetuate it. One Hill and Knowlton employee argued that none of the corporations should "seek a competitive advantage by inferring to its public that *its* product is less risky than others. (No claims that special filters or toasting, or expert selections of tobacco or extra length in the butt, or anything else makes a given brand less likely to cause you-know-what.)" Advertising executive Joseph Seldin agreed, remarking that the tobacco companies had worked themselves into a corner, "in effect promoting brands on a my-brand-gives-less-cancer-than-your-brand basis." While no ad campaign was that blatant, many implied their brands were safer than others. A 1954 *Life* ad for Philip Morris announced that it was the only cigarette made with "Di-GL," "the great scientific discovery that protects you from certain harsh irritants found in *every other* cigarette. No *other* cigarette . . . *with or without filters* . . . can remove all these irritants." The H&K staff concluded that the obstacles facing the TIRC included the "impression in the public mind implanted and aggressively cultivated over the years by much cigarette advertising that cigarette smoking in some way is bad for the health."[39]

Advertising also alienated one of the industry's most important publics, health care professionals. H&K questioned an R. J. Reynolds ad containing information on a survey that claimed "more doctors use Camels than any other cigarette." People who read the ads did not know, an H&K memorandum reported, that "interviewers had placed in the doctors' hotel rooms on their arrival [to a conference] cartons of Camel cigarettes. The chances are that the doctors ran out of cigarettes on arrival, and conveniently put a pack of Camels into their own pockets." The survey researchers then asked doctors what kind of cigarettes they had in their pockets. Public relations executive John Ducas worried that this kind of scam was "not the most effective way to build cordial relations with a group whose support is almost required." Indeed, the *Journal of the American Medical Association* had complained about cigarette advertising several times in the 1950s before banning it in 1954, and *Advertising Age* crusaded against misleading health claims throughout the 1950s. The agency did not intervene in tobacco advertising because manufacturers told John Hill that product promotion was one activity "that might very clearly fall within the purview of the antitrust act," and the tobacco industry continued its dubious advertising practices until the federal government intervened.[40]

Ads disseminating information about filter-tip cigarettes did apparently affect consumer behavior by the end of 1954. Some chose to sacrifice the taste and style of a favorite brand in order to smoke a "safer" cigarette. Others tried to stop smoking all together, indicating some believed the scientists, but Ochsner worried, "it's the cigarette huckster, not the scientist, who is likely to control the industry's claims" in an "advertising barrage for ever-new miracle filters—filters that will not only filter out the nicotine in tobacco smoke but even the carcinogens which the cigarette industry claims aren't there!"[41]

News Media Coverage
of the Health Scare

Both the scientists' and the advertising and public relations experts' interpretations of smoking were available to the press. The early disbelief among many journalists about charges made against cigarettes clearly affected their coverage of the health scare, but by 1954 the research indicting tobacco convinced some editors and reporters that tobacco was to blame. A review of coverage in specialty publications and in general circulation newspapers indicates that regardless of personal beliefs, editorial coverage of the Tobacco Industry Research Committee was generally positive. If reporters were skeptical about the honesty of the manufacturers' effort, they kept their doubts out of the news.

Many specialty publications ignored the controversy altogether, or mentioned it only in passing. Despite presumed interest on the part of tobacco growers, agricultural periodicals like the *Farmer*, *Farm Quarterly*, and *Farm Journal* did not cover the health scare in 1953 or 1954. Targeted at an African American audience, *Ebony* ignored the issue, and such women's magazines as *McCall's* and *Ladies' Home Journal* likewise devoted none of their pages to cigarettes. The liberal Catholic *Commonweal* mentioned the health scare in a three-paragraph note on a Cancer Society study. "With their hold on people, cigarettes may win out after all," the magazine said. "Certainly, with our Prohibition experience behind us, it would be foolhardy to forbid their sale." Other religious publications, like the Jewish magazine *Commentary*, avoided discussion of the scare. Only *Christian Century* questioned the manufacturers' decision to form the TIRC, arguing that "the cigaret people had better try again."[42]

Another set of periodicals, those produced for public relations and advertising agents, covered the issue in great detail, but almost solely from the standpoint of how the health scare affected the industry. *Printers' Ink* articles focused on sales figures, provided in annual surveys considered the most authoritative source available, and on advertising dollars spent by the tobacco companies. *Tide* wondered if other industries—cigars, confectionery—might be able to take advantage of "cigaret troubles," and contemplated the "record-breaking budgets" that would accompany the new marketing battle for "filter supremacy." *Advertising Age* regularly printed articles that included information critical of cigarettes and of the ways they were sold. In addition to its campaign against misleading health claims, *Ad Age* published articles about tobacco critics who asserted that the industry had disregarded conclusive evidence that smoking caused cancer.[43]

In contrast to many of the special-audience publications, virtually all of the nation's daily newspapers carried information on the health scare, and according to Hill and Knowlton's records, newspapers favored the formation of the Tobacco Industry Research Committee by a 13 to 1 margin. An analysis of editorial opinion, based on a sample of 671 articles collected by a clipping agency after the TIRC's announcement ad ran, found that only 9 percent of the papers expressing opinions on the TIRC were unfavorable, predicting biased research, while 65 percent were favorable without reservation. For example, neither the *New York Times* nor the *Wall Street Journal* questioned the integrity of the industry's move in news or editorial columns. Only about seventy articles indicated a belief that conclusive proof against smoking already existed. North Carolina's *Raleigh News and Observer* criticized formation of the committee, but only because its editors feared people would be skeptical of research produced by scientists linked to the industry.[44]

Of greater significance is a comparison of the ways newspapers dealt with the two competing interpretations of the health scare itself, "smoking is hazardous" versus "there is a scientific controversy about smoking." The release of Hammond and Horn's American Cancer Society study, presented at a medical meeting in San Francisco in 1954, afforded the TIRC its first opportunity to counter a charge from the researchers with its own statement. A review of coverage in the *New York Times*, the newspaper of record, and two newspapers with opposing political stances, the *St. Louis Post-Dispatch* and the *Chicago Daily Tribune*, shows what some newspapers did with the two frames.

The *New York Times*'s coverage of Hammond and Horn's study was both lengthy and thorough. "Cigarette smokers from 50 to 70 years of age have a higher death rate, from all diseases, as much as 75 per cent higher than that of nonsmokers," read the lead sentence of the first story about the study. The article then discussed the study's results, the doctors' backgrounds, and the methods used to uncover the findings. It also reported that another doctor presented an experiment showing exposure to cigarette smoke did not cause cancer in rats. Although the rats lived only 85 percent as long as a control group, the cause of death was tuberculosis rather than cancer. Finally, the paper noted that a spokesman for the TIRC "said the committee had no statement to make" in response.[45]

The following day the *Times* printed two follow-up articles that suggested that a medical controversy existed. The first was based on a statement by Clarence Cook Little, appointed to head the Scientific Advisory Board just a week before, commenting on the ACS study. Although noting that the doctor called the report "preliminary," the article summarized the study as a "statistical examination covering the last two and a half years." A second story, "Doctors Puff Away," followed. "While many doctors puffed on cigarettes in meeting rooms and hotel lobbies," the story said, the outgoing president of the American Medical Association "voiced the belief that the case linking cigarettes and cancer had 'not been proven.'" The doctor stressed, however, "that, in refusing to see any proof of a connection between cigarettes and cancer, he was not 'suspecting' the report of Drs. Hammond and Horn." Another physician said, "Most doctors seem impressed with the magnitude and the technical caliber of the study. They regard the statistical results as valid and as the strongest evidence to date against smoking," but he did not know of any who had given up smoking because of the report. Doctors, like everyone else, had reason to ignore the evidence.[46]

The *St. Louis Post-Dispatch* and the *Chicago Daily Tribune* also presented the Cancer Society study on the front page and offered the TIRC response the following day on inside pages. The *Post-Dispatch* announced, "Survey Shows Cigarette Smokers Die Sooner Than Non-Smokers," in its story, written by a staff writer. The doctors "said they had not expected to have significant results for another year, but that the findings from analysis of deaths so far showed such significance," the newspaper reported, "that it was decided not to delay their publication." The *Tribune's* story, taken from the Associated Press, varied little. It did emphasize more strongly that society "officials made clear that they feel the results of the study indicate cigarets involve risks also for younger men and for women who smoke." The following day's stories in both papers originated from the wire service. In the *Post-Dispatch* a story headlined "Smokers' Death Survey Called 'Preliminary' by Tobacco Group" quoted Little's statement and led with the comment, "The tobacco industry said today more study is needed to determine the causes of cancer and heart disease." The *Tribune* added a note that tobacco stocks had declined, and referred readers to a story in the business section on that aspect of the smoking scare. Regardless of the increasing availability of evidence that smoking caused cancer, these papers included both frames in their stories.[47]

Science Writers and the Health Scare·

Despite the generally positive reception the TIRC received in the press, by September 1954 the staff at Hill and Knowlton considered science writers an "obstacle" to their program, saying an "influential section of science writers" prejudiced against cigarettes were "able to color and slant stories in magazines and daily press." The TIRC tried to counteract this by planning August and September meetings for Little, TIRC chairman Hartnett, and a host of publishers, editors, and science writers from major publishing groups, including Arthur Hays Sulzberger of the *New York Times*, William Randolph Hearst Jr., Jack Howard of Scripps-Howard, and Roy Larsen of the Luce publications. Although the papers cited here do not support the notion of "slanted stories," perhaps the very fact that articles continued to appear signified to the public relations specialists that the science writers were critical of the industry. Bert Goss told Hill that his biggest concern with reporters "is the fact that they correctly report inaccurate or misleading charges by famous scientists."[48]

Any perceived journalistic skepticism toward the Tobacco Industry Research Committee is striking because Americans were very optimistic about science and medicine during the 1950s. A 1957 survey by the National Association of Science Writers showed over 80 percent of the 1,919 respondents believed the world was better off because of science, whereas only 2 percent said it was unquestionably worse. Furthermore, about half of those who felt positive about science cited improved health and better medical treatment as important factors. Scientists were also optimistic about their work. Although not all agreed science could solve world problems, the bulk believed in science and progress. In 1954 even Alton Ochsner thought smoking might be made safer. The "critical areas of investigation," he wrote, included "the problem of how to make smoking a less lethal agent in lung cancer incidence and a less deadly killer in heart disease." If science writers were skeptical, it was not because the public or scientists lacked faith in the ability of science to solve the cigarette problem but because of a suspicion of the TIRC in particular.[49]

Nevertheless, TIRC statements continued to appear in the press. Journalists who may have distrusted committee reports were constrained from reporting their suspicions by their roles within the science and the journalism communities. Science journalists acted as a bridge between the researcher and many other groups, so one of their duties was to translate complex scientific theories, data, and terminology for nonscientific audiences with varying levels of knowledge. Linking such diverse communities required understanding of science as well as journalism, but science journalists had disparate backgrounds in the topics they covered. Some had no education in science, while others had only general college courses. Cigarette research included animal experimentation, statistical analysis, and medical reports such as autopsies, requiring a reporter to have at least basic knowledge in a number of areas to cover just one topic in the news.[50]

The journalistic conventions of objectivity and balance constituted the most important constraint during the health scare, as reflected in the *New York Times* stories about the Hammond-Horn report. Science writers suffered from the same problem as fellow reporters who covered Senator Joseph R. McCarthy during this period: convention required that reporters print what a person said without questioning the reliability of sources or their statements. Even the *Journal of the American Medical Association*, which had banned industry advertising in its columns, covered the formation of the TIRC objectively. Editors and reporters much like John Hill believed objectivity suited the free press because, in a democracy, all points of view should be aired, the truth determined in the marketplace of ideas. Ironically, these conventions, which aim to help readers, actually restricted journalists' ability to evaluate the information they reported or the sources who provided it. Hill and Knowlton portrayed the committee as an independent source of scientific information rather than the PR arm of the industry, and reporters did not challenge that image.[51]

Deadline pressure made the balance rule even more significant. Science writers "tend to rely most on 'authorities' who are either most quotable or quickly available or both," one science reporter explained. To provide balance, reporters tried to interview authorities who would contradict each other, not necessarily those who were the best researchers or those who represented a broad range of views. By mid-1954 journalists in the elite press, including newsmagazines and wire services, knew they could rely on the TIRC to provide an alternate opinion.[52]

Resigning the Account

In 1969 Hill and Knowlton quietly resigned the tobacco industry account. John Hill, himself a smoker, defended H&K's position well into the 1960s, telling one public relations scholar, "The industry has appropriated

$20,000,000 for health research, and I am amazed that you would belittle what has been done in this field." Evidence indicates that Brown and Williamson, Liggett and Myers, Philip Morris, and undoubtedly the rest of the tobacco industry knew by the 1960s that nicotine was addictive and that cigarette tar was carcinogenic, based on its own research. Hill and Knowlton executives sat in on strategy meetings with tobacco executives and company PR directors six months prior to the release of the surgeon general's report, planning the industry's response with the assumption that the report would be negative. Moreover, W. T. Hoyt, the TIRC executive director and Hill and Knowlton staff member, deliberately withheld information about cigarettes from the surgeon general's advisory board and from the Scientific Advisory Board in 1963. The increasing availability of reliable medical evidence therefore cannot have been the source of the agency's problem with the account.[53]

During the early 1960s, one historian reports, Hill and Knowlton found itself increasingly pitted against its own client. "On the one hand," Richard Kluger reports, "it cautioned the industry against excessive displays of truculence or just plain putting its foot in its mouth." For example, H&K opposed a proposed statement that 97 percent of smokers never got lung cancer, both because it was inaccurate and because it was an admission that 3 percent did contract the disease. On the other hand, Kluger continues, when H&K executives advised the industry voluntarily to adopt an advertising code or to put warning labels on cigarette packages, the industry ignored their recommendations.[54]

H&K's diminishing role in policy making was the primary impetus for resignation. H&K had, in 1947, resigned another account, the National Retail Dry Goods Association, because of its staff's unwillingness to allow the public relations agents to participate in policy making, which the agency believed had led to poor policy and bad public relations. Resigning an account was therefore unusual but not unprecedented. Beginning in 1966, the tobacco industry began to fund a new type of grant, "special projects" that were awarded by its lawyers, without the peer review of the Scientific Advisory Board, and that focused on projects that could produce results for use in the industry's legal defense. Hill and Knowlton apparently objected to this activity, because it was ethically wrong, or because the attorneys had subsumed so much of H&K's role as counsel, or both. Executives took a long look at the account and decided to resign.[55]

Hill and Knowlton's foray into tobacco industry public relations had two important long-term effects. First, the agency's resignation, after it had maintained such a vital role as counsel for so many years, left at least some tobacco executives wary. When the Tobacco Institute considered hiring a new agency in 1970, Brown and Williamson voted against the proposal. An executive cited the company's number one reason: "The Hill and Knowlton experience." The resignation must have been more acrimonious than the lack of press coverage at the time would suggest.[56]

Second, Hill and Knowlton's strategy gave the industry a defense it used to stonewall its opponents for many years. A 1972 Tobacco Institute memorandum summarized the industry's twenty-year approach as a "holding strategy" consisting of three parts:

—creating doubt about the health charge without actually denying it
—advocating the public's right to smoke without actually urging them to take up the practice
—encouraging objective scientific research as the only way to resolve the question of health hazard.

Three years later, a tobacco executive admitted that the TIRC's successor organization, the Council for Tobacco Research, was an integral part of the industry's survival strategy. The CTR was, he said, the "best and cheapest insurance the tobacco industry can buy, and without it, the industry would have to invent CTR or would be dead."[57]

Vestiges of H&K's 1954 strategy could still be seen forty years later. During the 1980s the industry did its best to sow doubt among scientists about research on passive smoking, which suggested that nonsmokers could be harmed by environmental tobacco smoke, with the hope that the news media would cover such research with skepticism. Cigarette makers continued to insist that the case against smoking had not been proved as late as 1994, when the top executives of the seven largest companies testified before Congress that cigarettes may cause health problems but that the evidence was not conclusive.[58]

The "research" approach H&K developed for the industry remained the most useful. During litigation against Kool cigarettes, Brown and Williamson was asked what the company had done to keep abreast of scientific findings about tobacco. "Our reply tells about the ten imminent [sic] scientists" on the Scientific Advisory Board, and about the research grants made through the TIRC and later the CTR, the memorandum said. "Stated another way, our answer says CTR is our window on the world of smoking and health research. This avoids the research dilemma presented to a responsible manufacturer of cigarettes, which on the one hand needs to know the state of the art and on the other hand can not afford the risk of having in-house work turn sour." The TIRC and later the Council for Tobacco Research allowed the manufacturers to avoid responsibility for research that "can become the smoking pistol in a lawsuit." It is no wonder, then, that evidence presented in a 1988 Federal District Court trial in Newark, New Jersey, led Judge Lee Sarokin to conclude that the TIRC had been a public relations front rather than a true scientific search for evidence. However, the strategy may yet come back to haunt the industry, because H&K's "Frank Statement," which promised that the manufacturers would put the public first, may figure in litigation strategies of individuals and states suing the industry.[59]

The Impact of Advertising and PR

Although both tobacco and antismoking interests relied on the media to disseminate their claims during the health scare, the tobacco industry had a tremendous advantage, money to purchase the services of skilled media professionals. H&K did not present any arguments on behalf of cigarettes that tobacco executives had not previously made in the press. But the PR specialists realized the importance of credibility and emphasized that information they supplied to reporters should come from an organization associated with research and well-known scientists rather than the industry or the agency. Creation of the TIRC meant that public relations professionals could coordinate the statements of the tobacco companies into complete, well-organized reports such as background memoranda for the press, while scientists released their findings piecemeal. An example of the tobacco industry's advantage in the battle for media coverage was the advertisement announcing the creation of the TIRC. The ad, a full page less one column, cost about $250,000 for space and production. It assured the manufacturers of high visibility, full quotation, and freedom from adulteration, and it gave the industry a single, coherent voice. Newspapers quoted from the ad extensively when they wrote stories about the new committee. The health groups undertook no similar activities.[60]

Another vital part of the industry's success is that beginning in 1954 it disseminated information that smokers wanted to hear, giving them a source of support for their habit. People who liked to smoke found a rationalization for it in tobacco industry publicity and advertising, and Hill and Knowlton actively promoted statements that suggested people should do whatever they wished until the controversy had been resolved. For example, the agency sent to newspaper editors reprints of a *New York Daily News* article that said, "the experts can't agree, so the layman is entitled to believe any expert he chooses, or to believe none of them." "Whether or not it was so planned," Consumers' Union concluded, the TIRC's "constant statements that the findings are not conclusive have kept the speculation alive, and there is little doubt that the steady smoker can find, in this conflict, the justification not to stop." Simply covering both frames made the assertion of a medical conflict a reality.[61]

It is difficult to determine how much, if any, effect the advertising and public relations campaigns had on public beliefs and behavior concerning smoking. In 1957 tobacco industry research indicated that two-thirds of the public believed that the government had not done enough to warn people about cigarettes, but they also believed cigarette manufacturers were not to blame. Some, notably *New York Times* reporter Philip J. Hilts, suggest that H&K's work "may have been one of the most remarkable saves by a PR pitch in the history of that young industry," ignoring factors other than the campaigns—the wide acceptance of smoking by most adults, the discomfort and difficulty of smoking cessation, and the ways people deal with fear-arousing communications (including ignoring them)—which might also explain events during the cigarette scare. Edward R. Murrow, for instance, smoked through two *See It Now* programs on lung cancer. "Mostly people admit into consciousness only those things which interest and promise to benefit them," public relations consultant Rex Harlow explained in 1957. "They exclude those things they don't like or don't want." People did not want to think about dying of cancer.[62]

Still, both beliefs about smoking and consumption patterns changed as the two sides presented their cases in the media. Belief among adults that smoking causes lung cancer rose from 41 percent in 1954 to 50 percent in 1957, only to fall back to 44 by 1958. In the year following the surgeon general's report, 1965, the total leaped to 66 percent. After dropping slightly during the health scare, consumption rose after 1954—although not, ironically, among advertising executives—and fell after the surgeon general's report in 1964. Since then, both tobacco consumption and the percentage of smokers has gradually declined. Therefore, it appears that TIRC and filter-tip advertising campaigns did at the very least contribute to continued use of tobacco by affecting both the types and the amount of information available to the public in the news media.[63]

PART THREE

Changes at Hill and Knowlton

CHAPTER SEVEN

A Voice with an Accent

Hill and Knowlton Abroad

In 1946 Sterling Drug's showboat sailed up isolated rivers in Latin America to communities "where most of the inhabitants can neither read nor write, and with music, entertainment and suitable flourishes, put on a show which somewhere extols the quality of certain drugs offered for sale on the spot." *Printers' Ink* believed the campaign was "in a class by itself," although it stands in sharp contrast to the style of public relations favored by John Hill. Nevertheless, Hill and other public relations executives recognized a trend. Immediately following World War II, many United States–based companies began to expand their horizons to include more of the rest of the world as their marketplace, and in so doing they sought innovative ways to reach their new audiences. Hill and Knowlton was not the only public relations agency to follow American business overseas, but it quickly became the undisputed leader of the pack.[1]

For Hill international expansion was more than just a way to get rich, which was fortunate given that H&K's foreign offices lost money for nearly a decade. Instead, he was convinced that American companies could ill afford to ignore their public relations abroad, any more than they could at home. Perhaps more importantly, Hill believed corporations had to overcome their own high profiles, which sprang from the fact that they represented "the most powerful, the most envied and possibly the most disliked democracy on earth." Anti-American propaganda spread by Communists throughout the Third World only complicated matters. Companies must "strive for acceptance and goodwill in foreign lands," Hill wrote. "To the extent that such efforts succeed, they will help advance the cause of international understanding." That understanding had to be earned by American companies, the nation's most important ambassadors.[2]

Unlike some other American businesses, Hill and Knowlton tried to respect the cultures of host nations, but it was a respect tempered by the cold war mentality that pervaded both the commercial and the foreign policy communities during the 1950s. The executives served, or at least tried to serve, as a moderating voice, but even for them "international understanding" generally meant acceptance of American free enterprise, not compromise or even dialogue. In short, H&K's approach did not change when agents applied it to other cultures. Agency forays into Europe, Asia, the Middle East, and Australia during the 1950s demonstrate again that at Hill and Knowlton, public relations amplified the voice of business, even when it spoke in foreign tongues.

U.S. Business Abroad
after World War II

Multinational corporations originated in nineteenth-century Europe for both political and economic reasons. Among the first multinationals were Bayer, a German company founded in 1863; the Swiss company Nestlé and the American company Singer, both formed in 1867; and Britain's Lever Brothers, which opened in 1890. These and similar companies chose to build facilities in other nations because by doing so they could decrease transportation costs, secure supplies of raw materials, and, often, avoid tariffs. Many of today's giant multinationals operated in several countries by the end of the nineteenth century, and foreign direct investment, led by the United Kingdom, increased dramatically from the 1880s through World War I. After the war the United States emerged as the most dynamic direct investor, although the British still dominated in terms of ownership. The Depression and World War II discouraged multinational entrepreneurship, but the war changed everything, one public relations agent recalled, leaving "a world of exhausted nations and one immensely strong one—the United States."[3]

With the American postwar economy booming and much of the rest of the world in shambles, government officials and business leaders quickly grasped the utility of foreign investment. Corporations looked at such factors as the shattered industries of Europe, rapid and reliable air travel, efficient telephone services, spiraling labor costs in industrialized countries, and rising worldwide demand for new products, and found foreign investment an attractive option. Congress also favored international commerce. The Hickenlooper amendment, for instance, empowered the government to discontinue economic aid to any country if it tried to nationalize any U.S. business. The General Agreement on Tariffs and Trade (GATT) facilitated trade by creating a common set of principles accepted by many non-Communist countries to govern international trade, as opposed to individually negotiated, mutually exclusive agreements.[4]

This favorable political economy occurred because the government and corporations all sought a worldwide liberal economic order. Not all legislation favored American business interests abroad. The extraterritorial enforcement of antitrust laws is one example of U.S. law that corporations—and some foreign governments—resented. However, most government policies both encouraged and protected corporate expansion after the war, because some government officials hoped the flow of funds would reduce the amount of government-sponsored grants and loans needed to rebuild European economies and others saw trade as a vital line of defense. In other words, trade was not purely economic. It was not, after all, permitted with Communist nations. "World peace through world trade" was, to many Americans, a sagacious formula.[5]

Even considering the advantageous environment, the growth of U.S. direct foreign investments after the war was astounding. In 1946 the book value of such investment was $7.2 billion. By 1950 the value had increased to $11.8 billion, and by 1957 to $25.2 billion; six years later, the amount passed the $40 billion mark. U.S. foreign direct investment grew faster than the U.S. economy as a whole, and so massive was the postwar onslaught of the dollar that some have called it "the American invasion." Watching the influx of American capital to Europe and beyond, John Hill reasoned that public relations problems would soon follow, and he prepared to solve those problems by putting into place a worldwide PR network, even before his clients asked for it.[6]

Hill and Knowlton Follows Business and Leads PR

Just how far ahead H&K was in international public relations is difficult to assess. If the literature on public relations history is incomplete, the story of its emigration from the United States is even less well documented, both in completeness and in accuracy. A few pioneers had international accounts early in the history of formal public relations. Carl Byoir and Ivy Lee both worked for German companies before World War II, and Hamilton Wright had clients in Europe and the Caribbean, even representing the government of Egypt. Edward Bernays opened an office in Vienna in 1925, although it is not clear how long it remained open. In contrast to PR, large advertising firms like McCann-Erickson and J. Walter Thompson had already established a strong international presence by the mid-1950s, but many smaller ad agencies were moving abroad at roughly the same time and apparently for some of the same reasons as Hill and Knowlton. *Industrial Marketing* described a "rash of international activity" in December 1958, explaining that as companies moved overseas they pressured their ad agencies to supply service there. McCann-Erickson, which had been in Britain, France, and Germany since the 1920s, also offered public relations services to their international clients. Among practitioners who knew John Hill, however, there is agreement that his was the first PR agency to move out of the United States with any degree of success.[7]

Hill's personal interest in international affairs intensified after World War II ended. Postponed due to the steel strike, his first tour of Europe finally took place in 1952, when Hill was sixty-two years old. There he found extraordinary potential for the counsel his agency could offer. "Everywhere, it seems, there is a mounting desire to find ways of improving understanding," he said in 1957, "between employees and employers, management and shareholders, the plant and the community, as well as between people across national borders." Europe needed public relations.[8]

Several other factors contributed to Hill's decision to move H&K beyond U.S. borders, and not only to Europe. He needed a new challenge. His firm had become the largest of its kind, he had signed new clients like Studebaker and Gillette, and H&K had bought out two smaller agencies. Although the agencies, Edward W. Barrett and Robinson-Hannagan Associates, initially ran independent of H&K, they brought such international accounts as the government of Japan, the Suez Canal Company, and the Nassau Development Board. All three involved working for foreign entities in the United States, demonstrating to Hill a growing interest in public relations worldwide. Important clients like Procter and Gamble began to express interest in international PR by 1954, especially regarding Thomas Hedley of Newcastle, its British subsidiary. At some point the agency had established an office in Bogotá, Colombia, for Avco, and in 1949 it developed a proposal to promote Colombian tourism and trade in the United States. Perhaps most importantly, H&K worked on oil accounts with interests all over the world, including Standard Oil of Ohio, which had retained Hill for some twenty-five years, and Texaco, which retained H&K in 1952. Public relations counselors Earl Newsom, Carl Byoir, and Selvage, Lee and Chase, among others, began to solicit international business during the 1950s, and a rumor that Byoir planned to set up an operation in Paris prodded Hill to make a decision about his own agency's expansion.[9]

An encounter with a European PR practitioner gave Hill the incentive to take action on his desire to pursue international business. After returning to New York following his tour of Europe, Hill through mutual acquaintance George W. Ball met Loet Velmans, a Dutch citizen with writing experience who had begun to dabble in public relations. The multilingual Velmans so impressed Hill that he hired him. Having decided to pursue foreign operations and finding the right man, H&K set about obtaining clients and building an infrastructure to support worldwide service while Velmans trained in the New York office.[10]

Public Relations Audit for Caltex

The public relations audit system that H&K had developed for the steel industry helped the agency secure its first international corporate account, California Texas Oil (Caltex), in 1953. Among the domestic clients brought in by the audit were American Cyanamid and the American Red Cross, each of which signed on for the survey and stayed on so that H&K could implement the programs it had recommended. Executives hoped a similar procedure would lure in multinational accounts. Caltex found itself in hot water in several different countries for a variety of reasons during the mid-1950s: cartel hearings in the United States, a leak about an oil discovery in Australia, and nationalist tensions throughout much of Southeast Asia. The oil executives wanted Hill and Knowlton to perform a large-scale audit of company public relations practices and policies relating to those problems. Although Caltex did not become a long-term client, the project convinced John Hill that the future of public relations lay across international waters, and it helped to establish the agency's international credentials in the eyes of other business leaders.[11]

The Survey and Its Findings

Loet Velmans and Merrick Jackson, who edited *Steelways* for the Steel Institute, conducted most of the Caltex survey, which reviewed the oil company's operations in eight countries. Jackson and Velmans covered 31,000 miles between 14 January and 31 March 1954, traveling to Bahrain, India, Ceylon, Indonesia, the Philippines, and Japan, remaining for about a week at each location. Additionally, vice-president Dick Darrow traveled to New

Zealand and Australia. The purpose of the trips was to gather enough information to address two questions:

1. Is there a need for public relations activities extending into certain of the areas throughout the world in which Caltex affiliates have interests and operations?
2. If this need is established, how should such activities be organized and put into effect?

Caltex was actually a group of companies, founded in 1936 when the Texas Company acquired half interest in the Bahrain Petroleum Company and joined with Standard Oil of California to form California Texas Oil. When the H&K survey began, over eighty companies comprised Caltex, which in 1952 owned a combined fleet of tankers and ships among the world's five largest and produced 135 billion barrels of oil per year. The mammoth survey covered only a small portion of Caltex operations.[12]

The executives conducted comprehensive interviews of national and community leaders in selected company locations. In Indonesia, for instance, Velmans and Jackson met with nearly seventy people, including editors and correspondents, government officials, business and financial leaders, members of Parliament, an attorney, a hospital director, a member of the faculty and an administrator from the University of Indonesia, three U.S. diplomats, a physician, a labor officer, a police commissioner, and over two dozen European and Indonesian staff members of the company. All told, H&K agents interviewed hundreds of people in their attempt to ascertain the political, economic, and social climate in which Caltex operated.[13]

The audit summary from Ceylon provides an example of the reports Jackson and Velmans sent back to New York. The agents found the government "strongly anti-Communist" with left-wing opposition "composed of a number of Communist splinter groups among which the Trotskyites are a powerful vocal force." The University of Ceylon was "a hotbed of Marxism," and labor unions were leftist if not Communist, but the "highly developed individualism of the Buddhist Ceylonese" gave the executives "some hope that the democratic forces on the island will outlast Communism." Economically, Ceylon was a poor country, with a low standard of living, "though by comparison higher than that of the other countries of South East Asia." Its people were literate, but evidence suggested to the agents that many tended to believe everything they read or heard in the news media. The agents detected apathy toward Americans, strong anti-British sentiment, and even stronger anti-Indian feelings, the island "having been invaded so many times from the Indian mainland." Both government and business leaders supported foreign investment, but that had remained a dream. Velmans and Jackson believed the government insisted on "Ceylonization" of company staff much faster than was practical, which would constitute a continuing problem for the conglomerate. While Caltex did not have a bad reputation, "there appears to be insufficient knowledge about the company's policies and practices, both in the business community and among the employees." They concluded that public relations, then unknown in Ceylon, could be an effective tool "for mobilizing favorable sentiment."[14]

After completing similar assessments of the other locations, the agency identified problems that Caltex faced across the board. Unstable economies in many of the oil-producing nations might lead to higher taxes, regulations, and restrictions. Not surprisingly, the executives concluded that nationalism constituted Caltex's biggest problem. Nationalism "manifests itself in anti-foreign sentiment, in critical questioning of the company's policies and in government dicta which are tedious and sometimes unrealistic," Hill and Knowlton reported to Caltex. "It asks for quicker promotion of nationals; early replacement of expatriates by nationals; capital participation by nationals; incorporation in the country of the operation; directorships and officerships for nationals. It supports labor demands."[15]

Nationalism occurred for many reasons, partly because of the actions of American companies, according to the PR agents. Jackson and Velmans blamed Caltex in part for nationalism's appeal. "Caltex is criticized for not identifying itself sufficiently with the nationals on whom it depends for support," a preliminary report said. "This is believed to be Caltex' [sic] major public relations problem." Unfortunately, the negative climate went much deeper. It had been created by decades of Western blundering, in Jackson's opinion. "The road to independence," he wrote in a June 1954 draft report, "was paved by mistakes over the last fifty years," adding, "Nationals generally regard the businessman as the exploiter."[16]

In its report to the oil company Hill and Knowlton softened this criticism by focusing on the result, the appeal of nationalist agitation against the company, rather than its causes. Rising literacy, the agents explained, left nationals subject to outside pressures and propaganda, especially from the "anti-foreign business block." Executives suggested that the company must present its point of view or leave "its public position more and more at the mercy of its critics." The company could not afford to isolate itself. Instead, it must foster communication or allow misinformation and rumors to spread.[17]

Caltex, Hill and Knowlton concluded, had to face the fact that only public relations, not force, could subdue nationalist unrest. "There may have been a time in our history," an agency report explained to the oil executives, "when unjustified seizure of American property abroad would have brought an American warship to the scene." Although President Eisenhower had authorized covert CIA intervention in Iran and Latin America during the mid-1950s, the agents counseled their clients not to rely on such intervention, for, when it came to business, "that time has passed." Now a company's only recourse was "to do what it can to create the best possible climate of official and public opinion toward the company itself." The conglomerate needed public relations, which could "reduce some of the unjust criticism by setting the record straight and by regularly reaching influential persons in these countries." [18]

The Recommendations

Several basic steps, Hill and Knowlton argued, could resolve the problems the audit had identified. Top management must accept responsibility for public relations, meaning that it should make a statement on Caltex's PR policies, principles, and objectives. Next, management should clarify the public relations responsibilities and authority of local management. The company should set up a separate public relations department under a director who would report to top management, and qualified personnel should be provided immediately where conditions were most dire.[19]

H&K's recommendations had some impact on Caltex policies but, much to Hill's frustration, the company did not retain Hill and Knowlton for its overall PR responsibilities. The oil company set up internal public relations departments and added government relations programs. Although the agency picked up work for Caltex in Australia, executives continued to pitch its worldwide service to Caltex officials for many months to no avail. "It is beyond my power of comprehension," Hill wrote to Velmans, "to understand how a company with the stake it has in Europe would not want to keep an outpost for counseling and for the observation of political, social and economic trends and undercurrents which are changing the face of the globe— and which are most certain to have an effect upon the company's business." Still, Hill grew more interested in international public relations, and he looked toward Europe as he moved to build a public relations empire that could attract multinationals and other clients.[20]

"Go European, Young Man"[21]

The first step in fashioning a worldwide public relations system involved creating a network of associated public relations firms throughout Europe. After long discussions with the public relations counselor to Procter and Gamble's British subsidiary, Alan Campbell-Johnson, Hill commissioned Loet Velmans to negotiate agreements with leading practitioners across the continent, whereby the new associates could work on their own accounts plus handle whatever work H&K sent their way. For the first year, H&K paid a retainer fee of $500 to each affiliate, with the understanding that they had a mutually exclusive relationship. Any charges in excess of that amount would be billed to the New York office at individually negotiated rates. The original team consisted of Alan Campbell-Johnson, Ltd., in Britain, Franck Bauer et Associes in France, Hollander and Van der Mey in the Netherlands, and Eric Cyprès & Associés in Belgium. Others were shortly added. This arrangement reduced overhead for H&K while ensuring effective counsel across Europe by representatives who spoke the language and shared the culture of the area. Finally, H&K established a subsidiary, Hill and Knowlton, Proprietary, mostly to handle Caltex affairs, in Sydney, Australia. George E. McCadden, an American who spent seven years working for United Press in Australia, headed the office. This network was in place by July 1954.[22]

The associates had impressive credentials, not so much in public relations as in related fields. Many had ties to journalism as well as to government. Campbell-Johnson, educated at Oxford University, had served as Lord Mountbatten's press attaché in India; Bauer worked for the BBC during World War II and had served as special assistant to a cabinet minister and the French postwar reconstruction agency; and Cyprès worked for the *New York Herald Tribune* in Europe and his partner had been press attaché to the Belgian prime minister, while Hollander and Van der Mey were former officials of the Dutch government. Several held journalism degrees.

Interestingly, however, the associates had few formal ties to European industry, evidence perhaps that few companies practiced formal public relations. Cyprès's tenure as the promotion and advertising manager at Socony Mobil Oil in Belgium for five years during the 1930s made him the most experienced of the group. Frans Hollander also had an advertising background. After studying journalism at the Sorbonne, he became an account representative for J. Walter Thompson in The Hague and continued to work in advertising during the 1930s. In both cases, military service interrupted advertising careers. As in the United States a few decades earlier, then, journalism, advertising, and press relations for the government provided entrée into the new field of European public relations.

After retaining the associates, Hill and his executives pondered opening an international headquarters, a serious commitment on H&K's part. On the one hand, Hill realized it would require significant time and attention from agency staff in the United States. European understanding of public relations was "very far behind that in the United States," so it would take time to build a profitable business. Most U.S. firms only wanted publicity, not full-service counsel, in Europe, and, of course, the project would involve a significant financial investment by the agency. On the other hand, Hill said, it would provide "a peg on which to build increased stature and prestige for the firm" and "a service in Europe for our American clients," at the same time enabling the agency to offer services for European clients in both Europe and the United States. H&K's management team weighed the decision carefully.[23]

The risky investment in the European headquarters finally took place, entirely on Hill's initiative. In December 1954 H&K sent Loet Velmans, recovered from the malaria he had contracted while on the Caltex tour, to Paris, where he established the international headquarters in his apartment. Velmans coordinated the flow of information among the various associates and the New York office, which continued to make important policy decisions. Hill made trips to Europe in 1954 and 1957, staying as long as two months, to review operations and recruit business, while Velmans handled the day-to-day administration. Although King favored hiring Velmans in New York, on the whole the management team thought his move to Europe a mistake.[24]

The associates' first project was to gather data on the cigarette scare in Europe. The New York office requested information on such issues as European cancer levels and awareness of the medical research. Britain's Alan Campbell-Johnson informed the New York office that press and public reactions had been "steady," and that investors were "quietly confident about the American situation," showing "no tendency to 'sell short' here," especially because of the success of king-size cigarettes. Frans Hollander, located in the Netherlands, later notified them of a theory that there was an association between lung cancer and the increase in electric shaving. The agency followed all the international reports with interest. As a result of conversation with the British associate, the agency modified the TIRC's white paper for public distribution.[25]

The agency and the associates tracked numerous leads which seemed to offer possibilities for overseas assignments, but with limited success. Executives sought business from both American multinationals and foreign organizations. Procter and Gamble, the Dutch airline KLM, the North Atlantic Treaty Alliance, and especially the World's Fair seemed the best prospects. KLM did hire the agency, but the New York office, not the European network, in January 1955. H&K's work for KLM began with a study of the airline's public relations problems in the United States for the purpose of setting up a long-term program.[26]

An assignment in September 1954, from the commission charged with planning the 1958 Brussels World's Fair, constituted a minor triumph for the agency, because it was the first account brought in by the associates.

When the commissioner general of the fair, Baron Moens de Fernig, planned a trip to the United States, he retained H&K to plan and publicize the event. The agency hoped to parlay that into a longer-term appointment for fair public relations in Europe and the United States, and Belgian associate Eric Cyprès, who had obtained the client in the first place, pressed for a continuing role. No commitment was forthcoming.[27]

One major obstacle to obtaining accounts was that public relations outside of the United States was nearly nonexistent. As late as 1955, for example, there existed no independent counseling agency in Italy. In 1952 only three or four Belgian businesses plus subsidiaries of five American companies had public relations departments, although both the prime minister's cabinet and the Ministry of Foreign Affairs had press or PR specialists. The German Public Relations Association had only 253 members as late as 1967, with just 81 working in agencies. Public relations was even less developed in other parts of the world. In 1968 one PR agent reported that no more than a dozen Malaysian companies used public relations to any major extent, although most government departments had publicity officers.[28]

In Australia and Great Britain public relations gained acceptance more quickly. The majority of publicly held companies and many professional and trade organizations had public relations consultants or departments in Australia by 1968, although most apparently sought assistance with publicity only. British public relations began in the early 1930s, and by the mid-1960s nearly every major corporation had a PR department. Virtually all government departments had press officers by World War II, in addition to those working in the Central Office of Information. Britain's Institute of Public Relations, founded in 1948 with 248 members, had more than 2,000 members in 1966.[29]

Interest in public relations was growing outside the United States, but it was still a new idea and not many Europeans believed that they needed public relations. One client that Hill personally tried to obtain, the West German steel industry, was not interested in retaining a public relations agency, despite any argument Hill made. Although not all Europeans were as reluctant, one West German industrialist believed public relations "was not yet required in Germany." Trade associations and industries already had significant influence over legislation, "German public opinion is already tremendously disposed toward industry," and there was little need for product promotion given that prices were essentially fixed by cartels. Loet Velmans found in 1954, however, that community relations and industry-education cooperation were two fruitful areas that H&K could explore with West German business leaders.[30]

Local public relations agencies faced the same attitude. As one West German public relations practitioner wrote to Hill, "To say that Public Relations is still in its infancy in Germany would be something of an exaggeration. There is no Public Relations thinking." Practitioners in Germany did not "fill a need," Hansjürgen Schubert told Hill. "Instead, we have to create a need by educating management and the public towards mutual frankness and respect." H&K's affiliates, with the exception of Campbell-Johnson in London, reported similar problems, although they tried to remain optimistic. "Although the concept of public relations in some French quarters is still vague and sometimes confused with propaganda or publicity," a promotional flyer for Bauer's agency said, "there is increasing evidence that a new climate is emerging."[31]

Another problem involved the associates' inexperience. The associates sometimes bickered over the fees H&K negotiated with international clients. More seriously, when Procter and Gamble France asked H&K's French affiliate, Franck Bauer, to develop a program proposal, he recommended a plan that Procter and Gamble's director of advertising believed envisioned "manpower, organizational, financial and general workload commitments that are virtually impossible at the present stage of development of our French business." Loet Velmans told Hill that, "instead of 'getting his foot in the door,' as advised," the ambitious Bauer had "submitted a budget that probably is equal to, if not in excess of all his other business together!" After negotiation, and undoubtedly a scaling back of his plans, Bauer landed the French account in April 1956. In November Cyprès earned a three-month trial with Procter and Gamble Belgium.[32]

Despite such small victories, Hill and Knowlton could ill afford to retain the associates, much less support Velmans in Paris, unless the network could obtain its own clients. Hill's skeptical management team seemed to have been correct about his decision to send Velmans to Europe. Although William Durbin, who headed the international operation from New York, later reported that "almost without exception, the local business of the associates prospered," international business was much slower in coming. By October 1955 Hill was so troubled by the lack of new accounts that the agency began to decrease its international efforts. Although he recognized the long-range advantage of Velmans's presence in Europe, Hill nearly recalled him to New York, telling Campbell-Johnson, "there comes a time . . . when the dictates of good management compel us to face up to the fact that each month we are putting out a considerable sum of money upon which there is no return." Even Velmans agreed. "If these last eight months have taught me one thing," he wrote to Hill in September, "it is that the public relations practitioner in Europe is a rather frustrated person."[33]

In the eleventh hour Cyprès came through with the World's Fair account.

The commissioners finally agreed to hire the agency for phase one, "Operation Boss," which promoted the speedy nomination of a United States high commissioner for the fair. President Eisenhower's appointment took longer than the agency had anticipated, but Hill explained to Baron Moens that the appointee, Howard Cullman, "is a heavy stockholder in the tobacco industry which is one of the very important clients of our firm, and I have known him for some years." The agency had no control over the selection of candidates, or the final appointment, but the firm's relationship with Cullman may have convinced the Belgians they had selected the right firm.[34]

The next phases of the World's Fair program, nicknamed operations "Build" and "Come," provided H&K's network with bigger challenges. The former referred to the construction process, the latter to promotion of the fair to potential visitors. The objective, Cyprès later explained, was to "make the project well-known to the public and to arouse interest in the Exhibition amongst Governments, travel agencies, public spokesmen, newspaper publishers, radio and television chiefs, all those who controlled communication channels and could enable us to reach the public" to entice tourists to Belgium. The fair was a tremendous success. It opened with an inauguration by the king of Belgium on 17 April 1958, the site dominated by the Atomium, a towering projection of a molecule that encouraged peaceful uses of atomic energy and better international relations. Over 40 million visitors toured pavilions constructed by more than fifty nations.[35]

Although the World's Fair did not bring an immediate flood of clients, Hill's international gamble paid off handsomely by the late 1960s. The establishment of the European Common Market, which created a single market in France, Italy, West Germany, Holland, Belgium, and Luxembourg, eased the transfer of goods and information in the very areas where the agency already had public relations offices. H&K continued to increase its coverage until in 1960 the network covered thirty countries and the international coordinating office moved to Geneva. American Cyanamid gave the network an eight-month audition in 1958, eventually agreeing to a longer-term deal; Monsanto, Citibank, and Alcoa followed. H&K then began to sever its agreements with the European affiliates, opening offices of its own, although several of the original associates remained on the agency's international management board, and by 1967 the international branch had thirty-five employees in seven offices serving sixteen clients. The headquarters later moved to London, and the system was tinkered with in other ways, but in Hill and Knowlton International, N.V., H&K had created a model for the multinational public relations agency that others soon imitated.[36]

It was not the only agency seeking international expansion, but Hill and

Knowlton's leadership in the rapidly growing field of international public relations became apparent at the first World Congress of Public Relations meeting, held in Brussels during the World's Fair. Eric Cyprès chaired the congress, which consisted of 250 practitioners, 22 from the United States, the remainder representing twenty-two other nations. Along with Cyprès, H&K's representatives included Bauer, Hollander, Velmans, and John Hill. Cyprès gave a lengthy description of Operations Build and Come, and his talk ended with "prolonged and enthusiastic applause," according to the official transcript. In 1967 and 1968 Hill and Knowlton published a first of its kind, two volume *Handbook on International Public Relations*, in which the international associates presented chapters on the state of PR in their nations.[37]

A comparison with Barnet and Reef Associates, another international public relations firm based in New York during the 1950s and 1960s, provides a yardstick to measure H&K's growth. Founded in 1958, Barnet and Reef quickly set up an international network of affiliates much like H&K had done four years earlier. By the end of its first year it had attracted such clients as Dow Chemical, Columbian Carbon, and American Machine and Foundry. By 1962 it had added Goodyear, Philip Morris, United Fruit, and John Deere, among others. At its peak in the early 1960s, the agency had associates in forty-eight countries, far more than H&K, which had begun opening its own subsidiaries, had at that time. Perhaps the biggest difference was in what the two agencies could offer their foreign clients. Barnet and Reef had a staff of fifteen in its New York headquarters, while Hill and Knowlton was the largest firm in the world.[38]

A Voice of Moderation

Corporations like those that retained Hill and Knowlton turned to public relations because multinationals operated at the mercy of their host countries. Business leaders were encouraged to think of their companies as guests who could be asked to depart at any time, leaving their luggage—buildings, furnishings, expensive equipment—behind. Nations could tax, regulate, expropriate, or expel any company, as when Egypt nationalized the French Suez Canal Company in 1956. Calls for the most frequently recommended solution to the threat, good corporate citizenship, became axiomatic. "What is meant by 'good corporate citizenship,'" noted one business writer, "is difficult to determine, but most officials of U.S. enterprises will say that it means paying proper regard to the interests of the host country." Nationalization was always a threat, but it was intensified when the owners were foreign, so corporations had to convince the host government that they contributed important benefits to the nation.[39]

However, multinational corporate citizens were by their nature a part of at least two cultures, and the local plant had to try to integrate with the host culture while satisfying the business demands of the owner culture. "Management efforts to achieve an efficient operation and a high level of profits in overseas operations will succeed," according to one 1960s book on international management, "only where overseas managers are able to combine an understanding of the unique problems encountered in cross-cultural relations with management practices that have proved their effectiveness in industrialized countries." Some companies failed to understand or respect local culture and traditions and therefore developed poor relations with communities in other nations. For example, in trying to keep costs low, some companies hired women, upsetting local custom or religious belief.[40]

H&K, like other businesses, had a multiple agenda in its international work, and that contributed to the agency's careful consideration of the cultures of its clients' host countries. The first job of business was to provide a service people wanted while making a profit for the stockholders, but Hill also believed public relations activities could and should help in the cold war fight against communism. "America's new role in world affairs," he explained, "has put vast new responsibilities upon the American people," and on business in particular. Hill was not alone in supposing that American business was a potent factor in the cold war, its leaders "ambassadors of the American way of life." An IBM public relations representative wrote in 1968 that a company creating a good image abroad "can often be a better ambassador than the appointed diplomats."[41]

Few Americans doubted the importance of winning international allies, and some, like *Fortune*'s William H. Whyte Jr., worried that the actions of American businesses abroad might increase international tension, thereby harming the democratic cause. In 1952 Whyte made a blistering attack on American business communication, including international communication. In *Is Anybody Listening?* he expressed fear that the free world might destroy itself if too many people accepted the myth that "for all our bathtubs and our cars and our skyscrapers we are without moral purpose; that we are the New Carthage—all money no spirit." Americans had not won over allies because "we have failed to determine what it is we wish to communicate," talking of "the manifestations of our success rather than the causes." Whyte's solution included foreign exchange programs, increased propaganda, and conversion of top managements in Europe, and increased participation of foreign nationals in the job of selling America to non-Americans.[42]

Hill likewise saw the cold war as partly a public relations case in itself, one all the more important after the Soviet Union launched the first satellite into space. "America has a tremendous international public relations problem on its hands," Hill wrote in 1957, "in overcoming the lead Russia has taken in the cold war as a result of the successful launching of the satellite, and its apparent missile advances." For a man who had fought long and hard to sell America at home, fighting communism abroad was simply an extension of patriotic duty. Advancing the concepts of free enterprise around the world was both a matter of good business and essential to victory in the battle with communism. Indeed, rumors that Hill and Knowlton International supplied information to the Central Intelligence Agency are entirely plausible. Hill would have seen the opportunity to assist the CIA by sharing insights and information gathered during his or his executives' trips abroad as a way to help his nation and democratic free enterprise worldwide.[43]

Profit and patriotism were without doubt Hill's primary motives, but Hill and Knowlton, compared with other American companies, displayed great regard for other cultures. The agency practiced what public relations scholar Carl Botan has called a polycentric model of public relations, where "host country practitioners are entrusted with carrying out the MNC's [multinational corporation's] plans and programs based on their own experiences and contracts," but the host country "is merely a site for fulfilling the MNC's needs." Evidence for the existence of this approach lies in H&K's insistence upon hiring foreign nationals even though policy was made in the New York office. Executives encouraged companies to hire locally, suggesting, for example, in their report on Ceylon that Caltex establish a program under the direction of a Ceylonese public relations assistant. Even Hill's decision to hire Europeans to run the continental offices indicated an appreciation for cultural differences.[44]

The agency's position on hiring foreign nationals is surprising given its conservative hiring practices at home. Only a few women advanced to staff positions during the 1940s and 1950s. Eloise Davison and Mary L. T. Brown each directed Hill and Knowlton's women's program, which developed special angles on H&K clients for women. Brown, for instance, created a campaign for the Steel Institute suggesting that "a steel door can save your life," because unlike wooden doors, steel could withstand an attack. Jane Stewart started at Hill and Knowlton as John Hill's secretary in 1945, but her public relations abilities led her to the presidency of Group Attitudes, H&K's research subsidiary, by 1961. There were apparently few, if any, Jewish executives or people of color on the staff, and even white men were subject to careful scrutiny. H&K executives noted concern about one job applicant who had "a good background" but was "handicapped by a large, black, handlebar mustache." John Mapes added that the applicant was otherwise "a perfectly normal individual neither affected nor effeminate," although he was unmarried. The man was hired, but generally speaking, Hill and Knowlton's policies were no different than those of the large companies it served.[45]

There was a pragmatic reason for these sometimes progressive hiring practices: as in advertising, many public relations specialists believed that targeting certain groups required special knowledge that only membership in that group could provide. Only Mary Brown could understand the fear of a woman alone in a big city, imagining a stranger coming through her inadequate wood door. And only people intimately familiar with a foreign culture could practice public relations there. William Durbin, a Hill and Knowlton vice-president who headed international PR in the New York office, explained that one of the biggest pitfalls in international operation was "assuming that it is possible simply to export a homegrown public relations program to other areas of the world without taking into account the facts of life in the areas in which the company operates." An awareness of cultural differences thus produced a more broad-minded international hiring policy than otherwise prevailed.[46]

Despite a level of traditionalism at home, H&K displayed remarkable sensitivity to citizens of Caltex's host nations. Recognizing that multinationals transferred not only capital and technology but intangibles like culture and ideas, Hill acknowledged that "foreign peoples may desire to emulate our standard of living and provide markets for our goods; but they do not wish, for the most part, to adopt a made-in-America way of life." Moreover, he added, "it is their standards, not ours, which deserve management's first attention in all foreign operations." In a draft outline for H&K's report, Jackson went much further, recommending that Caltex not show white people in advertisements, advance nationals as soon as possible, offer improved educational facilities, procure locally, become familiar with native languages, and associate more with the nationals.[47]

Furthermore, H&K insisted on a more open communication policy than most businesses practiced. One author on international management, for example, wrote in 1969 that antiforeign investment attitude was deeply embedded in nationalistic traditions, so the most effective strategy was to avoid public attention. In contrast, in a supplemental survey of Caltex's periodicals, performed in 1955, Hill and Knowlton considered the needs of illiterate employees in poor nations like Bahrain and Indonesia, suggesting that publications be complemented by "periodic meetings, films with local language sound tracks, picture posters on bulletin boards, informal briefings by supervisors," and so on.[48]

The executives went far beyond recommendations on communication practices, however. They also wrote a credo for Caltex's international business operation, which the local companies could adapt to suit their needs, providing a mission statement for the company. Caltex "does not seek to make a profit at the expense of the country which has given it lodging," the credo said. "It believes its operations are being carried on with a full and sincere regard for the interests of the country; that it is providing the country with a greater net return than that which the country could obtain if it were to do the work itself; and that its presence there increases the company's strength, economic stability and standards of living." The executives contended that Caltex should provide every country the maximum economic, educational, and social benefit, employ and train nationals to advance to supervisory rank, and purchase goods and services locally.[49]

Of course, all of this may have been mere lip service. Because H&K was never retained to implement the Caltex program—perhaps in fact because of the approach it recommended—it is impossible to know how serious the executives were about implementing some of the more radical (in the eyes of oil executives) recommendations. Moreover, the agency never spelled out exactly how it would accomplish lofty goals like maximizing economic, educational, and social benefits.

However, even proposing open communication and consideration of host peoples' needs to a multinational oil company, and presumably to other international clients, suggests that the firm served as a moderating voice. Hill and Knowlton repeatedly encouraged business leaders to improve conditions in host countries rather than simply deplete resources; this is what "corporate citizenship" entailed. But Hill went much further. He wanted corporations to win over foreign allies by earning their admiration, which could occur only if the company understood what people thought. "As we have learned in our public relations work here," he wrote upon returning from Europe in 1954, "we must know what others think of us, why they think that way and what their interests are before we can communicate effectively with them." He recommended that companies give expatriate staffers language instruction, because "once the barrier is broken through, there can be more association between foreigner and national, usually to mutual advantage." And, he said he believed that a business leader should determine "how best he can coordinate his company's goals with those of the country."[50]

But the voice of moderation was not a model of two-way communication. The agency still employed an imbalanced relationship that favored the client organization over its publics. "Knowing other cultures' rituals, languages, social norms, and values is necessary but not sufficient preparation for forming international community relationships," public relations scholar Stephen Banks argues. "It is necessary also to remain open to the possibility of conducting business within others' worldviews and effectiveness criteria." H&K sought not so much mutual understanding as understanding for the purpose of persuasion. Information from the field would help decision makers in the United States determine the policies and practices the multinationals should undertake. For instance, in the 1955 audit of Caltex's publications, H&K concluded that poor communication between local operations and Caltex's headquarters restricted the "generation and flow of editorial ideas and materials from New York to the field." This was not a suggestion to listen to the demands and interests of the people living in Caltex's host countries, whether nationals or expatriate Americans. H&K wanted to improve conditions in nations where its clients operated, but the agency, not the people who lived in the client's country of operation, would determine how best to accomplish that. The voice of business spoke with a distinctly American accent.[51]

CHAPTER EIGHT

Hill and Knowlton since 1955

I n 1990 Hill and Knowlton was the largest public relations agency ever known. Although it had slipped behind Burson-Marsteller in billings during the 1980s, H&K and its controversial new CEO, Robert Dilenschneider, had recaptured the top position with a vengeance. Dilenschneider bought out the agency's old nemesis, Carl Byoir and Associates, as well as nine other public relations and lobbying firms, to give H&K top billings once again. In 1989 it reported that its clients—such as IBM, Xerox, and AT&T—included 25 percent of the world's largest companies, 35 percent of the *Fortune* 500 companies and nine of the top ten of *Fortune's* global 100. It had 1,900 staff members working in sixty-five offices in North and South America, Europe, the Middle East, the Far East, Australia, and New Zealand. In 1990 it merged with the high-powered lobbying firm Wexler Reynolds, whose principals included former officials from the Nixon, Carter, and Reagan administrations.[1]

But the practice of public relations, both inside and outside the agency, had changed dramatically. Corporate public relations sophistication had increased, with many organizations employing internal PR departments. This had two important consequences. First, few agency executives had the kind of access to client management that Hill, Mapes, Goss, and others had enjoyed during the middle decades of the twentieth century. Now, a public relations practitioner served as an intermediary between the agency and the policy makers. Second, many corporations no longer needed long-term counsel, but only assistance on short-term projects and crisis management.

At the same time, the pressure for agency growth was tremendous. These elements together drove Dilenschneider in New York and Robert Keith Gray in Washington to develop a different approach to client choice. Whereas Hill had accepted only certain types of clients, they asserted that almost everyone deserved representation, much like every citizen is considered deserving of legal counsel. This new approach allowed the agency to accept clients that many of Hill's colleagues believe he would have rejected, including the Catholic Bishops' pro-life campaign and the Citizens for a Free Kuwait. It even acquired another tobacco account, RJR Nabisco.

In other words, Hill and Knowlton's rapid growth came at a cost. The agency was not a firm that John Hill would have admired. It had lost its reputation for high ethical standards, conflict stalked the agency, and counsel to top management on corporate policy no longer occurred as a matter of course, if at all. During the 1990s public debate about the firm's personnel, clients, and techniques filled newspapers and airwaves to an extent unprecedented in Hill and Knowlton's sixty years of existence. The machine Hill built was used for everything about public relations that he hated most. The result was a disheartening loss of clients, staff, and preeminence. Asked to speculate on what Hill might have thought about H&K's new and uncomplimentary high profile, one of his friends mused, "John would have been so pained. So pained." In fact, perhaps only Hill's example could rescue the agency from its downhill slide.

Hill's Strategy for Long-Term Success of the Agency

H&K's founder consciously set up an agency that would survive him. "John Hill knew how to build a complete organization," Bert Goss said. "Most of the public relations pioneers were unable to do this. . . . only Carl Byoir and John Hill were successful in building large organizations." Harold Burson, whose agency eventually passed H&K in billings, believes Hill's greatest contribution was that he saw public relations as "more than a single office consultancy built around one person." Hill and Knowlton "demonstrated that you could operate on a global scale by delegating responsibility, that it could be run as a business." It is not possible to discern exactly how important a model Hill provided without further study of other postwar public relations agencies, but it is clear that H&K, with its combination of size and endurance, was a new kind of beast.[2]

The most important key to H&K's success was its ability to attract and keep blue-chip accounts, and one element in that success was innovation in

John Hill in 1956. He kept horses at his Towners, N.Y., farm and, according to friends, rode at least once a week. (Courtesy of the State Historical Society of Wisconsin)

public relations practices. H&K pioneered among agencies in relations with schools and educators with its program for the steel industry and had led agencies in developing international practice. The agency also changed the way many firms billed their clients when, in the late 1940s, it hired Price Waterhouse to set up a system of standard fees and staff-time charges rather than the somewhat haphazard method of setting different rates for different clients. In 1966 the firm created an Environmental Health Unit to elevate environmentalism to top management policy consideration. "Our job is not to oppose or fight progressive measures in the public interest," Hill explained, "but to keep clients informed on developments affecting them and to keep the records straight regarding their policies." H&K also experimented with new types of research, borrowing from advertising the idea of testing copy during the 1959 steel negotiations, and with computers in the 1960s. Few of these innovations were Hill's ideas; many came in conjunction with Goss or others. But the decision to implement them was ultimately Hill's.[3]

Innovations were important, but one of the agency's main attractions was its reputation for integrity and professionalism, a reputation based on both Hill's character and the agency's performance. Competitor and friend Farley

John Mapes, center, was H&K, Inc.'s second largest stockholder during the agency's earliest years. Although he left in 1950, Mapes returned to the agency to head the steel account in 1956. (Courtesy of the State Historical Society of Wisconsin)

Manning claimed Hill was "a great man who undoubtedly did more to advance public relations than any other person in the history of the business." Long-time corporate PR expert Howard Chase called him "one in a very small field of genuine counselors." One of Hill's successors at H&K believed he was "the reigning King of public relations during his active years." Consultant Chester Burger said when he began his career in public relations, "Hill and Knowlton was the standard-setter" that people perceived as "high level corporate counsel and advice and operations," and Hill was regarded as having "just a very plain, decent honesty about him." And Harold Burson recalled Hill as having "a tremendous reputation," the agency "a blue-chip list of accounts."[4]

That reputation remained only as long as Hill's personally trained successors stayed at the helm of H&K. Hill set up a chain of command to follow him—men he trusted and had molded in his own style. What would have been an orderly succession was disrupted, however, in several ways. Hill's heir apparent, Kerryn King, left the agency in 1952 to become director of public relations at Texaco, where he eventually achieved the rank of senior vice-president of public affairs. John Mapes, whom Hill regarded as a protégé and "more than anything else . . . a relative," lost his opportunity to head the agency when he left to open his own firm, even though H&K eventually brought him back. Hill turned to Bert Goss, who became president in 1955, although Hill stayed on as an active chairman. Goss died in his early sixties of Lou Gehrig's disease. Even Dick Darrow, whom Hill did not fully endorse but who followed Goss as president, died before Hill did in 1977. After a confusing three-person chairmanship, Loet Velmans, H&K's first international employee, emerged as president in 1976 and CEO in 1980. The agency did not stagnate during these somewhat turbulent years. According to an H&K news release, the agency doubled in size every four years from 1976 to 1984, and it maintained its reputation for ethical and expert— if bland—representation. After Velmans retired, the agency and its reputation began to change. Hill and Knowlton would survive, but not in a way Hill would have imagined.[5]

Clients and Activities: 1955–1986

In addition to international expansion, Hill and Knowlton grew during the 1950s and 1960s by acquiring smaller agencies and opening subsidiaries. H&K bought the Edward Barrett and Robinson-Hannagan agencies, and it eventually absorbed those agencies' accounts. In 1956 the firm bought Group Attitudes Corporation, the research company founded by John Mapes when he left H&K in 1950, and made it a subsidiary housed in the Hill and Knowlton offices. In the mid-1960s the agency created still another subsidiary, H&K Marketing Services Corporation, which provided product promotion for corporate marketing programs. Both subsidiaries could serve clients other than those that retained H&K.[6]

Although he remained an active part of the agency's management committee, Hill gradually took a less active role in day-to-day management of the agency. In 1955 he turned the presidency over to Goss. From that point, much less is known about the inner workings of the agency. Based on examination of several events after 1955, it appears that Hill's immediate successors, Goss, Darrow, and Velmans, continued to consider amplification of the voice of business the basic role of public relations.

The natural gas controversy of 1956 gave the agency the most public exposure it had had since the La Follette hearings after the 1937 steel strike. Hill and Knowlton's client sought public support for a bill to exempt the industry from federal regulation. The program began in 1954, when the Supreme Court handed down a decision that placed all natural gas producers who sold the commodity for interstate commerce under control of the Federal Power Commission. The producers argued that low gas prices were the product of free competition, and that regulation would ultimately hurt the consumer most by raising prices and by creating disincentives to looking for new sources of natural gas.[7]

H&K, public relations critic Irwin Ross wrote, "tackled the PR problem with its accustomed thoroughness." As they had done for steel, aircraft, and tobacco trade associations, the PR executives helped the newly organized Natural Gas and Oil Resources Committee (NGORC), under the leadership of Leonard F. McCollum of Continental Oil, develop a public relations program. The indispensable Bert Goss supervised a staff of as many as eighteen agents in addition to such veteran industry PR men as Kendall Beaton of Shell and Kenneth W. Rugh of Phillips Petroleum. Together they designed a campaign that mobilized corporations and individuals within the industry to tell their story to opinion leaders through speeches, pamphlets, and news releases, national advertising, radio and television programs, and background memoranda, even enlisting the support of AISI-member steel companies, who were major consumers of natural gas. In eighteen months, NGORC spent over $1.5 million.[8]

The campaign proceeded with apparent success until a bombshell dashed NGORC's hopes. A study of press clippings found that 1,718 editorials favored the industry, compared to just 513 that were unfavorable and 210 neutral. The House of Representatives had passed the Harris-Fulbright bill, which was favorable to the industry, and the Senate was considering it. Then, Senator Francis Case, Republican of South Dakota, announced that two lawyers representing an oil company had tried to convince him to vote for the bill by offering a $2,500 campaign contribution. The lawyers were not connected to Hill and Knowlton—in fact, the company that had retained them was not even a member of NGORC—but the agency found itself under Senate investigation for its role in the industry's campaign. The McClellan committee, charged with examining Case's charges, "found nothing improper with the public relations campaign." In fact, H&K sent copies of news articles about Bert Goss's testimony to editors in the advertising and public relations trade press because they exonerated the agency of any wrongdoing. The Senate passed the bill, but President Eisenhower refused to sign it, even though he was "in accord with its basic objectives," because he feared the scandal would "create long-term apprehension in the minds of the American people." Reflecting on the situation later, Hill wrote, "operation successful—the patient died."[9]

Another controversial client was the Pharmaceutical Manufacturers Association, which retained Hill and Knowlton during Senator Estes Kefauver's Subcommittee on Antitrust and Monopoly hearings, which began in 1959 and examined prices, drug testing, and advertising practices in the prescription drug industry. The agency emphasized the high cost of research, the good works of the manufacturers, and the need to get new drugs on the market quickly, and executives urged doctors and company employees to write to their legislators in opposition to new drug regulations. As usual, H&K relied on speeches, reprints of congressional testimony, news conferences, and brochures to reach the public with news about the hearings. The drug companies also hired lobbyists to plead their cause. However, as in the NGORC situation, an external event, the thalidomide scandal, sabotaged H&K's ability to help forestall government regulation of the industry.[10]

The campaign for the drug manufacturers revealed the continuing importance of Hill and Knowlton's role in creating and promoting one unified voice for an industry. Bert Goss, in a speech presented before the American Pharmaceutical Association in 1963, took task with the industry for using the government's role of trustbuster as a competitive weapon. "The people in the FTC and the anti-trust division freely state that they are surfeited with complaints from competitors, that is, from businessmen and professional people," he said. "What they appear to overlook is that the eventual effect of their action is a boomerang on themselves. . . . If this point could be made abundantly clear, we could hope for a more circumspect and constructive approach" to the problem. Pharmacists, he counseled, should unite under the banner of professionalism to stop such destructive in-fighting.[11]

The steel industry also kept the agency embroiled in some of the most exciting events of the era. Labor issues remained predominant, especially during the 1959 steel strike, which lasted 116 days. With plant capacity utilization falling, in part because of the recovery of the German and Japanese steel industries, steel executives argued that wage increases could not be paid for by greater worker efficiency. Costly, outmoded work rules would have to be changed. Hill and Knowlton executives promoted such opinions, while union leaders charged the industry with trying to turn back the clock, to destroy their position at the bargaining table. In the end the union accepted a wage freeze and promised two-and-a-half years of labor peace in exchange for company commitments to bear the full cost of insurance, hospitalization, and other benefits, as well as preservation of work rules the union favored.[12]

The industry's 1962 attempt to raise prices against President John F. Kennedy's objections was reminiscent of Truman's struggles with the industry, except that Kennedy won. U.S. Steel and the other large manufacturers retracted their announcement that they would increase prices after Kennedy's blistering attack on the companies. The issue involved individual companies, not the AISI, but the events affected how people felt about the industry as a whole. Perhaps most disheartening for H&K was a poll taken in November of that year which indicated "a heavy public leaning toward more, not less, government interference in the affairs of the industry." Such findings took their toll on Hill's confidence in the efficacy of his decades-long free-enterprise campaign.[13]

Despite such setbacks, Hill and Knowlton reached the apex of public relations respectability during the 1960s. A survey of the staff in 1963 showed a diverse and talented group. The average staff member had fifteen years experience in public relations. Most of the account executives were former public relations directors from a variety of industries and institutions, and more than three-fourths had worked in journalism. Altogether the staff had written forty-four books and had contributed articles to over 100 publications. Twelve had been teachers, and three had doctorates, with several others holding law degrees. There was a Pulitzer Prize winner, an ex-FBI agent, and a musical comedy writer, and others with experience in radio acting, cartooning, and television production. Of U.S. staff members, thirty-three could read or write French, nineteen German, eighteen Spanish, three Russian, three Italian, and one each Arabic, Greek, and Dutch. These agents worked in such specialized departments as education, women's interests, press relations, radio and TV, graphics, and technical writing. "We try to teach our account people that their function isn't necessarily to know all the answers," Dick Darrow, president of the firm in 1968, explained, "it's to serve as the quickest and most effective pipeline for drawing on the accumulated training and experience of all the staff we have assembled."[14]

Hill and Knowlton executives took great pains to promote the agency as an industry leader. Hill published two books, made dozens of speeches, and wrote articles for trade papers and industry magazines, and he encouraged his staff members to do the same. They spoke at industry meetings, wrote articles in public relations periodicals, and attended conferences. Collectively, H&K executives published books on such topics as international public relations and investor relations, and the agency also published its own research results, such as a book on careers in education based on a study conducted by Group Attitudes for the education department.[15]

During the 1970s and early 1980s, when Darrow and Velmans headed the agency, H&K continued to play a role in some of the most important events of the day. The agency campaigned against President Carter's proposed Consumer Protection Agency, and it represented Metropolitan Edison, which hired H&K the week after an accident at the utility's Three Mile Island nuclear power plant. It also represented the American Trucking Association, which sought deregulation during the Carter administration, in what was then the biggest public relations and lobbying campaign ever.[16]

Client Choice and the Bottom Line, 1987–1992

After the agency had become part of an advertising and public relations conglomerate, controversies involving Hill and Knowlton were of a different character. During Hill's time the agency was usually criticized because people disliked its clients' politics. Afterward, it became notorious for clients it chose to represent, and journalists and public relations practitioners alike called into question its ethics.

Hill and Knowlton joined the trend toward public relations and advertising agency mergers in 1980. The company was acquired by the JWT Group, which included the advertising agency J. Walter Thompson. The merger of the top advertising agency with the top public relations agency took place in part because H&K's leadership had been given assurances that it would continue as a separate entity. Although it is clear that the pressure to make money increased, if the JWT merger resulted in any meddling with agency practices, the problem never became public. The same could not be said of H&K's next owner. In 1987 the WPP Group, a holding company headed by British financier Martin S. Sorrell, acquired JWT. Sorrell's hostile takeover, described as "the most bloody" in the history of advertising, ended H&K's independence. Executives accused Sorrell of demanding growth and increased income to such an extent that they began to guard the bottom line more jealously than the agency's reputation.[17]

Under this tremendous pressure to succeed, Velmans' successor, Robert Dilenschneider, broke from Hill's model of quiet competence with numerous self-promotional activities. He wrote a book, *Power and Influence: Mastering the Art of Persuasion*, which he publicized by making the rounds of television talk shows. He also appeared in a *New York Times* profile that was a 1990 version of the *Harper's* profile of Ben Sonnenberg that John Hill had once mocked. "In a business that has traditionally produced quiet leaders," the *Times* said, "Dilenschneider is a blustery, outgoing character with a bit of the old Hollywood huckster in him, a man who has taken it upon himself to singlehandedly pull public relations from behind the curtain and thrust it in the public eye."[18]

In response to Sorrell's demand for growth, Dilenschneider began to accept clients on a per-project basis rather than for the long-term counsel that Hill had insisted upon. "I think he believes you die if you can't grow," one of H&K's senior vice presidents later said of Dilenschneider. He therefore accepted such accounts as a crisis program for Georgia-Pacific's takeover of the Great Northern Nekoosa Corporation from 1989 to 1990. The program addressed only the immediate issue of the takeover, not the company's overall relations with important publics. As one journalist noted, "clients like these have helped fuel the expansion" that Dilenschneider sought, "but they have diminished the white-shoe cachet that Hill & Knowlton so long enjoyed."[19]

The decision to accept per-project clients was due in part simply to changes in the practice of corporate public relations. Hill and Knowlton had sometimes served as a client's entire public relations department, so the H&K executive in charge of the account essentially became a part of the management team. This was the case of Hill with Avco, Goss with the aviation industry, Mapes with steel, and Darrow with Gillette. By the 1980s and 1990s, such relationships were extremely rare. As early as 1968 Dick Darrow admitted, "we as public relations people have probably overdone our naive insistence that we have some inherent right" to sit at the policy table. Two decades later most companies had internal public relations representatives who served as intermediaries between counsel and top management. If H&K had accepted only the clients who were willing to let the agency take such an active role, it would not have survived.[20]

Client choice became questionable in a second way when Dilenschneider discarded the agency's long-standing policy of refusing political and religious accounts. H&K under Hill did not accept religious institutions or foreign or domestic political groups as clients. For this reason the firm turned away the Republican National Committee, although Hill and some of his executives had worked for individuals like Taft, as well as the governments of South Africa and Angola, and, on several occasions, Ferdinand Marcos.

On the other hand, Hill and Knowlton had accepted some government accounts, those regarding tourism and economic development and approved by the U.S. State Department. In 1963, for instance, the government of Saudi Arabia retained H&K for a campaign to "maintain better understanding in the United States of the economic and social progress being made" in that country. The agency recommended that the government establish an official news service which could maintain regular contact with the U.S. press and release information fully and efficiently. Of particular interest, according to H&K, were stories on "medical care, education, urban services, agriculture, mining, settlement of nomads and establishment of a modern system of government." However, even these types of government clients were sometimes reconsidered. Although it was one of the agency's largest accounts, H&K severed the relationship with Saudi Arabia, apparently due to King Faisal's decision to join Arab regimes in the 1967 Arab-Israeli War, although he had previously been considered a moderate reformer.[21]

The new H&K likewise did not accept every account. During the 1980s it reportedly turned away potential clients connected to nearly every scandal that appeared in the news: dictators Muammar el-Qaddafi and Marcos, junk bond king Ivan Boesky and Irangate arms merchant Adnan Kashoggi, the Mafia, the Colombian drug lords, and Panama's General Manuel Noriega. The governments of Libya, Chile, and Guatemala were also reportedly turned away. Dilenschneider claimed the firm had lost $10 million in revenue due to business declined for ethical reasons.[22]

However, the agency did begin to accept clients that it would have refused under the old policy. In an era of fierce competition, Dilenschneider was faced with the choice of losing H&K's leading status or accepting political and religious accounts. He opted for the latter; John Hill might have chosen principle over profits.

Religious Accounts: Catholic Bishops and Scientology

H&K accepted an evangelist, Larry Jones, and the Ba'hai as clients, but a much more unsavory client brought the first round of public attention to Dilenschneider's agency. The Church of Scientology, founded by science-fiction writer L. Ron Hubbard, was publicly accused of being not a religion but "a hugely profitable global racket that survives by intimidating members and critics in a Mafia-like manner." Eleven of its top members had been sent to prison in the early 1980s for burglarizing and wiretapping dozens of agencies that had been investigating and attempting to prosecute the group for illegal activities. Critics accused the church of being a cult, former members sued for mental and physical abuse, and others charged it with recruiting followers for the sole purpose of bleeding them financially dry. According to one source, H&K's service to Scientology ranged from bailing members out of jail to helping the church cosponsor the Goodwill Games. Trout and Ries, a Connecticut marketing consultancy, said it "advised them to clean up their act, stop with the controversy and even to stop being a church." Yet H&K accepted the church's multimillion dollar account shortly after Hubbard's death in 1986, resigning it only when a 1991 *Time* cover story focused a spotlight of negative publicity on the church and its PR firm. Bad press continued when the church sued H&K and its parent company, WPP Group, a suit that was quietly settled in June 1994. Altogether, the episode indicated things had changed at Hill and Knowlton.[23]

Another religious client, the Bishops Pro-Life Committee of the United States Catholic Conference, an antiabortion organization that retained Hill and Knowlton in March 1990, also attracted attention to the agency. The committee, headed by Cardinal John O'Connor of New York, sought a campaign aimed at Catholics and non-Catholics alike to promote the church's antiabortion position. Staff members learned about the new client by reading about it in the newspaper—hardly the ideal employee relations for a public relations agency to practice. Several women executives reportedly quit, and over 160 of the 400 staff members in the New York office signed a petition condemning the way the new account had been handled.[24]

Censure for H&K's decision to accept the pro-life account rose from all sides. Unflattering headlines like "When a PR Firm Could Use a PR Firm" appeared in the press. "Criticism flared in the public relations community" as well, reported *Newsweek*. "Competitors offered to work free for Catholics for a Free Choice." Many Catholics argued the money could be better invested in underfinanced parishes, convents, and schools. After spending $3 million, the bishops severed their relationship with the firm. Like Scientology, the account indicated an alteration of H&K's client policy.[25]

Political Accounts: Kuwait

Hill and Knowlton also broke with tradition by accepting foreign governments as clients for political campaigns in the United States. The agency represented both China and Turkey, countries that had frequently been accused of violating human rights, although both nations had diplomatic ties with the United States at the time. The client drawing the most attention and criticism was the Citizens for a Free Kuwait (CFK). The group's president was Dr. Hussan Al-Ebraheem, a professor of international politics at Kuwait University and former government education minister. He refused to release the names of the other board members for security reasons, although H&K described them as "a group of Kuwait doctors, lawyers, professors and businessmen with financial support from the Kuwaiti government." Other reports described the organization as a front for the Kuwaiti royal family and "a group of wealthy Kuwaitis and other Arabs in Europe." According to Justice Department records, about $18,000 of CFK's budget came from seventy-eight individuals in the United States and Canada, while $11.8 million came from the Kuwaiti government. Although the group's exact membership is unknown, its mission was clear: to build public support for President George Bush's plan for American military intervention in the crisis in Kuwait after Iraq invaded the smaller country in August 1990.[26]

H&K's Washington office directed the program, with upward of seventy people working on the account there. Both Bob Gray, who headed the office, and Craig Fuller, H&K's chief operating officer and former chief of staff to then Vice-President George Bush, had close ties to the White House, and Fuller was frequently spotted there during the crisis—so much so that one critic claimed that during the war H&K "operated as an annex of the Bush White House." The agency created print and video news releases, held Kuwait Information Day on twenty college campuses and a National Pray Day, offered workshops for foreign principals on giving press conferences and interviews, ran an advertising campaign, produced a nightly Arabic radio program for broadcast from Saudi Arabia, and monitored media coverage. It commissioned a poll in major world cities on opinions about the invasion and support for Kuwait, and it prepared exhibits for the United Nations Security Council and the U.S. House Foreign Affairs Committee. Agents also released hostage letters to the media. The agency tried to combat images of Kuwait as being undemocratic and of its citizens fleeing for Europe while Americans fought for their freedom, but H&K found Americans were most receptive to atrocity stories. Two of its video news releases, on Iraq's invasion and subsequent human rights violations in Kuwait, were the second and fourth most frequently used releases of 1990, reaching a combined audience estimated at nearly 100 million television news viewers.[27]

Iraqi atrocity stories were not difficult to find. Soldiers were said to have stabbed a pregnant woman with a bayonet, moved sick and elderly patients from their hospital rooms, removed patients from life-support machinery, or denied them medical treatment. Less horribly, the Iraqis were accused of seizing anything of value from Kuwait, "hospital equipment, treasures from the national museum, building materials, even street lights." Without doubt, many of these stories were correct, but, journalist Arthur Rowse noted, "all were relayed without question as accurate—often with an assist" from Hill and Knowlton.[28]

Support for CFK's cause was both quickly and strongly forthcoming. Newspaper editorial opinion "was heavily tilted" in favor of Kuwait, with twenty-four of the twenty-five largest newspapers editorializing for the military liberation of Kuwait. Both the National Association of Manufacturers and the Chamber of Commerce pledged their support. But "in reality H&K's job was not difficult," a critic of the agency wrote. "Once the President committed half a million American troops to foreign soil, the overwhelming majority of the country supported him." Then, too, Hill and Knowlton was not alone in promoting Bush's policy. An even larger PR apparatus was also at work: the White House, the Pentagon, the State Department. Many had accepted the Bush administration's view of the invasion before H&K ever began work on the account. A week after the invasion a newsmagazine published a story titled "Iraq's Power Grab," featuring a cartoon sketch of an octopus with Saddam Hussein's face and photographs of Kurdish citizens of Iraq who had been gassed under his orders. Support for the government's position was such that the Military Families Support

Network and the Physicians for Social Responsibility were reportedly unable to purchase television airtime for advertisements opposing the war.[29]

After the war, however, two ethical questions were raised about H&K's work for Citizens for a Free Kuwait. First, critics speculated on the extent to which the agency's work may have helped to distort the picture by influencing witnesses or disguising their identity. Some charged the agency with spreading "false tales of Iraqi atrocities to instigate the Persian Gulf war." *TV Guide* reported that H&K selected and coached Kuwaiti refugees, so that only "those with the most compelling tales—and the ones most in keeping with the agenda of Hill and Knowlton's client—were made available to news organizations," thereby limiting "journalists' ability to independently assess claims of brutalities."[30]

One H&K-coached witness engendered most of the criticism. A Kuwaiti teenager, identified only as "Nayirah," testified before Congress that she had seen Iraqi soldiers tear premature babies from their incubators, leaving them on the cold hospital floor to die. This gave credence to an Amnesty International report that 312 premature babies had died after being removed from their incubators, and few in the American press or government questioned the report or Nayirah's testimony. However, a year after the war, the *New York Times* reported that Nayirah was not simply a fifteen-year-old refugee, she was also the daughter of Sheik Saud Nasir al-Sabah, Kuwait's ambassador to the United States and a member of the royal family. The *Times* questioned whether Nayirah had actually been in Kuwait at the time she claimed to have witnessed the atrocities, although the U.S. Embassy in Kuwait City later confirmed that she had been. Another "Kuwaiti refugee" who testified before the U.N. Security Council in November was Fatima Fahed, who was married to Sulaiman Al-Mutawa, Kuwait's minister of planning, and was a well-known television personality in Kuwait. Many questioned Hill and Knowlton's decision not to reveal their true identities.[31]

A second set of questions about H&K's representation of CFK surrounded its relationship with two members of Congress. Tom Lantos, Democrat of California, and John Edward Porter, an Illinois Republican, had "a close relationship with Hill and Knowlton," according to the *New York Times*. Both were members of the Congressional Human Rights Caucus, which had been organized with help from an H&K vice-president and was housed at a reduced rate in H&K's Washington office, and the two men had once headed the organization. H&K's political action committee had contributed $500 to Lantos's 1988 election fund, and CFK had donated $50,000 to the caucus after Iraq's invasion. "It's plainly wrong for a member of Congress," the *Times* editorialized, "to collaborate with a public relations firm to produce knowingly deceptive testimony on an important issue." H&K denied that it had produced "deceptive testimony," arguing Nayirah had, "although her life was in danger as a member of the royal family, volunteered under an assumed name" to work in the hospital. Porter averred that he did not know Nayirah's identity, and Lantos denied that his relationship with Hill and Knowlton was relevant to his decision not to reveal it.[32]

After the *New York Times* broke the Nayirah story, coverage was extensive. Television newsmagazines such as *20/20*, *Crossfire*, and *60 Minutes* aired programs on H&K's role. Newspapers and magazines likewise jumped on the story. Many noted that six senators cited the incubator story to justify their support for the war in a vote which was won by a margin of five. Coverage was critical to say the least.[33]

Hill and Knowlton's standard response to questions about the ethics of its representation of CFK was that everything Nayirah said was true and she therefore deserved to be heard. But critics suggested that had her identity been known, her accusations would have faced greater skepticism. John Martin, a reporter for ABC News, interviewed key hospital officials after the war ended. "They acknowledged that some infants had died as a result of the chaotic conditions, including a shortage of nurses," according to Martin's report, "but said no infants had been dumped from their incubators." Additionally, such organizations as Middle East Watch and Amnesty International decided not to promote the story because the evidence was so sketchy. It is unlikely that what Nayirah said was the whole truth.[34]

Other Controversies of Client Choice

Even accounts that received much less public attention could be considered troublesome. The agency worked for Exxon after an Alaskan oil spill, then the worst in history, and for Stanford University during a scandal in which the school was accused of overbilling the federal government on research projects. Another client involved Hill and Knowlton with the Bank of Credit and Commerce International (BCCI), which was implicated in the Iran-Contra arms shipment scandal. Robert Gray was a director in the BCCI-controlled First American Bank in Washington, for which the agency had registered as a lobbyist from 1988 to 1990. H&K, along with fifty other defendants, was sued by BCCI's depositors for painting BCCI as a legitimate business, but executives asserted that they too had been deceived by the client. The agency went on to represent Clark M. Clifford, former secretary of defense, who faced court battles for his position as chairman of First American.[35]

Finally, Hill and Knowlton's client choice was problematic because it lost accounts due to conflicts of interest. H&K lost its $1 million Smithkline Beecham account, because the client objected to H&K's work for Scientology, which campaigned against the use of certain drugs. It also lost the $500,000 Quaker Oats account because it also handled Kellogg, which pulled its business after Dilenschneider embarrassed the company by praising its former CEO, whom the company had just forced out, in his book. The agency signed on for the pro-life campaign despite also working for Warner-Lambert and Baxter Travenol Lab, both of which manufactured contraceptive devices the Catholic Church opposed. It seemed that nearly every decision executives made regarding account selection involved the agency in some kind of dispute.[36]

Cleaning Up Its Own Image

The rapid-fire ousters of two CEOs added fuel to the fire of news coverage of the agency, although the steps were taken to rehabilitate H&K's tarnished image. In June 1991 Dilenschneider was stripped of most of his operating responsibilities, despite having raised the agency's revenues from $114 million to $197 million. In September Dilenschneider either resigned or was fired, and his character was much maligned in the press. "The man seemed to have a tragic flaw," one magazine observed. "The more powerful he became, the more he believed in his own greatness." The scandals had been too much.[37]

Robert Gray became the next chairman of H&K, but he, too, quickly became embroiled in controversy. His brief tenure at the top was ended by an unflattering biography, *The Power House*, which Gray says is so full of lies and inaccuracies that he sued the author and the publisher. The book described Gray's career at H&K, and at his own agency, Gray and Company, which he opened when he left with H&K clients and staff in protest of the JWT merger. He sued H&K, but within a few years the agency bought Gray out for $21 million and returned him to the Washington office, where he brought in several of the most controversial accounts—the bishops, the Kuwaitis, and BCCI. The biography, which accused Gray of unethical business behavior, ties with the CIA, and outrageous personal behavior, attracted attention mostly for reporting a rumor that President George Bush had had an affair with one of his aides. Gray resigned from H&K in October 1992. "He had been under pressure because of Hill & Knowlton's financial problems, loss of clients and negative publicity from its controversial clients in recent years," the *New York Times* reported.[38]

All of this led to what the *Wall Street Journal* called the "boldest round yet of Hill & Knowlton–bashing by other PR executives." Consultant Alfred Geduldig, for instance, accused the agency of practicing "propaganda" and "exaggeration," while the editor of one trade publication reported "a widespread feeling within the industry" that H&K had "brought some discredit on our business." The author of Gray's biography asserted that "it seemed like H&K would take almost any client and do whatever the client wanted even if it was counter to their advice," ending the importance of the counseling function for which the firm had been renowned. The agency once considered the standard-setter was now the scapegoat.[39]

Back to the Future

Dilenschneider's and Gray's choices in clients reflected a larger debate within the public relations community. As one public relations educator has written, "There are two schools of thought on the issue of client representation. One says you shouldn't work for someone you don't believe in. The other says that clients deserve representation in the court of public opinion." John Hill favored the former approach, but the new H&K chose the latter. In defending the firm's decision to accept the Catholic account, Dilenschneider said that "no group in our society should be denied the right to free expression under the First Amendment or prevented from seeking advice on how best to exercise that right." Trento argued that "to Gray's protégés, refusing a client for personal reasons was itself unethical and unprofessional." Gray qualified that statement, saying Hill and Knowlton's approach was that "a client deserves representation if his goals are not either unpatriotic, immoral, or illegal." This was "not a matter of morality," but because "I can't sell a client's issue if I can't sell it in terms that will be acceptable to the person I'm trying to sell it to." "It's not a moralistic judgment whether or not we should represent this company because they produce a product we many not like or that company because they seek a legislative agenda that's not ours—that's crazy," he said. "That's not our right."[40]

The new approach had serious consequences that were reflected in H&K's finances and its status in the public relations community. A trade journal gave Hill and Knowlton a grade of C-plus for its performance during 1991, criticizing it for putting its top talent on high-profile work and leaving its retainer accounts to junior people, for sniping between Dilenschneider and Gray, and for the mass defections of personnel. Although one report suggested H&K had actually profited from publicity about Kuwait, according to another trade paper by 1993 Hill and Knowlton had fallen to third place among agencies, behind the number one agency by $50 million in net fees and with 500 fewer employees. The change was due partly to Burson-

Marsteller's 1.93 percent growth, but more to H&K's 14 percent plunge. The Washington office had fallen 30 percent, Chicago almost 60 percent. By category of specialization, Hill and Knowlton led in only three areas: financial and investor public relations, beauty and fashion, and travel. Moreover, by 1993, a combination of factors led WPP Group shares to drop from $24 to $3, the company barely making a profit.[41]

The changes were also reflected in employee morale, which had plunged to an all-time low. "I don't know of anyone working there who isn't dreaming of getting out," said a senior executive who left after the agency accepted the antiabortion account. H&K had long been known for its ability to retain its employees, in part due to employee stock ownership and a profit-sharing plan pioneered in public relations by H&K. But in the midst of all the other problems came employee revolt. Many left the firm to start their own businesses, and some took H&K clients with them. The agency sued several of its former employees, including one group that left to form Capitoline International, a Washington lobbying firm. That company's founder said, "It has become increasingly clear that H&K isn't a place where public relations professionals wish to work," and Hill and Knowlton lost its suit.[42]

Hill and Knowlton's success had been due to a number of converging factors—the social context of the Depression, World War II, and the cold war, and their effects on business leaders of the era; Hill's personality and philosophy of public relations; the ability of his management team and successors to maintain his legacy; and the agency's reputation for offering high-level counsel and ethical representation. By the time Velmans retired, changes in the business world and the public relations community meant that many of these factors were disappearing, and by the time Thomas E. Eidson and Howard Paster replaced Dilenschneider and Gray, they were gone.[43]

Hill and Knowlton maintained a much lower profile after the resignations of Dilenschneider and Gray as it attempted to return to a style of public relations more like John Hill's. The primary goal was to "clean up Hill and Knowlton's image." When Howard Paster, a former aide to President Bill Clinton, replaced Gray as the Washington office's general manager in August 1992, the *Washington Post* described the difference: "More pro bono work. More involvement in the community. Greater caution about clients. Fewer parties and social activities. A lower profile." Both Paster and Thomas Eidson in the New York office made it clear that client choice was paramount. "One clearly cannot accept clients because they have a checkbook," Paster told the *Post*. "When the story becomes who the client is, you're distracted from serving the interests of your other clients." Eidson similarly told the *Wall Street Journal* that, while the firm would not shy away from clients strictly because they were controversial, "we're going to be much sharper, much more careful, in the type of prospect we go after."[44]

H&K also returned to the practice of seeking new clients through innovation and by prioritizing client needs. Agency research found that its large size deterred new clients because it connoted insensitivity, high cost, and slow response by a staff of generalists. According to *Public Relations Journal*, CEO Eidson therefore supervised a movement of specialization within the agency. A new marketing and communication group designed to address gay and lesbian audiences is one example. Beginning in 1995 fourteen employees in seven cities worked for the specialty group with such clients as an AIDS research program at Rockefeller University and the Los Angeles Gay and Lesbian Center. H&K also stepped up its activity in Asia, especially China, Hong Kong, and Taiwan, and its Dallas office brought together African American and Hispanic agencies to help clients reach multicultural markets.[45]

Hill and Knowlton could not turn back the clock, but the back-to-basics approach seemed to be effective. It is no longer possible for a large agency to work on a policy-only level, so H&K and other public relations executives no longer have the considerable influence that Hill, Goss, Mapes, and Darrow once took for granted. But, by 1995, H&K had climbed back into second place on the list of advertising-public relations agencies, with net fees of over $141 billion and 1,250 employees, behind only Burson-Marsteller's pace of almost $212 billion and 1,860 employees. By 1997 even some competitors conceded that the firm's image had improved. Hill and Knowlton's successful return to its former approach to public relations indicated that John Hill had set the standard not only for other agencies during his time but for his own agency over time.[46]

CHAPTER NINE

Hill and Knowlton and Postwar America

Hill and Knowlton made significant contributions to the development of public relations practice during the decades following World War II. Hill proudly described some of them in his 1963 book, *The Making of a Public Relations Man*: "development of a broad range of specialized public relations services staffed by experts," "establishment of Hill and Knowlton international offices," "application of cost accounting and modern budget procedures in the practice of public relations," "recognition of community relations as an important part of corporate and industrywide public relations," and "creation of a professional-attitude research division in order to measure the dimension and quality of public relations problems." These strategies and techniques changed the state of public relations, but H&K's impact on society ran far deeper.[1]

Hill and Knowlton believed its mission was twofold: to amplify the voice of industry when its leaders had specific messages to send, and, at the same time, to educate Americans about the role of big business generally. Amplifying the voice of business meant simply taking the thoughts and words of industry leaders and making them heard in the public, political, and media arenas, and H&K was undeniably successful in doing so. Its contribution to the "selling of America" is less obvious, but H&K's work did have a significant impact because of its influence on its own clients.

The agency was able to affect media discussion of issues affecting its clients on innumerable occasions, demonstrated most clearly in the case of tobacco. By creating a seemingly independent organization that was actually a public relations stratagem, H&K took advantage of the conventions of objectivity and balance, arguing that there existed a medical controversy, as opposed to a clear-cut health hazard. The agency even affected the quantity of news by convincing at least some journalists not to pursue the story. It also influenced media discussion simply by providing reporters with information such as statistical data or opinions of the industries it represented. Although the agency successfully influenced the frames used in the media for nearly every client, setting the media agenda was more difficult. When H&K attempted to warn the public of the impending danger of the collapse of aircraft manufacturing, for instance, it was ignored until other advocates made the issue relevant.

The agency was somewhat less successful at influencing political discussion of important issues. In the butter case H&K affected what political actors said by focusing on one aspect of the issue, the possibility of fraud, essentially narrowing the debate. The agency was most effective in providing information and frames of interpretation to advocates already in agreement with its clients. This included supplying the results of the fraud survey to the dairy state advocates and statistics on the aviation industry to the Finletter and congressional policy boards. The agency rarely set the political agenda. Rather, it responded to problems created when medical researchers, reporters, the margarine manufacturers' PR agency, and others made statements that caused members of Congress and presidential administrations to become interested in an issue.

Influencing public discourse and opinion proved the most difficult, for people were not unthinking recipients of H&K's messages. The historian Howell John Harris concluded that business propaganda had little effect on the climate of public opinion during the 1950s, noting that opinion polls showed continuing suspicion of business throughout the decade. Hill and Knowlton was able to affect discussion of public issues—whether regarding the steel industry, cigarettes, or aviation—but primarily by adding to the frames of interpretation used in public debate. It could not prevent and never tried to stop other groups from contributing to public debate as well. During the 1952 steel strike, for example, individuals had access to opinions and interpretations offered by the industry, the union, and the Truman administration, as well as journalists and members of the judiciary and Congress. Moreover, public discourse was often affected as much by external events as by PR campaigns. In the aviation campaign, outside factors like international tensions affected what people thought and said more than the public relations program did; with butter, personal experience, cost, and availability of the product were important variables. At times H&K campaigns did appear to be effective, but usually when people already agreed with the position the agency advocated.[2]

H&K's educational campaign also yielded mixed results. In the early 1950s *Fortune* magazine's William H. Whyte Jr. published a series of articles and then a book on what he saw as the dismal failure of corporations to communicate with the people, despite the millions of dollars they had spent "selling America to Americans." *Is Anybody Listening?* he asked. "The bulk of this 'Free Enterprise' campaign was an insult to the intelligence and, as many businessmen themselves suspected, a prodigious waste of time and money to boot," Whyte concluded. "Nobody seemed to be listening." Two years later, *Time* likewise argued that "the sad fact is that industry has lost ground in its public-relations campaign."[3]

Hill and some of his executives also questioned exactly how much they had accomplished. Bert Goss saw in the 1960s a credibility gap between business and the people analogous to that between politicians and their constituents. "The task of communications to narrow" that gap, he said, was "a major one," adding, "small wonder that business has struggled with it for decades and has achieved such moderate success." A decade later, Hill himself brooded, "As I think of the past, I become convinced that perhaps the most serious mistake made over the years was that business talked too much to itself and about itself and its needs, and too little about what all this means to people. So people are not listening." These doubts led Hill to modify his own philosophy of public relations. Hill wrote that he had come to believe that PR "is a never-ending and often frustrating endeavor to build a two-way bridge of understanding between people." Hill and Knowlton, however, had never practiced that model of public relations, nor did it after Hill's death.[4]

However, the historian Richard Tedlow has contended, trade association public relations did make some contribution to gaining public acceptance for the system, although its precise impact cannot be measured. Certainly business leaders believed their campaigns had been effective, at least enough to continue financing them. Said one steel executive, "I am convinced that the program that the industry carried on" since 1946 "has created a different viewpoint in the public's mind about the steel industry and to a considerable degree about all basic industry." During the 1950s, public relations practitioners like Hill agreed. "Today, the planned political attacks against industry no longer flow weekly and monthly out of the capital. There is no longer a close liaison between the political power and various union leaders, of the kind that kept management beleaguered for years," he wrote in 1955. "Profits are no longer under attack. Constant threats of excessive regulation, or unfair competition from government, have ceased. On almost every front, industry finds itself operating in an improved climate of public opinion for which at least some measure of credit is owed its own sound public relations concepts of recent years."[5]

PR clearly played a major role in government-industry accommodation after the war. Time and again Hill and Knowlton helped its clients with hearings before congressional and presidential boards, preparing testimony on labor relations, prices, expansion, and other basic issues, and then publicizing that testimony as widely as possible. Led by John Hill, H&K executives consistently repeated their messages about free enterprise, insisting that profit was paramount and that business decisions should be made by markets and managers, not by federal regulation—unless the industry for some reason (fraud in the case of butter, the need for steady contracting in the case of aircraft manufacturing) needed regulation in order to compete fairly or survive at all. H&K's role in the policy making of its clients meant that it contributed significantly to this process of accommodation.

The agency sought to amplify the voice of business, and it did. Did that make any difference for social and political action? It depended on the issue and the support for the client's side that preexisted H&K's campaigns. The agency's mobilization of noisy support for the aircraft industry, for instance, may have given some members of Congress a pretext for voting for the higher appropriations for the Air Force, something they actually wanted to do for budgetary and other reasons. In the case of tobacco the changes in media content did seem to affect personal decisions about smoking, and once the health scare died down calls for social and political action had little appeal. But in neither of these cases did the agency's programs change opinions. Instead, they offered information that people were already interested in hearing. With butter, on the other hand, influencing political debate had negligible effect on the outcome for consumers, because both consumers and members of Congress agreed that the law must be revised, and H&K could not alter their opinions.

The agency's mixed success in affecting social and political action was less important than the unintended and indirect effects its campaigns had on its clients and on the American people. Contribution to the creation of a climate of intolerance in the postwar era is one example. Nearly every statement emanating from the Steel Institute warned of the threat of creeping socialism, while the aircraft manufacturers subtly invoked the threat of communism, and events seemed to prove the agency right. Truman's attempt to redirect public attention to steel prices by seizing the industry inadvertently gave the industry an illustration of the danger of socialism that it had for twenty years claimed was imminent. If the president could order the takeover of an industry by executive fiat, perhaps the federal government really was dictatorial and untrustworthy. The industry's warnings, Truman's actions, and events in Korea, coupled with the tension many Americans already felt about the Soviet Union, may have made some more vulnerable to the accusations made by Joe McCarthy and other red-baiters, especially regarding Communists in the government. John Hill and his executives never intended to support such stridency, but they were honestly worried about the role of the federal government and therefore talked about it ceaselessly.

Another indirect effect came through Hill and Knowlton's ability to unify an industry and its supporters into one coherent voice. The executives frequently were able to fuse disparate groups, companies, and individuals into a single force fighting for a common cause. The agency realigned dairy farmers with their leaders on oleo tax policy; helped steel companies and plants contribute to industrywide public relations objectives; brought together military, industry, and civilian groups interested in air power; and urged many other industries to undertake similar activities—chemical, petroleum, and pharmaceutical, to name three. This unity gave industries an advantage against less organized opposition, such as the anticigarette medical researchers of the 1950s. Groups that lacked high-quality public relations representation were vulnerable to attack.

The campaigns also provided business leaders with a justification for their own behavior. Richard Tedlow argues that the free-enterprise campaigns created the appearance of public support if not the reality. This gave business executives license to take certain actions under the rationale that they had the support of public opinion, even though opposition groups made the same claim. The industry, the union, and the Truman administration for instance all used their mail, which had often been prompted by public relations campaigns, to argue that the people supported whatever position they each held in the 1952 steel strike. This alone was a meaningful effect.[6]

But perhaps the most important effect was brought about through the reinforcement of the opinions of H&K's clients and people who were similar to them. Roland Marchand points out that public relations materials such as institutional advertisements could boost executive morale and win respect for sponsors, but the public relations campaigns also fortified executives in the face of battle. During the 1952 steel strike, few opinions were transformed. Yet steel executives believed that they had a strong case against federal intervention in business decision making and that their winning the fight was a moral and legal imperative. They pressed on, therefore, until they had achieved their goals. What they said to one another reinforced their own determination to defy the Truman administration—making H&K's job of amplification all the more important. For the general public this reinforcement culminated in a months-long crisis and a steel strike when the nation was waging battle against a dreaded enemy.[7]

Whyte's question, "Is anybody listening?" is a pertinent one. Although neither he nor John Hill and his executives realized it, the answer was yes. Business executives heard the agency's messages loud and clear. Hill and Knowlton's campaigns affected the general public, but mostly by affecting its own clients and people who already thought like they did.

1937 (Hill and Knowlton in Cleveland)

Akron Chamber of Commerce
American Iron and Steel Institute
Austin Company
Berger Manufacturing Company
Block Company
Cleveland Bakers Club
Cleveland Chamber of Commerce
Eaton Manufacturing Company
Electric Vacuum Cl.
Euclid Avenue Association
Greater Akron Association
Great Lakes Exp.
Hill and Knowlton Special (steel research project)
Midland Steel
National City Bank Cleveland
Otis Steel
Petroleum Industrial Committee
Pickand Mather
Republic Steel Corporation
Retail Merchants Board
Standard Oil Company, Ohio
Trundle Eng. Company
Warner-Swasey Company
Youngstown Sheet and Tube

[*Source*: La Follette Committee Hearings, Exhibit 6305, p. 15523.]

1947–1948 (Hill and Knowlton, Inc., of New York)

Aircraft Industries Association
Air Power League
American Institute of Steel Construction
American Iron and Steel Institute
Aviation Corporation

Consolidated Vultee Aircraft
Erie Railroad Company (shared with Cleveland for part of year)
General Chemical Company
Jacobs Aircraft Engine Compnay
Lithaloys Corporation
National Association of Manufacturers
National Fertilizer Association
National Retail Dry Goods Association
Shipbuilders Council of America
Swank, Inc.

Added within the next year:
Butter producers group (American Butter Institute/National Cooperative Milk
    Producers Federation/National Creameries Association)
General Chemical
Hewitt-Robins, Inc.
National Air Council

[*Source*: "Analysis of Fees Received during Liquidation Period," Box 27, Folder 12,
JWH; "Report to Stockholders of Hill and Knowlton, Inc.," Box 27, Folder 1, JWH.]

1953

Aircraft Industries Association
American Iron and Steel Institute
Avco Manufacturing Corporation
California Texas Oil Company
Cudahy Packing Company
Licensed Beverage Industries
Manufacturing Chemists' Association
Procter and Gamble Company
Studebaker Corporation
Texas Company

[*Source*: John Hill to Victor Emanuel, 16 July 1953, Box 5, Folder 2, JWH.]

1955

Aircraft Industries Association, Inc.
Allied Stores Corporation
American Iron and Steel Institute, Inc.
American National Red Cross
American Potash and Chemical Corporation
Australian Oil Refining, Ltd.
Avco Manufacturing
Board of Trade of the City of Chicago
Boys Republic
California Texas Oil Company, Ltd.
Caltex Oil (Australia) Proprietary, Ltd.
Cities Service Petroleum, Inc.

Clary Corporation
Coca-Cola Company
Coca-Cola Export Corporation
Compagnie Universelle du Canal Maritime de Suez
Electric Auto-Lite Company
Embassy and Consulate General of Japan
Galbreath Corporation
Gillette Safety Razor Company
Glassware Institute of America
Greater New York Association, Inc.
Licensed Beverage Industries, Inc.
Nassau Development Board
Natural Gas and Oil Resources Committee
New York City Omnibus Corporation
Olin Mathieson Chemical Corporation
Owens-Illinois Glass Company
Procter and Gamble Company
Southern Company
Studebaker-Packard Corporation
Texas Company
Tobacco Industry Research Committee
Trans Australia Airways
Waltons-Sears (Australia)
West Australian Petroleum Proprietary, Ltd.

[*Source*: Box 42, Biographical Clippings; and "Clients of Hill and Knowlton, Inc. and Affiliates," Box 5, Folder 2, JWH. Includes clients of Robinson-Hannagan Associates, which H&K had just purchased; Edward W. Barrett and Associates; and Hill and Knowlton, Proprietary, Ltd.-Sydney, Australia.]

1966

U.S. Clients:
Allied Chemical Corporation
American Institute of Steel Construction
American Iron and Steel Institute
American League of Professional Baseball Clubs
American Petroleum Institute
American Potash and Chemical Corporation
Armstrong Cork Company
Avco Corporation
Boys Republic
Budd Company
California Computer Products, Inc.
Chemical Industry Council of Southern California
Cities Service Company
Citizens Tax Council, Inc.
Colonial Pipeline Companay
Cummins Engine Company, Inc.
Dobbs Houses, Inc.

El Paso Natural Gas Company
Ernst and Ernst
Ethyl Corporation
Falstaff Brewing Corporation
Farm Service Industries Committee
Gillette Company
Lead Industries Association, Inc.
Licensed Beverage Industries, Inc.
Life and Casualty Insurance Company
Lily-Tulip Cup Corporation
Marathon Oil Company
Murchison Brothers
New York Life Insurance Company
New York University
Owens-Illinois, Inc.
Packard Bell Electronics
Procter and Gamble Company
Richardson-Merrell, Inc.
Savings Banks Association of New York State
Schlumberger Limited
Southern Railway System
State Education Department of New York
Tobacco Institute, Inc.
Union Pacific Railroad Company
United Gas Corporation

International Clients:
Alcoa International, Inc.
First National City Bank
Gillette Company
Hong Kong Chamber of Commerce
Hoover Worldwide Corporation
Hughes Aircraft Company
Imperial Tobacco Company of Canada Limited
Marathon International Oil Company
Ministry of Tourism, Bahamas
Monsanto International
Newsprint Information Committee of Canada
Philips Phonographic Industries
Procter and Gamble Company
Saudi Arabia
World Airways, Inc.

[*Source*: Donald W. Riegle Jr., "Hill and Knowlton, Inc.—II," Harvard Business School Case Study (1966), Box 6, Folder 9, JWH.]

Abbreviations Used in the Notes

AISI   American Iron and Steel Institute Papers, Hagley Museum and Library, Wilmington, Del.

B&W   Brown and Williamson Papers, University of California–San Francisco (accessed through http://www.library.ucsf.edu./tobacco)

B-V   Boeing-Vertol Division Papers, Hagley Museum and Library, Wilmington, Del.

COHC   Columbia University Oral History Collection, New York City

EAG   Evarts A. Graham Papers, Washington University, St. Louis, Mo.

HSTL   Harry S. Truman Library, Independence, Mo.

JWH   John W. Hill Papers, State Historical Society of Wisconsin, Madison, Wis.

MJ   Merrick Jackson Papers, State Historical Society of Wisconsin, Madison, Wis.

PAPC   President's Air Policy Commission, Harry S. Truman Library, Independence, Mo.

PM   Philip Murray Papers, Archives of the Catholic University of America, Washington, D.C.

PSF   President's Secretary's File, Harry S. Truman Library, Independence, Mo.

RAT   Robert A. Taft Papers, Library of Congress, Washington, D.C.

SHSW   State Historical Society of Wisconsin, Madison, Wis.

SS   Stuart Symington Papers, Harry S. Truman Library, Independence, Mo.

Truman OF   Truman Official File, Harry S. Truman Library, Independence, Mo.

WLRB   Wisconsin Legislative Reference Bureau, Madison, Wis.

Introduction

1. "John W. Hill," n.d. [1961], Box 42, Biographical Clippings, JWH. The Hill papers consist of client files and correspondence relating to most of the agency's largest accounts during the 1940s and 1950s. Materials such as personnel and financial information are not included.

2. "Public Relations: A Communication System Ripens," 67. If indeed the agency's clients' sales were $50 billion that percentage is correct, given that the GNP was about $500 billion in 1959 (*Statistical Abstract of the U.S.*, 324). It is impossible to calculate

now, however, because no complete client list is available. Billings for public relations agencies were not as a rule made public. Ross, "Inside Public Relations," 9 July 1958, Box 42, Biographical Clippings, JWH; "Public Relations Today," *Business Week* (2 July 1960), 6, Box 42, Biographical Clippings, JWH. See Wise, "Hill & Knowlton's World of Images," 101, for listings of the largest agencies in terms of staff, clients, offices, and revenue.

3. "Public Relations Today," 7, Box 42, Biographical Clippings, JWH; "Public Relations: A Communications System Ripens," 66.

4. Autobiographical works include Lee, *Publicity*; Bernays, *Biography of an Idea*; and Hill, *Corporate Public Relations* and *Making of a Public Relations Man*. General histories include Galambos and Pratt, *Rise of the Corporate Commonwealth*; Raucher, *Public Relations and Business, 1900–1929*; Tedlow, *Keeping the Corporate Image*; Olasky, *Corporate Public Relations and American Private Enterprise*; and Ewen, *PR!*. Histories of public relations agencies include Cutlip, *The Unseen Power*; Bennett, "Carl Byoir"; and Hamel, "John W. Hill."

5. McQuaid, *Uneasy Partners*, 36; Fones-Wolf, *Selling Free Enterprise*, 287.

6. Hill, *Making of a Public Relations Man*, 169.

7. John W. Hill, "Forty Years of Public Relations," in Hill and Knowlton, Inc., *Current Thoughts*, 218.

8. Barrett, preface to Hill, *Making of a Public Relations Man*, vi.

9. Marchand, *Advertising the American Dream*, 84; Goss, "How to Reduce Business' Credibility Gap," 396.

10. Hill, *Corporate Public Relations*, 131.

Chapter One

1. Hamel, "John W. Hill," 1–9; Hill, *Making of a Public Relations Man*, 8–15.

2. Hill, *Making of a Public Relations Man*, 12–13, 19.

3. Temin, *Lessons from the Great Depression*, 21, 33; Leuchtenburg, *Franklin D. Roosevelt and the New Deal*, 19; Nichols, "Good Reading for Reporters," 31 October 1962, Box 42, Biographical Clippings, JWH; Hill, *Making of a Public Relations Man*, 31.

4. Hill, *Making of a Public Relations Man*, 38, 44–45, 64; Chandler, *America's Greatest Depression*, 1.

5. Hill, *Making of a Public Relations Man*, 32; "The Men Who Make Steel," AISI.

6. "U.S. Corporate Management," 47; Gordon, *New Deals*, 280; Leuchtenburg, *Franklin D. Roosevelt and the New Deal*, 177; Hill, *Corporate Public Relations*, 17. For a survey of activities, see Stratton, "Public Relations in Steel," 107–11.

7. On steel labor prior to Little Steel, see Brody, *Steelworkers in America* and *Labor in Crisis*.

8. The National Labor Relations Act (49 Stat. 449 [1935]), the Wagner Act, created the National Labor Relations Board to help regulate disputes. Sweeney, *The United Steelworkers of America*, 27; Harris, *Right to Manage*, 97.

9. Phelps and Jeuck, "Criticisms of the National Labor Relations Act," 31; Fones-Wolf, "Industrial Recreation," 238–41; Zieger, *The CIO*, 35, 54, 57–58; Nelson, *American Rubber Workers*, 128–30; Cohen, *Making a New Deal*, 294, 304.

10. Fones-Wolf, *Selling Free Enterprise*, 25; Stalker, "The National Association of Manufacturers"; Tedlow, *Keeping the Corporate Image*, 62–64; Krooss, *Executive Opinion*, 25; Grafton, "Propaganda from the Right," 257.

11. "Emergency Advertising," 43; "Strike Copy in Seattle," 80; "'Who Can Win?,'"

16; "'Nobody Wins a Strike,'" 92; Marchand, "The Inward Thrust of Institutional Advertising," 188–96; Marchand, "The Fitful Career of Advocacy Advertising," 142; Hill, *Corporate Public Relations*, 5.

12. The ad appeared in the *Cleveland Plain Dealer*, 1 July 1936, 6. U.S. Senate, *Violations of Free Speech and Rights of Labor*, 10162 (hereafter La Follette hearings).

Gridley, in "Weaknesses of Strike Copy," wrote that "no one studying strike advertising can do anything but applaud the foresightedness of the American Iron and Steel Institute" for placing the ad before any strikes started (88). An employee of a clipping agency found 321 editorials about the ad: 36 defended labor outright, 47 deplored the situation or expressed alarm, and 238 were "temperate" (Crowell, "The Editorial Slant on Steel," 378). United Steelworkers of America Education Department, *Then and Now*, 62.

Hill was not the only PR agent involved in the strike. John Price Jones also worked for steel clients (Cutlip, *Unseen Power*, 241), and the NAM ran ads and hired an agency to prepare radio publicity in strike towns (Blumenthal, "Anti-Union Publicity," 677, 682).

13. Zieger, *The CIO*, 59; "The Corporation," 59; Sweeney, *United Steelworkers of America*, 28–29; Brody, *Labor in Crisis*, 180–81; U.S. Bureau of the Census, *Historical Statistics*, 693; Thompson, "C.I.O. Expanding on Two Big Fronts," E7. Jones and Laughlin Steel Corporation, 57 U.S. 615 (1937), was the test case in which the Supreme Court upheld the National Labor Relations Act.

14. Harris, *The Right to Manage*, 97–99; Grace, "Industry and the Public," 681.

15. "The Industrial War," 168. On Girdler see, for example, *Fortune*'s "Republic Steel," which said, "the story of Republic is the story of the struggle, so far successful, of a supremely able management against supremely great odds" (76). Hill, *Making of a Public Relations Man*, 30. Hill met Girdler when his client, Central Alloy Corporation, merged with numerous others to form Republic.

16. La Follette hearings, Exhibit 3571; Bernstein, *Turbulent Years*, 435; Powers, *Cradle of Steel Unionism*, 110; quoted in Tedlow, *Keeping the Corporate Image*, 99.

17. Sofchalk, "The Chicago Memorial Day Incident"; Bernstein, *Turbulent Years*, 495–96; Zieger, *The CIO*, 62–63. Both the La Follette Committee and the Citizen's Joint Commission of Chicago found the laborers blameless ("Aftermath of a Massacre," 174). Auerbach, "The La Follette Committee," 447; "Girdler Repeats His Biggest 'No,'" 14.

18. Baughman, "Classes and Company Towns," 177, 190–91; "Report of the Chairman," in Congress of Industrial Organizations, *Proceedings of the First Constitutional Convention*, 32; Zieger, *The CIO*, 63.

19. Hill, *Making of a Public Relations Man*, 47, 49. H&K press releases and brochures are reprinted in the La Follette hearings exhibits (text only, 15534–62). See also the cover stories of *Steel Facts*, October 1934 and May 1935.

20. "The Real Issues," La Follette hearings Exhibit 6563, 15764–66. See also *Steel Facts*, April, July, and September 1937.

21. Hill, *Making of a Public Relations Man*, 55; Girdler, "The C.I.O. versus American Democracy."

22. Auerbach, "La Follette Committee," 443.

23. La Follette hearings, 9736–37, 9739, 9760, 13879, 13887; Girdler, "What's Ahead in Industrial Relations?," Box 122, Speeches—Republic Steel, AISI. Girdler was correct in asserting that many of the pickets were outsiders: at South Chicago on Memorial Day, of the sixty-eight arrested only fourteen worked for Republic; of the dead, four worked for Inland, four for Carnegie-Illinois, and one for the Works Progress Administration ("Girdler Repeats His Biggest 'No,'" 15).

24. Broun, "L'Affaire Sokolsky," 360; La Follette hearings, 10321; Sokolsky, "The

CIO Turns a Page," 314, and "Giants in These Days," 691–700. Sokolsky pointed out that he had made public the connection in his column (see "Sokolsky Makes Reply" and Sokolsky, "Creeds and Faiths").

25. Hill, *Making of a Public Relations Man*, 58; La Follette hearings, 10310, 10329; Hamel, "John W. Hill," 170; Tedlow, *Keeping the Corporate Image*, 101.

26. "Steel," 285; La Follette hearings, 10314–16, 10331–40. The companies were Republic, Youngstown Sheet and Tube, National, Bethlehem, Inland, and Armco (La Follette hearings, 13870, 11202–3). For a discussion on the mechanics of community pressure against unions, see Zahavi, *Workers, Managers, and Welfare Capitalism*, 155–58.

27. Manning, personal correspondence; Hill, *Making of a Public Relations Man*, 108, 113. For an example of Emanuel's glowing recommendations of H&K to a potential client, see Emanuel to Dr. C. W. deKiewiet, 4 October 1950, Box 5, Folder 2, JWH. Hill, *Making of a Public Relations Man*, 111–12; Hamel, "John W. Hill," 48. In 1948 nine H&K staff members worked actively on the Avco account, which received additional assistance from the publicity, art, and other departments (Hill to Emanuel, 20 July 1948, Box 87, Folder 4, JWH).

28. Hamel, "John W. Hill," 48–49. See correspondence in JWH under Emanuel's name in both the Correspondence and the Client files and in RAT chronologically under Emanuel's name. According to an H&K catalog of mailing lists, Emanuel had a personal mailing list of 137 names (17 November 1952, Box 37, Folder 14, JWH). Hill to Emanuel, 28 October 1948, Box 87, Folder 4, JWH.

29. "Memorandum on Hill and Knowlton, Inc.," n.d. [1950], Box 42, Biographical Clippings, JWH; Hill to Allen, 23 February 1950, Box 1, Folder 6, JWH. For examples of client solicitation, see Hamel, "John W. Hill," 87–90. Allen was also used to impress current clients (see Hill to A. M. Rochlen, 2 October 1953, Box 45, Folder 7, JWH). Hill, *Making of a Public Relations Man*, 111; "Robinson-Hannagan Associates," Box 42, Biographical Clippings, JWH.

30. Hamel, "John W. Hill," 52; Gras, "Shifts in Public Relations," 128.

31. Freeman, "Delivering the Goods," 573. The Little Steel formula emerged in Cases 30, 31, 34, and 35, 1 War Labor Report 325. On labor during the war, see Lichtenstein, *Labor's War at Home*.

32. Hill, *Making of a Public Relations Man*, 37. New York billed $30,640.82 while Cleveland brought in only $15,866.66 for that month ("Fees—1945," Box 6, Folder 11, JWH). By one account, the New York office had thirty-five employees by 1946 ("Frances Campbell Reports How It Was . . . ," Box 6, Folder 10, MJ). Memorandum on Hill and Knowlton, Inc., n.d. [1951], Box 99, Folder 8, JWH. When Knowlton retired in 1964, Hill insisted that Hill and Knowlton of Cleveland change its name.

33. Pendleton Dudley to George Hamel, n.d. [1965], Box 7, Hamel Papers.

34. Ross, *Image Merchants*, 35; Bowen and Clark, "Reputation by Sonnenberg," 39; Hill to T. J. Ross, 31 January 1950, Box 37, Folder 9, JWH; Bernays, *Biography of an Idea*, 387; quoted in Donald W. Riegle Jr., "Hill and Knowlton, Inc.—II," Harvard Business School Case Study (1966), Box 6, Folder 9, JWH; Wise, "Hill and Knowlton's World," 143–44.

35. Wise, "Hill & Knowlton's World," 140; Kelley, *Professional Public Relations and Political Power*.

36. Hill, "Industry's Iron Curtain," 3; Burson interview; "Merrick Jackson: Remembers H&K in 40s, 50s," Box 6, Folder 10, MJ.

37. Stalker, "National Association of Manufacturers," 165; Tedlow, *Keeping the Corporate Image*, 98.

38. Hill, *Corporate Public Relations*, 63.

39. *Abrams v. U.S.* (1919), 250 U.S. 616; Hill, *Corporate Public Relations*, 6–7.

40. Lee, *Publicity*, 41; Lee, "The Problem of International Propaganda"; Ewen, *PR!*, 409.

41. Hill, "The Future of Public Relations," in Hill and Knowlton, Inc., *Public Relations*; Bert C. Goss, "The Image and Politics," in Bristol, *Developing the Corporate Image*, 148.

42. Hill, "Telling the Facts," Box 39, Folder 7, JWH. The July 1937 issue of *Steel Facts* noted that production dropped due to strikes, but its lead story was "Steel Employees Average $10 More per Week Than Other Workers."

43. Hill, "Industry's Job in Public Relations," Box 39, Folder 7, JWH.

44. Hill, "Organizing for Public Relations," Box 39, Folder 7, JWH.

45. Grunig and Hunt, *Managing Public Relations*, 22; Rudge, "Two-Way Communications," 13.

46. Golden, "Survival Lessons," 49; Broughton, *Careers in Public Relations*, 12. Once Hill knew the agency was in the running for a new account, he pursued it with vigor; see, for example, Hill to H. O. C. Ingraham, 24 July 1951, Box 99, Folder 8, JWH.

47. "Notes for the Wisemen Dinner," 17 November 1958, Box 18, Folder 7, JWH; James Irwin to the Wisemen, 10 March 1978, Irwin Papers. Irwin writes that General Foods's Verne Burnett gave the group its name when John Long of Bethlehem Steel flew the entire group to Secaucus Valley in company DC-3s. Over cocktails that evening, Burnett said the junket should be an inspiration in helping the group find a name. They'd made a pilgrimage to Bethlehem, Burnett said, "How about 'Wisemen'?"

48. Merrick Jackson to Ed Doherty, 14 June 1989, Box 6, Folder 10, MJ.

Chapter Two

1. Draft of President's Report, n.d., Box 5, Drafts of President's Report (1947), All-American Aviation, Inc., Papers, HML; John E. P. Morgan to W. Stuart Symington, 13 June 1946, Box 1, Correspondence, SS.

2. Mingos, "Birth of an Industry," 25–69. By the end of 1945, contracts worth $21 billion had been canceled.

3. In the decade following the war the AIA typically spent just under one-third of its budget on public relations, but in 1947 the manufacturers appropriated half of their $700,000 budget to PR (AIA Public Relations Budget for 1956, Box 52, Folder 11, JWH).

4. A complete list of AIA members as of September 1947 is included in Box 6, B7-1, PAPC. The largest manufacturers in the immediate postwar era were Beech, Bell, Boeing, Consolidated Vultee, Curtiss-Wright, Douglas, Fairchild Engine and Airplane, Grumman, Lockheed, Glenn L. Martin, McDonell, North American Aviation, Northrop, Republic, Ryan Aeronautical, and United Aircraft and Transport (Rae, *Climb to Greatness*, 190).

5. Bonney, "Aviation Public Relations," 576–88; "Aircraft Manufacturing in the United States," in Cleveland and Graham, *Aviation Annual of 1946*, 90–91; Ramsey, "Aircraft Industries Association," 160–77. Wilson remained active in the association as chairman of the board.

6. Lee, *Aviation Facts and Figures* (hereafter AIA 1956), 20, 7, 30; this is an AIA annual publication. "Report of the President," AIA Annual Report, 4 December 1947, Box 44, Folder 6, JWH.

7. Pollard, *Economic Security*, 228–29, 24; Truman, "Special Message to the Con-

gress," 19 December 1945, *Public Papers of the Presidents of the United States: Harry S. Truman, 1945*; Reardon, *Formative Years*, 313–15; Doenecke, *Not to the Swift*, 161–66; Griffith, "Old Progressives and the Cold War," 334–47; Herken, *Winning Weapon*, 215.

8. "Reminiscences of Ira C. Eaker" (1974), 36, COHC; Yergin, *Shattered Peace*, 201.

9. Rae, *Climb to Greatness*, 196; Davis, *Postwar Defense Policy*, 149; "A Program to Bring the Keller Report before Congress and the Public," 7 August 1947, Box 106, Folder 3, JWH. As with the aircraft manufacturers, the Shipbuilders Council had begun working with H&K during the war on peacetime plans. Report of Activities, 1947–1948, Box 106, Folder 4, JWH; Hill, *Making of a Public Relations Man*, 105.

10. Rae, *Climb to Greatness*, 174; AIA 1956, 7.

11. "AIA Report of the President for 1945 and Program for 1946," Box 30, AIA-1949, B-V.

12. "AIA Report of the President for 1945 and Program for 1946," Box 30, AIA-1949, B-V; "Proposed Revision of the Public Relations Program," 26 July 1951, Box 30, AIA-1951, B-V; Hooks, *Forging the Military-Industrial Complex*, 241–61; Mrozek, "Truman Administration," 75; Vogel, "Why Businessmen Distrust Their State," 51.

13. Lee, "Public Relations," 10–11; "AIA Report of the President for 1945 and Program for 1946," Box 30, AIA-1949, B-V; Hill, *Making of a Public Relations Man*, 101.

14. Hill, *Making of a Public Relations Man*, 102. The Public Relations Advisory Committee consisted of Deac Lyman of United Aircraft, John Canady of Lockheed, Lee Taylor of North American, Rocky Rochlen of Douglas, Ken Ellington of Republic, and about a dozen others.

15. Vander Muelen, *Politics of Aircraft*, 1, 5.

16. Burson interview; "Outline of Public Relations Activities," May 1947, Box 52, Folder 10, JWH; "Proposed Public Relations Budget," 18 January 1949, Box 62, Folder 7, JWH; "AIA Report of the President for 1945 and Program for 1946," Box 30, AIA-1949, B-V; "Memorandum for Mr. Symington" from Col. John B. Montgomery, 17 August 1946, Box 1, Correspondence, SS; Hill to Murray, 23 November 1943, Box 46, Folder 3, JWH.

17. Wilson, "The Moral Edge," 546.

18. Hilgartner and Bosk, "Rise and Fall of Social Problems," 53–78; Gitlin, *Whole World Is Watching*, 7.

19. Hill, *Corporate Public Relations*, 135; Elder and Cobb, *Political Uses of Symbols*, 173, 13–14, 160–61.

20. The Air Coordinating Committee was created by Executive Order 9781 in March 1945. "Washington Outlook," 6; "General Echols' Air Policy Program" in P.R. Memo 47-14, Activity Report for 18 January to 17 February 1947, Box 43, Folder 11, JWH.

21. Along with Finletter, the commissioners were George P. Baker, vice-chair, Palmer Hoyt, Henry Ford II, and Arthur D. Whiteside; Ford resigned early in the investigation and was replaced by John A. McCone. Finletter had served in the Army in World War I, and Baker on the Army's air staff during World War II. Hoyt was publisher of the *Denver Post*, and Whiteside was president of Dun and Bradstreet; McCone's company had been associated with the AAF during the war, but was more closely connected with oil refining, chemistry, and shipbuilding than aviation.

22. President's Air Policy Commission, *Survival in the Air Age*, 7–8; "Statement of Thomas K. Finletter," Box 6, Reports, Weihmiller Papers; Memorandum to Finletter (from McCone), n.d., Box 25, F2-3, PAPC; Box 26, F4-1, PAPC; S. Paul Johnston to J. Edgar Hoover, 3 November 1947, Box 26, F4-2, PAPC; Borowski, *A Hollow Threat*, 28; Rae, *Climb to Greatness*, 193.

23. Congressional Air Policy Board members from the Senate: Albert Hawkes (N.J.),

Homer Capehart (Ind.), Edwin Johnson (Colo.), Ernest McFarland (Ariz.); from the House: Charles Wolverton (N.J.), Karl Stefan (Neb.), Alfred Bulwinkle (N.C.), Paul Kilday (Tex.). U.S. Senate, *National Aviation Policy*, 4, 7.

24. P.R. Memo 48-10, Activity Report for 2 December 1947 to 23 January 1948, Box 43, Folder 11, JWH; Goss to Eugene Wilson, 23 January 1948, Box 54, Folder 5, JWH.

25. Mention of preparation of remarks is made, for example, in P.R. Memo 47-44, Activity Report for 21 April to 28 May 1947, Box 43, Folder 11, JWH; Sam S. Tyndall to R. H. Sutherland, 24 September 1947, Box 44, Folder 2, JWH; H&K news release on PAPC testimony, 28 September 1947, Box 6, B7-1, PAPC; "Report of the President," AIA Annual Report, 4 December 1947, Box 44, Folder 6, JWH; Goss to Hal Davis, 21 August 1947, Box 44, Folder 2, JWH.

26. Hill, *Making of a Public Relations Man*, 103; Goss to Sen. Styles Bridges, 20 September 1948, Box 46, Folder 12, JWH.

27. Symington to Finletter, 28 October 1947, Box 18, C2-8, PAPC; "The Betrayal of Air Power" (April 5, 1948), 50, (April 12, 1948), 54, and (19 April 1948), 66; "Expansible Industry or Mothball Fleet?," 50. For a thorough description of these events, see Bailey and Samuel, *Congress at Work*, 357–81.

28. Wilson Oral History (1962), 808–9.

29. "Special Public Relations Program for AIA," 20 September 1946, Box 52, Folder 10, JWH.

30. Cohen, *Press and Foreign Policy*, 120; McCombs and Shaw, "The Agenda-Setting Function of Mass Media," 176–87.

31. P.R. Memo 48-10, Activity Report for 2 December 1947 to 23 January 1948, Box 43, Folder 11, JWH; Goss to Echols, 26 April 1949, Box 46, Folder 13, JWH; "Air Policy," 58.

32. Goss to Doris Fleeson, 24 February 1949, Box 46, Folder 13, JWH; P.R. Memo 47-44, Activity Report for April 21 to May 28, 1947, Box 43, Folder 11, JWH. The client files do not contain lists of press contacts until later, but a 1956 weekly summary indicated contact with twenty-eight different reporters on stories regarding costs, effects of strikes on the industry, production rates, guided missiles, procurement, traffic control, Russian aircraft, and security policies ("Press Contacts—week of July 16–20, 1956," Box 43, Folder 9, JWH). Echols to Chet Shaw, 3 July 1947, Box 46, Folder 3, JWH.

33. Samuel S. Tyndall to Hill, Goss, and Mapes, 21 March 1947, Box 53, Folder 10, JWH.

34. P.R. Memo 48-10, Activity Report for 2 December 1947 to 23 January 1948, Box 43, Folder 11, JWH; P.R. Memo 47-103, Activity Report for 1 September to 1 December 1947, Box 43, Folder 11, JWH. H&K came in under budget.

35. Price, "On the Public Aspects of Opinion," 665; McLeod, Pan, and Rucinski, "Levels of Analysis," 56–59.

36. "Outline of Public Relations Activities for the Fall and Winter," 28 May 1947, Box 52, Folder 10, JWH; Goss to Hill, 12 February 1947, Box 44, Folder 2, JWH.

37. "Outline of Public Relations Activities for the Fall and Winter," 28 May 1947, Box 52, Folder 10, JWH; Echols to Harry Woodhead, 7 May 1947, Box 46, Folder 3, JWH; Echols to Gen. Bonner Fellers, 5 September 1947, Box 46, Folder 3, JWH; Goss to Fellers, 14 January 1947, Box 53, Folder 13, JWH; Samuel S. Tyndall and R. H. Sutherland to Hill, 9 June 1947, Box 46, Folder 9, JWH.

38. "Report of the President," AIA Annual Report, 4 December 1947, Box 44, Folder 6, JWH; Goss to Sen. Hal Davis, 3 February 1947, Box 52, Folder 9, JWH; AIA, *Aircraft Year Book for 1948*; P.R. Memo 47-103, Activity Report for 1 September to 1 December 1947, Box 43, Folder 11, JWH. Two AIA-sponsored books were Taylor and Wright, *Democracy's Air Arsenal*, and Hinton, *Air Victory*.

39. Goss to Fellers, 14 January 1947, Box 53, Folder 13, JWH; Bottoms, *The VFW*, 110.

40. Goss to Hill, 30 October 1947, Box 46, Folder 10, JWH; Goss to Hill, n.d., Box 44, Folder 5, JWH; "How Potent Is the Legion?," 7.

41. "Report on the American Legion–AIA Community Air Power Program," 6 January 1947, Box 44, Folder 5, JWH; "Current Activities of the American Legion Program," 29 May 1947, Box 43, Folder 11, JWH; "The First Quarter's Results," n.d., Box 44, Folder 5, JWH; "The Community Air Power Program," n.d., Box 44, Folder 5, JWH.

42. Watson, *Office of the Secretary of the Air Force*, 56, 58; Goss to William Wagner, 7 January 1947, Box 44, Folder 1, JWH. See correspondence in Box 1, Folder 7, JWH.

43. "Report of the President," AIA Annual Report, 4 December 1947, Box 44, Folder 6, JWH; P.R. Release 47-34, Box 52, Folder 14, JWH.

44. J. B. M. to Symington, 5 September 1947, Box 1, Correspondence—Air Policy Commission, SS; Goss to Col. C. J. Brown, 15 January 1947, Box 44, Folder 1, JWH.

45. "Strengthening of Air Power Gets Big Vote in Survey," for release 20–21 February 1949, Box 1, American Institute of Public Opinion Papers; David C. Lewis to Truman, 23 August 1947, Truman OF 1639, 1285-D; Dr. Bullard to Truman, 15 April 1948, Truman OF 1639, 1285-D.

46. Goss to Col. C. J. Brown, 15 January 1947, Box 44, Folder 1, JWH.

47. "Dates," P.R. Release 47-30 for 6 May to 16 June 1947, Box 52, Folder 14, JWH; "Weekly Washington Bulletin," Box 47, Folder 6, JWH (only two copies remain in the Hill collection, from 1945 and 1946, so it is not clear how long the agency continued to send them to the companies); P.R. Memos, Boxes 49–51, JWH.

48. *Washington Information Directory*, Box 54, Folder 4, JWH; "Background Information on the President's Temporary Air Policy Commission and the Joint Congressional Policy Board," September 1947, Box 44, Folder 2, JWH.

49. P.R. Memo 47-103, Activity Report for 1 September to 1 December 1947, Box 43, Folder 11, JWH. See also Goss to Hill, draft "Memo to Committee," 30 December 1946, Box 46, Folder 9, JWH; Goss to Leland Taylor, 26 October 1948, Box 46, Folder 12, JWH.

50. Goss to W. D. Eckert, 21 June 49, Box 46, Folder 13, JWH; Goss to Charles Frazer, 15 January 1948, Box 46, Folder 11, JWH; *Editorials on the Crisis in Air Power*, Box 44, Folder 2, JWH; Goss to Fellers, 14 January 1947, Box 53, Folder 13, JWH; Louis E. Starr to VFW Comrades, 23 January 1947, Box 43, Folder 11, JWH; Goss to Clyde Mathews, 14 January 1947, Box 53, Folder 13, JWH. Along with *Planes* articles by senators, H&K reprinted copies of a *Collier's* series titled, "Will Russia Rule the Air?" P.R. Memo 47-23, Activity Report for 17 February to 18 March 1947, Box 43, Folder 11, JWH.

51. AIA 1956, 7, 20; Damon, "Airline Outlook," 460.

52. Smith, *The RAND Corporation*; Rand Corporation, *Rand 25th Anniversary Volume*, v; Friedman, "The Rand Corporation," 61–68.

53. "The Aircraft Industry, 1903–1953," Box 43, Folder 8, JWH.

54. Kelly, *Miracle at Kitty Hawk*; Corn, *Winged Gospel*, vii. Goldstein, *The Flying Machine and Modern Literature*, analyzes stories about flying from Leonard da Vinci to the moonwalk.

55. AIA 1956, 61–62.

56. "AIA Report of the President for 1945 and Program for 1946," Box 30, AIA-1949, B-V; P.R. Memo 47-14, Activity Report for 18 January to 17 February 1947, Box 43, Folder 11, JWH. See copies of three speeches in Box 53, Folder 9, JWH.

57. Bluestone, Jordan, and Sullivan, *Aircraft Industry Dynamics*, 27. Corridors were twenty-mile-wide air lanes protected by written agreement. AIA, *Aircraft Year Book for 1949*, 119; Yergin, *Shattered Peace*, 377, 387.

58. Sherry, *Preparing for the Next War*, 207; De Seversky, "The U.S. Air Force in

Power Politics," 477; Millis, *The Forrestal Diaries*, 514; Kennett, *History of Strategic Bombing*, 182–85.

59. Schilling, "The Politics of National Defense: Fiscal 1950," 45; Robert A. Taft to Abe McGregor Goff, 17 January 1948, Box 893, Air Force-1948, RAT; Sherry, *Preparing for the Next War*, 224. See Gallup news releases on defense spending and universal military training for 11 January and 27 December 1946; 16 February, 23 March, 13 June 1947; 19 January and 9 April 1948—support for universal military training consistently ran at about 70 percent (Box 1, American Institute of Public Opinion Papers). Millis, *The Forrestal Diaries*, 426; Hartmann, "President Truman and the 80th Congress," 172.

60. Yergin, *Shattered Peace*, 358; Bilstein, *Flight in America*, 185; news releases for 24 March 1948 and 4 July 1948, Box 1, American Institute of Public Opinion Papers; Monroe R. Brown to C. Hart Miller and Frank N. Piasecki, 24 August 1951, Box 30, AIA-1951, B-V.

61. Goss to Stowers, 19 November 1947, Box 53, Folder 14, JWH; Goss to Stowers, 1 April 1948, Box 46, Folder 10, JWH; Tyndall to Hill, Goss, and Mapes, 21 March 1947, Box 53, Folder 10, JWH.

62. "The Wildest Blue Yonder Yet," 95. See also, Baldwin, "What Air Power Can—and Cannot—Do," 5–7+; "Shall We Have Airplanes?," 77–81+; Wilson Oral History (1962), 813; Yergin, *Shattered Peace*, 339–41; Baker Oral History (1974), 53; Eisenhower, "Liberty Is at Stake," 229.

63. Gaddis, *The Long Peace*, 42; Tracy D. Mygatt to Truman, 12 May 1948, Truman OF 1639, 1285-D.

64. Proposed Revision of the Public Relations Program, 26 July 1951, Box 52, Folder 10, JWH. The AIA retained H&K well into the 1960s, but the client files describing their programs in the Hill Papers end in the late 1950s.

Chapter Three

1. Harry Botsford to John Mapes, 6 February 1947, Box 62, Folder 16, JWH.

2. Marchand, *Advertising the American Dream*, 82.

3. Galbraith, *American Capitalism*, 2, 87; U.S. Bureau of the Census, *Historical Statistics*, 693; Council on Wage and Price Stability, *A Study of Steel Prices*, 9, 17; American Iron and Steel Institute, *Steel's Competitive Challenge*, 14; "Rise of 54% in Manufacturing Products," 5.

4. "Industry's Public Relations Job," 75; Tedlow, *Keeping the Corporate Image*, 151; "Meeting Community Responsibilities," Box 5, Folder 4, MJ.

5. "Industry's Public Relations Job," 76; Galbraith, *American Capitalism*, 2, 4; Tedlow, *Keeping the Corporate Image*, 120.

6. Link, "How to Sell America to Americans," 3–7+; Carr, "Translating the American Economic System," 3; Johnston, "Free Enterprise Now Faces Crisis and Opportunity," 19–20; Drepperd, "Begin Selling 'Free Enterprise' in the Kindergarten," 20+; Irwin, "Tell the Public Why America's Future Depends upon Free Enterprise!" 17–18+; Wells, "Remain Silent and Die," 9.

7. Griffith, "The Selling of America," 394–95, 400. In 1939 Hill and Knowlton participated in an Ad Council campaign for steel scrap collection, and John Hill would later serve on the council's board of directors (Hill, *Making of a Public Relations Man*, 63). Companies like Alcoa promoted "free enterprise" at least in part because they feared antitrust action (Baughman, "*See It Now* and Television's Golden Age," 107; "Wooing the Eggheads for Alcoa," 116).

8. H&K's institutional advertising service began in January 1947 (Hill to Emanuel, 20 January 1947, Box 87, Folder 2, JWH). Tedlow, *Keeping the Corporate Image*, 138, 120.

9. Green, *World of the Worker*, 194; Zieger, *American Workers*, 104, 108–11; McQuaid, *Uneasy Partners*, 26; Irons, "American Business and the Origins of McCarthyism," 76.

10. Vaizey, *History of British Steel*, 118, 128, 150; Abromeit, *British Steel*, 114–16; Heal, *Steel Industry in Post War Britain*, 76; "What Socialized Steel Means," 24–25. See also "Battle for Britain's Steel," 88–90.

11. Hill to Mapes and Jackson, 27 June 1949, Box 69, Folder 6, JWH; "U.S. Steel Corporation: II," 127–28; Goss to Hill, 12 March 1948, Box 71, Folder 16, JWH.

12. Harris, *Right to Manage*, 185; "Getting Better Acquainted: Reviewing the Year's Public Relations Activities, 1947–48," n.d., Box 71, Folder 9, JWH. Ryerson, "Belabored Steel Puts Up Million," Box 102, Clips (2), AISI.

13. "Steel Industry Becomes More Vocal," Box 102, Clips (2), AISI; memoir, Box 4, Folder 5, MJ; Botsford to Hill, 19 November 1946, Box 58, Folder 11, JWH. The film *Steel — A Symphony of Industry* had been produced in 1936, and by December 1946 it had been seen by over a million theatergoers and almost 900,000 in schools, service clubs, and the like (Mapes to Walter S. Tower, 16 December 1946, Box 62, Folder 1, JWH). "PR Comics," 58; no copy of the book appears in JWH, but correspondence on it is located in Box 62, Folder 15. "Important Questions . . ." ad in *Tide* 23 (8 April 1949), 1; news release for 19 October 1947, Box 75, Folder 9, JWH; background memos, Box 61, Folder 1, JWH; "Community Relations Program," 10 September 1947, Box 71, Folder 15, JWH; Hill, *Making of a Public Relations Man*, 63–64.

14. See, for example, copies of the advertisements in "Confidential Report to Member Companies," 15 December 1945, Box 58, Folder 11, JWH.

15. "Steel—Pacemaker for Peacetime," and "Steel Spends a Billion Dollars," Box 62, Folder 1, JWH.

16. Advertisements, Box 58, Folder 11, JWH.

17. "A Report of the Activities of the American Iron and Steel Institute in Washington," 24 April 1946, Box 71, Folder 8, JWH; "Washington Backgrounds," Box 80, Folder 3, JWH. Work in Washington increased until the 1970s, when the AISI moved its headquarters there, established its own public relations staff, and dropped H&K (Gray interview).

18. Burson interview; Lazarsfeld, "Who Influences Whom," 32+; Lazarsfeld, Berelson, and Gaudet, *People's Choice*.

19. "Steelways Mailing List," 18 January 1949, Box 62, Folder 7, JWH.

20. "Getting Better Acquainted: Reviewing the Year's Public Relations Activities, 1947–48," Box 71, Folder 9, JWH; Starch survey, 5 March 1956, Box 78, Folder 5, JWH; Merrick Jackson, "An Industry Fights Back," Box 5, Folder 3, MJ.

21. Harry Botsford to John Mapes, 6 February 1947, Box 62, Folder 16, JWH.

22. Galbraith, *American Capitalism*, 155; Botsford to Mapes, 6 February 1947, Box 62, Folder 16, JWH; "Community Relations Program," 10 September 1947, Box 71, Folder 15, JWH. See reference in "Suggested Letter from Institute Members," 11 June 1947, Box 62, Folder 16, JWH.

23. Miller, "National and Local Public Relations Campaigns," 305–23.

24. Hill to T. M. Girdler, 12 July 1948, Box 63, Folder 1, JWH.

25. Fones-Wolf, *Selling Free Enterprise*, 159; Irwin, "Winning Better Public Relations with the Community," n.d., Box 1, Irwin Papers. See also Irwin, "Winning Better Relations with the Community," 170–92.

26. "Notes for Mr. Hill," 15 March 1948, Box 63, Folder 1, JWH; "Outline for Community Relations Meeting," 16 March 1948, Box 63, Folder 1, JWH.

27. Purcell to Hill and Mapes, 11 June 1947, Box 62, Folder 16, JWH; Purcell to Hill and Mapes, 6 June 1947, Box 62, Folder 16, JWH. The field agents held meetings to discuss problems, get information on new materials, and review the program ("Community Relations Field Staff Meeting No. III," 24–25 May [1948], Box 63, Folder 1, JWH).

28. Purcell to Hill and Mapes, 6 June 1947, Box 62, Folder 16, JWH; Crenshaw to Hill, 11 August 1947, Box 62, Folder 16, JWH.

29. All nine booklets are located in Box 4, Folder 9, MJ. "Editor's Assistant," No. 1, November 1947, Box 63, Folder 11, JWH. The agency offered stories in mat format, which the editors could easily use to set the story in type. "Elements of a Steel Company's Community Relations Program," n.d. [1947 or 1948], Box 63, Folder 1, JWH; Baughman, *The Republic of Mass Culture*, 42.

30. John A. De Chant to Don Knowlton, 4 February 1948, Box 69, Folder 3, JWH. Harry Lundin's office was in Hill and Knowlton of Cleveland's offices, but H&K, Inc., paid for his office and his own secretary. "Hill and Knowlton, Inc.," Harvard Graduate School of Business Administration Case Study, 1956, Box 6, Folder 9, JWH.

31. "The Public Relations Audit," n.d. [1950], Box 73, Folder 4, JWH.

32. "Getting Better Acquainted: Reviewing the Year's Public Relations Activities, 1947–48," Box 71, Folder 9, JWH. Steel executives became increasingly active in making speeches at platforms arranged by the agency. By 1951 H&K was arranging dozens of national and regional speeches by company leaders and AISI officials ("Speakers' Bureau Schedule," 29 June 1951, Box 76, Folder 9, JWH). American Iron and Steel Institute, *AISI Yearbook: 1948*, 602–8.

33. Whitmore, "Public Relations—A Two-Way Street," 21; "Getting Better Acquainted," Box 71, Folder 9, JWH.

34. "Community Relations Program," 10 September 1947, Box 71, Folder 15, JWH; "Iron & Steel Program," 50; "Getting Better Acquainted," Box 71, Folder 9, JWH.

35. Jackson to Goss, 11 April 1951, Box 73, Folder 4, JWH; PR Audit for Crucible Steel, February 1951, Box 73, Folder 4, JWH.

36. Jackson to Goss, 11 April 1951, Box 73, Folder 4, JWH. See "Meeting Community Responsibilities," May 1953, Box 5, Folder 4, MJ.

37. Progress Report of Public Relations Activities, 14 December 1949, Box 28, Folder 6, JWH; "Outlines for the Staff from the Starch Survey," 5 March 1956, Box 78, Folder 5, JWH. "An Industry Fights Back," speech before the annual meeting of the Book Paper Manufacturers Association, 30 March 1950, Box 5, Folder 3, MJ.

38. Davison, "The Third-Person Effect in Communication," 3; Ross, *Image Merchants*, 265.

39. Progress Report of Public Relations Activities, 14 December 1949, Box 28, Folder 6, JWH; Hill to E. T. Weir, 1 September 1949, Box 81, Folder 12, JWH; Hill to Charlie White, 1 September 1949, Box 82, Folder 1, JWH; McDonald to Hill, 14 October 1949, Box 82, Folder 4, JWH; Washington Plan, n.d. [1949], Box 82, Folder 5, JWH; Suggestions for Community Action, n.d. [1949], Box 81, Folder 11, JWH; Hill to John Stephens, 27 July 1949, Box 82, Folder 2, JWH.

Columbia letter to stockholders and employees, 28 October 1949, Box 81, Folder 11, JWH; Inland letters to employees and advertisement schedule, Box 81, Folder 9, JWH; Bethlehem employee newsletter, 20 September 1949, Box 80, Folder 17, JWH. On the field men, see, for example, Garrett A. Connors to Hill, 1 September 1949, Box 81, Folder 7, JWH, and Clarence Randall to Hill, 1 September 1949, Box 81, Folder 9, JWH.

40. Mapes to Hill, 13 January 1947, Box 62, Folder 7, JWH; "Proposed Public Relations Budget," 1 January 1949, Box 62, Folder 7, JWH; Merrick Jackson to Hill, 9 September 1946, Box 71, Folder 8, JWH; "Program for Furnishing Materials to Schools," 10 June 1948, Box 75, Folder 6, JWH; Armco Steel news release, n.d., Box 64, Folder 7, JWH; Warren Nelson and Donald Van Cleve to Walter Tower, 11 January 1951, Box 64, Folder 6, JWH; Warren Nelson to Hill and Goss, 7 June 1951, Box 64, Folder 6, JWH; Hill, *Corporate Public Relations*, 118–30.

41. See reports in Box 61, Folder 14, JWH.

42. Saugus restoration began in 1949; see Box 75, Folder 1, JWH; "Comments on Profit Ad; Pittsburgh Area," n.d., Box 71, Folder 16, JWH; Hill to Moreell, 23 August 1949, Goss to Moreell, 26 August 1949, and Goss to Moreell, 30 August 1949, Box 81, Folder 8, JWH.

Chapter Four

1. Paul T. Truitt to J. Howard McGrath, National Association of Margarine Manufacturers editorial cartoon booklet, 10 January 1949, Box 33, Oleo 194, McGrath Records; John G. Mapes to Russell Fifer, excerpt of script, 17 March 1950, Box 56, Folder 1, JWH. The show ran on NBC's radio network.

2. "Butter," 491; "Butter or Oleomargarine—Who Needs Protection?," 317; "U.S. Treasury Urges Repeal," 1. In 1948 colored margarine was taxed ten cents per pound, white margarine one-quarter cent per pound.

The standard account of the legislative history of the margarine industry is Howard, "Margarine Industry in the United States." For a comparative study, see van Stuvenberg, *Margarine*, 281–327.

3. "Staff Responsibilities and Assignments," n.d. [1947], Box 7, Folder 1, JWH.

4. Schwitzer, *Margarine and Other Food Fats*, 59. The original oleomargarine was made from beef fat, felt gritty, and was barely edible ("Just as Good," 24); Riepma, *Story of Margarine*, 2, 124–25; Tousley, "Marketing," 235; Howard, "Margarine Industry," 317. The margarine industry–sponsored study by Drs. Harry Leichenger, George Eisenberg, and Anton Carlson was widely publicized.

5. "Margarine Taxes," 43–44; Vine, "It's a Showdown—Butter vs. Oleo," 43; Charles Ellsworth to staff, 10 April 1948, Box 55, Folder 1, JWH; Good, speech before the American Butter Institute annual meeting, quoted in "Butter Institute," 52; Mapes to Fifer, 2 February 1949, Box 55, Folder 13, JWH. The Milk Industry Foundation director had good reason for his action; an analysis of more than 200 newspaper clippings on the dairy industry that appeared in January and February 1949 showed "price and oleo are far and away the most popular subjects," with most of the headlines "more unfriendly than friendly" ("More on Public Relations," 32).

6. Ball and Lilly, "The Menace of Margarine," 496; "Margarine vs. Butter," 32; "Fun with Margarine," 124; "Latest on Oleo," 350; script for 7 April 1948, Box 184, Kaltenborn Papers. A Gallup poll indicated 69 percent of the public favored repeal; 58 percent of those who used only butter favored repeal; and 39 percent of all farmers favored repeal (Gallup news release for 13 March 1948, Box 54, Folder 12, JWH). Snyder, "Wisconsin, Top Dairy State, Is Using Oleo in Record-Breaking Gulps," *Madison (Wisconsin) Capital Times*, 26 May 1948, WLRB.

7. "Margarine Loses Again," 62; Russell Crenshaw, Background Memorandum, 12 April 1948, Box 55, Folder 1, JWH; "Butter," 491; U.S. Congress, House, *Congressional Record*, 26 April 1948, vol. 94, pt. 4, 4842–78; Morris, "House Votes to Repeal Oleo Taxes," 1.

8. "Temporary Plan," n.d. [April, 1948], Box 56, Folder 4, JWH; Charles Ellsworth to staff (emphasis in original), 10 April 1948, Box 55, Folder 1, JWH.

9. "Temporary Plan," n.d. [April, 1948], Box 56, Folder 4, JWH. In a background memo, H&K contrasted the dairy witnesses before the House Agriculture Committee, including dairy farmers and a dairy cattle breeder, the dean of an agricultural college, a representative of dairy cooperatives, and two dairy union officials, with those for oleo: American Federation of Labor's lobbyist, soybean processors and growers association representatives, and retail and grocers association representatives ("Butter vs. Imitations," 1949, Box 55, Folder 1, JWH).

10. Hill to Holman, Fifer, and Gordon, 28 April 1948, Box 55, Folder 7, JWH; Mapes to Goss, 15 November 1948, Box 57, Folder 6, JWH. Selvage and Lee used the same tactic for the margarine makers ("Where Do We Go From Here?," 142).

11. "Work Progress Report," March–April 1949, Box 56, Folder 3, JWH; Goss to Holman, 3 May 1948, Box 55, Folder 7, JWH; Senator Eugene D. Millikin to Taft, 13 May 1948, Box 733, Oleomargarine 1948–49, RAT; U.S. Senate, *Oleomargarine Tax Repeal Hearings* (hereafter 1948 Finance hearings); *Congressional Record Daily Digest*, 27 May 1958, vol. 94, pt. 14, D396.

12. Thomas E. Martin (Iowa) to Taft, 21 May 1948, Box 898, Margarine Tax 1948, RAT; Reid F. Murray (Wis.) to Taft, 15 May 1948, and Alexander Wiley to Taft, 11 May 1948, Box 733, Oleomargarine 1948–49, RAT; 1948 Finance hearings.

13. "Outline of Continuing Program," n.d. [May 1948], Box 56, Folder 14, JWH; U.S. Congress, Senate, Statement of Senator Wiley, *Congressional Record*, 15 June 1948, vol. 94, pt. 7, 8245, 8247.

14. "Oleo Tax Repealer Dies," 2; "Outline of Continuing Program," n.d. [May 1948], Box 56, Folder 14, JWH.

15. Mapes to Goss, 10 March 1949, Box 56, Folder 3, JWH; Russell Crenshaw to Bert Goss, 15 November 1948, Box 6, H&K Correspondence—Memos, JWH.

16. Pabst, *Butter and Oleomargarine*, 39; survey, May 1948, Box 55, Folder 2, JWH; "⅓ of These Restaurants Served Oleo as Butter," Box 54, Folder 11, JWH; "Yellow Belongs to Butter," 142; Mapes to Holman, 6 December 1949, Box 55, Folder 3, JWH.

17. "How You Can Keep Butter Dollar$ Flowing into *This* Area," Box 56, Folder 12, JWH; "Fact Finding Survey" notes, Box 56, Folder 10, JWH. H&K also cited a survey that showed 51 percent of the sample approved of a law that provided for the sale of white oleo and removed all taxes, because, the agency concluded, "people are afraid of fraud" ("Butter Brings Out the Facts," draft of advertisement, 22 December 1949, Box 54, Folder 11, JWH).

18. Teletype from Goss, 21 September 1948, Box 56, Folder 3, JWH; "A Joint Statement," 28 October 1948, Box 56, Folder 6, JWH; Lewis C. French, "Oleo 'Retreat' in State Told," *Milwaukee Journal*, 15 December 1948, WLRB; "State Farmers More Tolerant of Oleo, Butter Substitute," *Green Bay Press-Gazette*, 5 November 1948, WLRB; "Butter-Oleo Battle Re-engaged," 4.

19. NAMM news release for 27 October 1948, Box 55, Folder 8, JWH; "Butter vs. Imitations," 1949, Box 55, Folder 1, JWH; see also WCA newsletter, 8 April 1949.

20. "No Margarine Compromise," 24; "More on the Margarine Fight," 4; "More on Public Relations," 32.

21. "An Aggressive Plan," 24; Mapes to Goss, 15 November 1948, Box 57, Folder 6, JWH; Goss to Fifer and Holman, 5 January 1949, Box 56, Folder 5, JWH.

22. "Outline of Continuing Program," n.d. [1948], Box 56, Folder 14, JWH; Goss to Holman, 11 February 1949, Box 56, Folder 3, JWH; Holman to Goss, 21 March 1949, Box 56, Folder 5, JWH; "Butter vs. Imitations," 1949, Box 55, Folder 1, JWH.

23. U.S. Congress, House, Regulation of Oleomargarine, *Congressional Record*, 31 March 1949, vol. 95, pt. 3, 3600–3631; "Butter vs. Imitations," 1949, Box 55, Folder 1, JHW.

24. 1948 Finance hearings, 213; U.S. Congress, Senate, Statement of Senator Wiley, *Congressional Record*, 4 April 1949, vol. 95, pt. 3, 3776–77; ads: "Who Gets Hurt?" and "To Prevent Fraud," Box 54, Folder 11, JWH.

25. "Report on Highlights of Oleomargarine Hearings," 8 April to 13 April 1949, Box 55, Folder 6, JWH. 1948 Finance hearings, 40, 28.

26. Howard, "Margarine Industry," table 21, 353a; "Unilever I," 88–92+; "Unilever's Africa," 57–65+; "Unilever III," 74–81+. H&K hired the International News Service to examine Unilever's finances, plans for expansion, and market shares (Goss to Louis Alwell, 6 April 1949, Box 56, Folder 3, JWH). Hunziker, *Butter Industry*, 146–47.

27. "Report on Highlights of Oleomargarine Hearings," 8 April to 13 April 1949, Box 55, Folder 6, JWH; 1948 Finance hearings, 254.

28. *Congressional Record Daily Digest*, 27 April 1949, vol. 95, pt. 18, D233.

29. Murray to Taft, 15 May 1948, Box 733, Oleomargarine 1948–49, RAT; "Just as Good," 24; Boyer, "Policy Making by Government Agencies," 274–75; Hunziker, *Butter Industry*, 32.

30. WCA newsletters for 15 August and 7 February 1949.

31. Lindow, "Creamery Operation Is a Profession," 38–39; WCA newsletters for 19 November 1948; 3 January, 24 February, 31 March, 8 April, 16 May 1949; and 16 July 1950.

32. WCA newsletter for 19 November 1948. Golden Guernsey Dairy Cooperative had changed its policy in February 1948 ("Bold Decision Turns Tide of Battle on Oleo Yellow," 260). "Annual Report of the President," in *Wisconsin Creameries Association Annual Convention and Annual Reports*, 29 September 1948; "Eat Lard, Oleo Foe Tells State Poor," *Milwaukee Journal*, 8 March 1948, WLRB.

33. U.S. Congress, Senate, Statement of Senator Wiley, *Congressional Record*, 17 February 1949, vol. 95, pt. 1, 1324; "Vote to Give to Fight vs. Oleo Group," *Sheboygan Press*, 5 December 1949, WLRB; the organization was the Sheboygan County Holstein Breeders' Association. U.S. Congress, Senate, Editorials and Resolutions submitted by Senator Wiley, *Congressional Record*, 21 March 1949, vol. 95, pt. 3, 2815.

34. See references to money in the WCA newsletters for 3 January, circular from Minnesota association [n.d.], 24 January, 7 February, 24 February, 2 April, 8 April, 25 June, 7 July, and 16 December 1949, and 20 January 1950. They collected $11,500 by September 1949 ("Annual Report of the President," in *Wisconsin Creameries Association Annual Convention and Annual Reports*, 28 September 1949). H&K was aware and concerned about the lack of funds (Charles Ellsworth to Hill, 27 June 1949, Box 55, Folder 11, JWH).

35. "Issues of Oleomargarine Tax Repeal," Box 733, Oleomargarine, 1948–49, RAT. This testimony, before the House Agriculture Committee, took place before the dairy groups retained H&K. See the food dealers' journal, *Wisconsin Food Dealer*, especially "Favor Passage," and "Tax Gouge." Also see "Seeks Repeal of Oleo Laws," *Milwaukee Journal*, 16 February 1949, WLRB; the petition drive was headed by the president of the Wisconsin Retail Meat Dealers Association.

36. "The Margarine Tax Fight," 14; "Oleo, Oil, Gas and Sulpher," *Green Bay Press-Gazette*, 26 January 1949, WLRB; "The Butter—Margarine War," *Wisconsin State Journal*, 25 March 1949, WLRB; "The Creameries Reply," *Wisconsin State Journal*, 31 March 1949, WLRB.

37. Riepma, *Story of Margarine*, 100.

38. "Oleo Lobby Has Launched Another Bitter Attack," 143. See also "Fight Fraud," "Bold Decision Turns Tide of Battle on Yellow Oleo," "Hour of Decision Has Arrived," and "Your Letters Will Decide Yellow Oleo Issue."

39. All the state's oleo plants had closed by 1936 (Howard, "Margarine Industry," table 19, 329a); Wyant, "Voting via the Senate Mailbag," 363; Sussman, *Dear FDR*, 151. J. Howard McGrath, Senatorial Records, Box 33, Oleomargarine H.R. 2245, HSTL. No examination of a Wisconsin senator's mail on this issue can be made: McCarthy's papers are unavailable to researchers and Wiley's, which include constituent mail on other issues, do not contain any on the butter fight. It is possible he received too much to save (Wiley Papers).

40. Holman, Fifer, and Gordon letter and booklet, 12 January 1949, Box 33, Oleomargarine 1949, McGrath Records; Benjamin Redmond of Kingsdale Dairies to McGrath, 18 January 1949, Box 33, Oleomargarine 1949, McGrath Records.

41. The extent to which Selvage and Lee had influenced this debate is unclear, but the NAMM won an award for the campaign ("Awards Made for PR," 56). Mentioning the legal frame were Representatives Taber, Welch, Eberharter, Whittington, Harris, Teague, and Kefauver; the political frame, Corbett, Taber, Sabath, Domengeaux, Larcade, Rivers. U.S. Congress, House, *Congressional Record*, 26 April 1948, vol. 94, 4835–41 (hereafter 1948 debate).

42. 1948 debate, Statement of Representative Sabath, 4838.

43. 1948 debate, Statement of Representatives Eberharter, 4838, and Whittington, 4839.

44. 1948 debate, Statement of Representatives Welch, 4838, Domengeaux, 4839, Whittington, 4839, Teague, 4840, and Kefauver, 4840.

45. 1948 debate, Statement of Representatives Eberharter, 4838, and Whittington, 4839.

46. 1948 debate, Statement of Representatives Sabath, 4838, Eberharter, 4838, and Hobbs, 4840.

47. 1948 debate, Statement of Representatives Eberharter, 4838, Whittington, 4839, and Kefauver, 4840.

48. U.S. Congress, Senate, Statement of Senator Gillette, *Congressional Record*, 5 January 1950, vol. 96, pt. 1, 74 (hereafter 1950 debate).

49. 1950 debate, Statement of Senator Fulbright, 74, 76–77.

50. 1950 debate, Statement of Senator Gillette, 78–79.

51. H.R. 2023, 16 March 1950, White House Bill File, Box 61, HSTL; Public Law 459, 81st Congress, 2d session, 16 March 1950. Truman received only seven messages on the issue, with just two entreating him not to sign (Truman OF 656, 174-G).

52. "Up Butter and at 'Em," 22. Land O'Lakes' sales dropped 17 percent in the year after the margarine act was passed (Ruble, *Land O'Lakes*, 9). Dales, "Ending of Oleo Tax Raises Use of Fats," 79; Howard, "Margarine Industry," 325; "Margarine Survey," 41; U.S. Department of Agriculture, *Agricultural Statistics*, 142; U.S. Bureau of the Census, *Historical Statistics*, 522; "Doom Prophets Sell Us Short," *Wisconsin State Journal*, 20 January 1950, WLRB; WCA newsletter for 7 July 1949.

53. WCA newsletter for 24 January 1949; "Farm Folks Veto Oleo Tax Repeal," *Wisconsin Agriculturalist and Farmer*, 15 October 1949, WLRB; "'Dairy Depression' Seen in Oleo Bill," 11; U.S. Congress, House, Statement of Representative St. George, *Congressional Record*, 31 March 1949, vol. 95, pt. 3, 3606; Krooss, *Executive Opinion*, 217–21; Stein, *Fiscal Revolution*, 217.

54. Ellsworth to Mapes, 7 December 1949, Box 55, Folder 11, JWH; "Farm Folks Veto Oleo Tax Repeal," *Wisconsin Agriculturalist and Farmer*, 15 October 1949, WLRB;

"Butter-Oleo Battle Re-Engaged," 4; "More on Oleo-Butter," 5; U.S. Bureau of the Census, *Historical Statistics*, 522; "U.S. Produces More Oleo Than Butter," 46.

55. U.S. Congress, House, Statement of Representative Abernathy, *Congressional Record*, 31 March 1949, vol. 95, pt. 3, 3609; U.S. Congress, House, Statement of Senator Fulbright, *Congressional Record*, 4 January 1950, vol. 96, pt. 1, 47; U.S. Congress, House, Statement of Representative Cooley, *Congressional Record*, 31 March 1949, vol. 95, pt. 3, 3618.

56. U.S. Congress, House, Statement of Representative Keefe, *Congressional Record*, 26 April 1948, vol. 94, pt. 4, 4845.

57. See in particular U.S. Congress, House, Statement of Representative O'Sullivan, *Congressional Record*, 31 March 1949, vol. 95, pt. 3, 3616–17, which reads like an H&K news release. Taft to Representative Thomas Martin, 26 May 1948, Box 898, Margarine Tax 1948, RAT.

58. "U.S. Treasury Urges Repeal," 1; "U.S. Oleo Tax Nearer Repeal," 4. H&K especially hoped to avoid bad press in the PR community; see Mapes to Glenn Griswold, 24 January 1950, Box 55, Folder 10, JWH. "Status of the Butter Public Relations Program," n.d. [April or May 1950], Box 56, Folder 1, JWH; "A Message on Oleo and Synthetics," 20 January 1950, Box 55, Folder 10, JWH.

59. Ellsworth to Mapes, 7 December 1949, Box 55, Folder 11, JWH.

60. Hill to Holman, Fifer, and Gordon, 28 April 1948, Box 55, Folder 7, JWH.

Chapter Five

1. Stebbins, "Truman and the Seizure of Steel," 20. For a similar argument on the free enterprise campaigns, see Tedlow, *Keeping the Corporate Image*, 204–5.

2. Hogan, *Economic History of the Iron and Steel Industry*, 1624–25; Zieger, *The CIO*, 300; Sweeney, *The United Steelworkers of America*, 98. Among the other points were the union shop, consideration of the guaranteed annual wage, and elimination of regional wage differentials ("1951 Wage Policy for the United Steelworkers of America," Box 105, PM). For a thorough review of these events, see Sawyer, *Concerns of a Conservative Democrat*, 255–75.

3. "Memorandum for Files," 2 April 1952, Box 4, Memoranda 1951–52, Enarson Papers, and "The OPS Position on Steel Prices," n.d., Box 28, Steel Strike April 16–30, Murphy Papers. "Statement by the President," 22 December 1951, Truman OF 1028, 342. An independent assessment of the steel industry conducted in August 1951 found that the eight leading companies had increased efficiency and raised prices so that the average annual return on equity in the postwar period amounted to 17 percent ("The Steel Industry and the Eight Leading Companies," August 1951, Box 34, Companies—Pamphlets, AISI). "Recommendations of the Wage Stabilization Board in the Steel Case," 20 March 1952, Box 114, WSB, PM; Sweeney, *The USWA*, 100; Hammond, "The Steel Strike of 1952," 286. "Resolution Adopted by International Wage Policy Committee," 21 March 1952, Box 114, WSB, PM; news release for 30 March 1952, Box 105, CIO Releases, PM; Shelton, "Steelworkers Will Fight," 501.

4. Krooss, *Executive Opinion*, 373; Sutton, Harris, Kaysen, and Tobin, *American Business Creed*, 118; Zieger, *The CIO*, 300; Randall, "Free Enterprise Is Not a Hunting License," 40; Enarson, "The Politics of an Emergency Dispute: Steel, 1952," 55.

5. Hill to Robert E. Gross, 15 October 1952, Box 45, Folder 5, JWH; Marcus, *Truman and the Steel Seizure Case*, 254; Harbison and Spencer, "Politics of Collective Bargaining," 705; Olds, "Some Observations on the Recent Steel Strike," address before the Denver Rotary Club, 21 August 1952, Box 123, Speeches—USS—Olds, AISI.

Industry frustration was caused by the fact that although it continually broke government price controls, it had to fight the same fight again every time the USWA opened negotiations. For 1943, see Steel Case Research Committee, *The Steel Case*, 1:5–7; for 1946, see Hill, "Industry's Iron Curtain," 3; for 1949, see "Steel Panel Is Revival of Discredited Procedure," 14.

6. Executive Order 10340, Truman OF 1214, 407-B, Steel Seizure; Hogan, *Economic History*, 1624–25; Hammond, "Steel Strike," 286.

7. Herling, *Right to Challenge*, 16–17; Brophy Oral History (1955), 332, COHC. Script for 5 May 1952, Box 193, Kaltenborn Papers; Blough Oral History (1975), 139; Harris, *Right to Manage*, 72, 74; Polenberg, *War and Society*, 165. Opinion polls about labor should be used cautiously, because one study found that such polls were inevitably biased against labor (Kornhauser, "Are Public Opinion Polls Fair to Organized Labor?," 498).

8. "Basic Facts in the Steel Wage Case," 14 April 1952, Box 82, Folder 14, JWH (hereafter "Basic Facts"). The memorandum includes ten pages of wage, profit, income, and investment figures used to support the arguments the industry presented. "Labor Relations and Public Relations," 304. Officers' Report, 1952 USWA *Proceedings*.

9. 1952 CIO *Proceedings*; "T-H Can't Be Rejiggered," 7.

10. "Statement by Philip Murray," 17 December 1951, Box 105, PM; "Facts about the Union Shop," n.d. [January 1952?], Box 108, Wage Negotiations 2, PM; "The Union's Side in the Steel Crisis," text of radio address from 7 April 1952, Box 108, Wage Negotiations 2, PM.

11. "Statement by Philip Murray," 17 December 1951, Box 105, PM; "The Union's Side in the Steel Crisis," text of radio address from 7 April 1952, Box 108, Wage Negotiations 2, PM; news release for 30 March 1952, Box 105, CIO Releases, PM.

12. Client list, 1950, Box 7, Folder 2, JWH; "Memorandum concerning Public Information Procedures and Activities," 6 January 1952, Box 83, Folder 13, JWH; Merrick Jackson to Hill, 26 May 1952, Box 83, Folder 9, JWH.

13. "Two New PR Firms," 58–59; James Selvage to Hill, 8 August 1950, Box 37, Folder 13, JWH; Hill to Mapes, 16 May 1952, and Hill to Ryerson, 15 May 1952, Box 7, Folder 3, JWH.

14. Fairless, "Whose Sacrifice?," Address before the Society of Industrial Realtors, 15 November 1951, Box 123, Speeches—USS—Fairless, AISI; "Statement of Steel Companies in the Wage Case," 4 April 1952, Box 83, Folder 15, JWH. Hill, *Making of a Public Relations Man*, 72; Admiral Ben Moreell, "A Steelmaker Discusses the Issues," text of radio address, 11 January 1952, Box 122, Speeches—Jones and Laughlin, AISI; "No Shortage Here," 3; "Your Stake in the Steel Crisis," text of radio address, 6 April 1952, Box 123, Speeches—USS—Fairless, AISI.

15. News release for 31 December 1951, Box 1, American Institute of Public Opinion Papers.

16. Rossiter, "The President and Labor Disputes," 120; Hamby, *Beyond the New Deal*, 454; McCullough, *Truman*, 898; Marcus, *Truman and the Steel Seizure*, 59; "Memorandum for the President," 15 November 1951, Box 2, Letters to the President, Clark Papers; memorandum, 21 April 1951, Box 1, Quarterly Reports, Clark Papers.

17. Copy of letter from Truman to Murray, 31 December 1951, Box 105, PM; Steelman Oral History (1963), 36.

18. For a complete review of legislative action, see "Government Action in the Steel Dispute of 1952," 1 December 1952, Box 1, Steel Dispute, Houston Papers.

19. "Can Wage Board Survive Dispute over Steel Case?," 70; "Steel Profits: How High?," 22–23.

20. Conn, "Steel," 14; Shelton, "Fair Offer on Steel," 293; scripts for 5, 14, and 21 December 1951, Box 192, Kaltenborn Papers.

21. The radio networks were ABC, CBS, NBC, and Mutual; the television networks were ABC, CBS, NBC, and Du Mont. News release for 8 April 1952, Truman OF 1028, 342.

22. News release for 8 April 1952, Truman OF 1028, 342; Truman, "Government Seizure of Steel Industry," *Public Papers of Presidents of the United States: Harry S. Truman, 1945*, 420–22. The president also asked Congress to provide legislation to deal with the steel problem (message to Congress, 9 April 1952, Truman OF 1028, 342). Although Truman had threatened seizure, many people expected him to invoke the Taft-Hartley Act, which may explain why the companies had refused to settle with the union (Marcus, *Truman and the Steel Seizure*, 79). See also John W. Davis to Republic Steel, 31 March 1952, Box 4, Memoranda 1951–52, Enarson Papers; the attorney advised Republic that in his opinion the president did not have the constitutional power to seize the industry.

23. Statement of Maurice J. Tobin, Officers' Report, 1952 USWA *Proceedings*, 156; "Statement by Secretary of Commerce Charles Sawyer," 8 April 1952, Box 110, General Memoranda, Sawyer Papers; Arnall to Sawyer, 17 April 1952, Box 112, Basic Steel—Office of Price Administration, Sawyer Papers.

24. Sawyer transcript, 3 May 1952, Box 110, Confidential Dictation, Sawyer Papers. Only Enarson urged enlistment of public opinion as a weapon against the industry (Enarson to Steelman, 2 July 1952, Box 4, Memoranda 1951–52, Enarson Papers). Murphy to Sawyer, 21 April 1952, Box 110, General Memoranda, Sawyer Papers; the brochure was "These Are the Facts," a reprint of Clarence Randall's speech discussed later.

25. Hill, *Corporate Public Relations*, 133–34; Hill, *Making of a Public Relations Man*, 69; Blackman, *Presidential Seizure in Labor Disputes*, 3, 281.

26. Ross, *Image Merchants*, 107–8; Hill, *Making of a Public Relations Man*, 79.

27. Ross, *Image Merchants*, 108; "Steel Companies in the Wage Case," 15 September 1952, Box 82, Folder 17, JWH. Management cooperated with the union to keep the mills running during the seizure (Department of Commerce news release, 15 April 1952, Box 111, Basic Steel Significant Documents, Sawyer Papers).

28. "Suggested Recommendations for Continuing the Industry Activity," AISI Post-Steel Wage Case Program 1952, Box 71, Folder 7, JWH; Ross, *Image Merchants*, 108; Heilbroner, "Public Relations," 28; Cheney, "Some Facts about Profits," 1–3; "Steel Output Drops to 12½% in Strike," 1–2; Henderer, *Public Relations Practices in Six Industrial Corporations*, 121–23; Box 80, Client Correspondence, U.S. Steel 1948–1951, and Box 81, Client Correspondence, U.S. Steel 1952–1958, Barton Papers. The ad supplemented such PR activities as a letter C. F. Hood, the company's executive vice-president of operations, sent to all manufacturing division employees of U.S. Steel (13 June 1952, Box 108, Wage Negotiations 2, PM).

29. Advertisements, Box 82, Folder 7, JWH; Cort, "The Church and the Steel Crisis," 170; Vorse, "Big Steel and the Little Man," 603–5. Advertising expenditures as of 31 August totaled $975,462; the total budget for companies in the Steel Wage Case as of 15 September was $1,676,662.

30. DiBacco, "Draft the Strikers," 68; C. M. White, "Of the Government, by the Government, and for the Government," text of speech before the American Steel Warehouse Association, 20 May 1952, Box 122, Speeches—Republic, AISI; "Statement by Mr. Randall," 8 April 1952, Box 83, Folder 15, JWH; text of statement by Clarence Randall, 9 April 1952, Box 83, Folder 15, JWH. The speech was broadcast over the same eight channels as Truman's speech. The PR agency arranged for the time, but said the words

were Randall's own. Text of statement by Clarence Randall, 9 April 1952, Box 83, Folder 15, JWH.

31. "Basic Facts."

32. Bernstein, "Political Ideas of Selected American Business Journals," 259; Vaizey, *History of British Steel*, 150; "Report to Board on Public Opinion," 8; Prechel, "Steel and the State," 653. See also, U.S. House, *Study of Monopoly Power*; "Management Looks at Public Relations," 450.

33. Marcus, *Truman and the Steel Seizure*, 83.

34. Text of statement by Clarence Randall, 9 April 1952, Box 83, Folder 15, JWH; "Basic Facts."

35. Stalker, "National Association of Manufacturers," 127; Sutton, Harris, Kaysen, and Tobin, *American Business Creed*, 116; "Basic Facts."

36. News release for 11 April 1952, Box 105, CIO Releases, PM; news release for 23 April 1952, Box 108, Wage Negotiations 2, PM.

37. Officers' Report, 1952 USWA *Proceedings*, 36.

38. Resolution No. 9, 1952 USWA *Proceedings*, 144; Statement of Delegate Joe Germano, 1952 USWA *Proceedings*, 153; Statement of Delegate Royster, 1952 USWA *Proceedings*, 159.

39. Officers' Report, 1952 USWA *Proceedings*, 37; text of Murray speech, 7 July 1952, Box 83, Folder 16, JWH; Statement of Delegate Sam Camens, 1952 USWA *Proceedings*, 160.

40. Zieger, *American Workers*, 131; 1952 CIO *Proceedings*, 180; text of Murray speech, 7 July 1952, Box 83, Folder 16, JWH.

41. News release for 9 June 1952, Box 108, Wage Negotiations 2, PM; Report of Philip Murray, 1952 CIO *Proceedings*.

42. Murray believed the AISI was using the advertisements to buy publishers' support; text of Murray speech, 7 July 1952, Box 83, Folder 16, JWH; "PRAC meeting," 8 May 1952, Box 72, Folder 5, JWH. Excerpts of editorial reaction, 10 April 1952, Box 83, Folder 14, JWH; no editorials favorable toward Truman were included, and all were drawn from moderate to conservative newspapers. "The Seizure Order," 28.

43. Comments of the two California editors who rejected the editorial: "Your editorial is poison. Only Stalin will be pleased" (Battersby to Hill, 19 May 1952, Box 84, Folder 2, JWH); and "Don't bust a blood vessel. The Republic will survive" (Battersby to Hill, 6 May 1952, Box 84, Folder 2, JWH). "Will Strikes Bring Socialism?," 15, 17.

44. "Steel Seizure Presents Congress with Its Greatest Issue of the Year," *Congressional Digest* 31 (May 1952), 129–30; "Truman and Steel," 32; "Corporate Profits Understated," 6.

45. "Steel: What Next, Mr. President?," 3; "Steel and the Press," 5; "Quizzing Randall," 99.

46. Sevareid, *In One Ear*, 231; Taft, "The Taft-Hartley Act," 195; Green, "The Taft-Hartley Act," 200–201; Patterson, *Mr. Republican*, 193, 357; "How the Taft-Hartley Law Protects You . . . ," Box 453, Guylay—February 1952, RAT.

47. Statement of Sen. Hubert Humphrey, 1952 USWA *Proceedings*, 204; news release for 5 June 1952, Box 111, Communications from Public Groups and Officials, PM.

48. Wyant, "Voting via the Senate Mailbag," 359, 365; Sussman, *Dear FDR*, 150–51.

49. Dexter, "What Do Congressman Hear?," 18; Wyant, "Voting via the Senate Mailbag," 365; Sussman, *Dear FDR*, 180.

50. Leigh Smith to Hill, 10 July 1952, Box 82, Folder 21, JWH; Smith to Hill et al., 6 June 1952, Box 83, Folder 2, JWH; Leigh Smith to Merrick Jackson, 15 July 1952, Box 82, Folder 21, JWH.

51. Copies of letters to Steel Companies in the Wage Case: H. B. Naylor, 25 June 1952; Kernan Roeson, 25 April 1952; and Margaret Theresa Carberry, 1 May 1952, Box 111, Communications in Support, PM.

52. Theodore Rozos to Murray, 8 April 1952, Box 111, Communications from Individuals in Support, PM.

53. Other frames were mentioned, including the WSB recommendations were fair (8), the industry was unfair (1), and the companies were not following the seizure order properly (2); Robert M. Fleming to Murray, 6 April 1952, Box 110, Letters from Individual Workers, PM.

54. Enarson to Steelman, 15 April 1952, Box 14, Steel 1952, Stowe Papers.

55. See for instance, letters from Frank A. Crawford to Truman, 18 April 1952; Roy E. Cast, 17 April 1952; and Mrs. J. E. Cinkar, 29 April 1952, Truman OF 1215, 407-B Steel Seizure 1952 C; Betty Harwood to Truman, 9 April 1952, Truman OF 1215, 407-B, Steel Seizure 1952 H.

56. Robert A. Anderson to Truman, 15 April 1952, and A. M. Burrer to Truman, 9 April 1952, Truman OF 217, 407-B, Steel Seizure 1952 A.

57. Marcus, *Truman and the Steel Seizure*, 195–96, 225, 227.

58. Stowe Oral History (1976), 26; transcript of news conference, 24 April 1952, *Public Papers of the Presidents: Harry S. Truman, 1952*, 294; Marcus, *Truman and the Steel Seizure*, 250–51; Sawyer, *Concerns of a Conservative Democrat*, 268; news release for 2 June 1952, Box 108, Wage Negotiations 2, PM; Lovett to Truman, 25 June 1952, PSF 136, Steel. Although his staff had considered possible actions if the Court voided the seizure (see "Steel Actions under Possible Court Decisions," n.d., Box 110, General Memoranda, Sawyer Papers), Truman had "confessed he would be terribly shocked, disappointed, and disturbed if the Supreme Court went against him" (Sawyer, *Concerns of a Conservative Democrat*, 267).

59. News release for 16 June 1952, Box 105, CIO Releases, PM. During the strike itself, the most common complaints among members and nonmembers alike were that the union leaders were arrogant or greedy dictators, that people should not be forced to join a union, that the Korean War effort should take precedence, and that the steelworkers desperately needed to get back to work because they were out of money (Box 113, PM).

60. News release for 24 July 1952, Box 83, Folder 16, JWH; Enarson, "Politics of an Emergency Dispute," 71; Donovan, *Tumultuous Years*, 390.

61. U.S. Bureau of the Census, *Historical Statistics*, 693; Stowe Oral History (1989), 87; Truman, *Memoirs*, 469–70; Bernstein, "Economic Impact of Strikes in Key Industries," 41; "Report to the President by the Director of Defense Mobilization," 1 August 1952, Truman PSF 136, Steel; CEA to Truman, 15 October 1952, Box 1, Quarterly Reports to the President, Clark Papers.

62. Description of study by the Psychological Corporation, Box 82, Folder 9, JWH. The sample included 200 residents (30 percent upper, 40 percent middle, and 30 percent lower socioeconomic status) of New Haven. Personal interviews were conducted between 7 and 10 May; the final ad had run on 28 April.

63. "Public Opinion Index," Dave Dillman to Hill et al., 17 April 1952, Box 83, Folder 8, JWH.

64. See, for instance, "Why Steel?" an AISI collection of newspaper editorial opinion regarding the steel price controversy of 1950, Box 70, Folder 7, JWH. Randall, "Steel," 34; Vorse, "Big Steel," 603; Suchman, Goldsen, and Williams, "Attitudes toward the Korean War," 173.

65. Walter S. Tower, "Subjugation or Liberation?" address before the American Iron and Steel Institute, 22 May 1952, Box 121, Speeches by Steel Men—AISI—Tower, AISI.

Results of an Opinion Research Company survey in the Taft papers are nearly identical (Claude Robinson to Taft, 30 April 1952, Box 811, Steel Dispute—1952, RAT). News release for 28 May 1952, Box 1, American Institute of Public Opinion Papers.

66. Hill, *Corporate Public Relations*, 134; Edward L. Ryerson, "Management Thinking and Public Relations," 25 September 1952, Box 102, Public Relations (2), AISI.

67. "An Appraisal of the Steel Industry," 13 June 1946, Box 70, Folder 8, JWH; Opinion Research Corporation survey, March 1955, Box 70, Folder 11, JWH; see also, Exhibit 4, "Hill and Knowlton, Inc.," Harvard Graduate School of Business Administration, 1956, Box 6, Folder 9, JWH.

68. Sevareid, *In One Ear*, 21; Marcus, *Truman and the Steel Seizure*, 34–35; news releases for 31 December 1951, 11 May 1952, and 21 June 1952, Box 1, American Institute of Public Opinion Papers.

69. Mills, *Power Elite*, 22; Memorandum, 5 October 1949, Box 81, Folder 13, JWH; Hill, "Public Relations Suggestions on Steel Strike," 23 July 1952, Box 83, Folder 21, JWH.

70. U.S. Congress, Senate, Statement of Senator Ferguson, *Congressional Record*, 16 April 1952, vol. 98, pt. 3, 4026, 4155; Leigh Smith to Bert Goss, 27 June 1952, Box 83, Folder 4, JWH; William Shaw to Sawyer, 24 April 1952, Box 110, Basic Steel Strike, Sawyer Papers; news release, n.d., Box 83, Folder 15, JWH; see NAM statement in Truman OF 1214, 407-B Steel Seizure.

71. "Steel: What Next, Mr. President?," 3; Morse later became a Democrat.

72. Statement of Sen. Hubert Humphrey, 1952 USWA Proceedings, 203.

73. Stowe Oral History (1963), 35; Murphy Oral History (1970), 461; Murphy added that he thought the reports had little influence. Enarson to Truman, 15 April 1952, Box 14, Steel 1952, Stowe Papers. The president responded to C. S. Jones; see news release for 27 April 1952, Truman OF 1028, 342 Steel.

74. Fones-Wolfe, *Selling Free Enterprise*, 109; Zieger, *The CIO*, 301; Shelton, "Fair Offer on Steel," 293; Conn, "Steel: The Price of Peace," 8; Claude Robinson to Taft, 30 April 1952, Box 811, Steel Dispute—1952, RAT.

75. News release for 19 July 1952, Box 83, Folder 16, JWH.

76. Resolution No. 1, 1952 USWA *Proceedings*, 119; Statement of Delegate Royster, 1952 USWA *Proceedings*, 159; Statement of Walter Reuther, 1952 USWA *Proceedings*, 319; Randall to Hill, 25 August 1949, Box 81, Folder 9, JWH; Hamel, "John W. Hill," 82.

77. Hill to Ryerson, 6 May 1952, Box 83, Folder 8, JWH; "Steel Takes Its Case to the Public," 30; "Steel PR Men Bombard the Press and Public," 37; "PR Men Give Pro & Cons on Steel Case," 42–43; R. A. Carrington to Hill, 14 May 1952; W. H. Grimes to Hill, 13 May 1952; Robert L. Bliss to Hill, 16 May 1952, Box 82, Folder 8, JWH.

78. Hill to C. M. White, E. J. Hanley, Admiral Ben Moreell, J. L. Mauthe, Hiland G. Batchellor, and E. T. Weir, 12 April 1952, Box 82, Folder 18, JWH. Byoir did not help his own cause when in 1951 he appeared before a group of weekly newspaper publishers and made comments critical of the steel industry (James Rowan to Hill, 23 April 1951, Box 82, Folder 18, JWH); "Memorandum to Mr. Ryerson," 17 April 1952, Box 83, Folder 8, JWH; "PR Men Give Pros & Cons on Steel Case," 42–43; Hamel, "John W. Hill," 79; L. Rohe Walter to S. S. Tyndall, 30 April 1952, Box 59, Folder 5, JWH.

79. Hammond, "Steel Strike," 290.

Chapter Six

1. Ochsner, "The Case against Smoking," 432; "Lung Cancer Views Aired," 1; "Big Tobacco Stocks Rally," 1.

2. "Public Relations Today," *Business Week* (2 July 1960), 11, Box 42, Biographical Clippings, JWH.

3. Harrison, "Tobacco Battered and Pipes Shattered," 554; Troyer and Markle, *Cigarettes*, 34. By 1909 states banning the sale of cigarettes included Arkansas, Illinois, Indiana, Iowa, Kansas, Michigan, Minnesota, Missouri, Nebraska, New Hampshire, North Dakota, Oklahoma, South Dakota, Washington, and Wisconsin. They were also heavily taxed in Tennessee and West Virginia.

4. Lombard and Doering, "Cancer Studies in Massachusetts," 481–87. See also Broders, "Squamous-Cell Epithelioma of the Lip," 656–64, and Arkin and Wagner, "Primary Carcinoma of the Lung," 587–91.

5. Friedell and Rosenthal, "Etiologic Role of Chewing Tobacco," 2130–35. See also Grace, "Tobacco Smoking and Cancer of the Lung," 361–64.

6. "Cigaret Habit" (November 1948), 1008, and "Cigaret Habit" (December 1948), 1287; Wynder and Graham, "Tobacco Smoking as a Possible Etiologic Factor," 329–36; Wynder, Graham, and Croninger, "Experimental Production of Carcinoma," 855–64; Doll and Hill, "Study of the Aetiology of Carcinoma of the Lung," 1271–86; Ochsner, DeCamp, DeBakey, and Ray, "Bronchogenic Carcinoma," 691–97, and *Smoking and Cancer: A Doctor's Report*; Hilts, *Smoke Screen*, 14.

7. Riis, "How Harmful Are Cigarettes?," 9; "Smoking Tobacco," 696; Eleanor Curtiss to Truman, 16 January 1950, Box 1036 Truman OF 348; Norr, "Cancer by the Carton," 7–9.

8. See, for instance, five paragraphs on Hammond and Horn's survey in "Smoking and Mortality," 37, and eight paragraphs on Wynder and Graham's survey in "Cancer in Heavy Smokers," 343; "Smoke Gets in the News," 20–21; Graham to Wynder, 6 February 1957, Box 103, Folder 762, EAG; "Smoking Mice Live Normal Span," 23.

9. Wynder to Graham, 4 December 1953, and "Walter Winchell's Statement," 13 December 1953, Box 103, Folder 762, EAG.

10. Fritschler, *Smoking and Politics*, 70; "Smoke Screen," 102; "In a Rabbit's Eye," 96–97. The commission's Cigarette Advertising Guides prohibited all references to the physical effects, except pleasure, of smoking unless claims were based on scientific proof (Calfee, "Cigarette Advertising Regulation Today," 264).

11. Bernays, *Public Relations*, 181. The groups did take steps to organize later in the decade. The "Study Group on Smoking and Health" issued a 1957 report that concluded, "the sum total of scientific evidence establishes beyond reasonable doubt that cigarette smoking is a causative factor in the rapidly increasing incidence" of lung cancer. (Report reprinted in "Smoking and Health," 1129–33). The group included representatives from the ACS, the American Heart Association, the National Cancer Institute, and the National Heart Institute. More influential was the National Interagency Council on Smoking and Health, formed at the behest of the surgeon general (Fritschler, *Smoking and Politics*, 122–25).

12. Snegireff and Lombard, "Survey of Smoking Habits of Massachusetts Physicians," 1042–45; Horn, Cameron, and Kipnis, "Survey of Medical Opinion toward Smoking," Box 3, Folder 26, EAG; Hammond and Horn, "The Relationship between Human Smoking Habits and Death Rates," 1316; "The Mortality of Doctors in Relation to Their Smoking Habits," 449–50.

13. Friedman, *Public Policy*, 64; Troyer and Markle, *Cigarettes*, 68–70.

14. Pat McGrady to Graham, 29 September 1948, Box 3, Folder 26, EAG; Graham to ACS, 29 June 1956, Box 3, Folder 25, EAG. Graham fired off a letter to the American Medical Association complaining about an editorial on cigarette advertising that had appeared in the AMA's *Journal*, because he felt only *JAMA* readers knew about it. An

AMA official responded that a general press release had been issued to the wire services and metropolitan papers (George F. Lull to Graham, 30 April 1954, and Graham to ACS, 1 July 1954, Box 3, Folder 26, EAG).

15. John A. Rogers to Graham, 10 December 1953, Box 3, Folder 26, EAG. On radio, see Graham to Marian Merrill Timmers, 16 April 1954; on television, ACS to Graham, 6 November 1953; on film, see ACS to Graham, 18 July 1954; Box 3, Folder 26, EAG. Graham to Charles S. Cameron, 18 February 1952, Box 3, Folder 26, EAG.

16. Graham to Cameron, 16 August 1951; Graham to Cameron, 28 December 1951; Cameron to Graham, 12 January 1953, Box 3, Folder 26, EAG. Graham was almost as inaccessible on the radio, saying, "Statistical studies, however, show no significantly greater increase in incidence of the disease in people who are excessively exposed to the exhaust fumes of automobiles than in others" (George E. Probst to Graham, 18 March 1954, Box 3, Folder 26, EAG).

17. Bud Littin to Roy Battersby, 26 May 1954, Box 111, Folder 1, JWH; Burger, "Credibility," 309–10. The results of the story should not have been surprising to *Reader's Digest*. In 1950 Brown and Williamson had plugged a *Digest* article to promote Viceroys ("'Digest' Tobacco Diatribe Turned into Viceroy Ad," 38).

18. By one report the manufacturers first approached Earl Newsom, who declined the account and referred them to H&K (Cutlip, "The Tobacco Wars," 27). Confidential Memorandum to John Hill, 14 December 1953, Box 110, Folder 10, JWH; "Background Material on the Cigarette Industry Client," 15 December 1953, Box 110, Folder 6, JWH; "Letter of Transmittal to Manufacturers," 22 December 1953, Box 110, Folder 10, JWH; Hill to Bert V. Chappel, 14 August 1953, Box 4, Folder C, JWH; Carl Thompson to Hill, 28 September 1954, Box 111, Folder 9, JWH. See also Pollay, "Propaganda, Puffing and the Public Interest," 39–54.

Hahn served as the first chairman of the TIRC from January to April 1954. O. Parker McComas took over from April to July 1954, then T. V. Hartnett became chairman, a position he filled until January 1969. Signing the advertisement were American Tobacco, Benson and Hedges, Bright Belt Warehouse Association, Brown and Williamson, Burley Auction Warehouse Association, Burley Stabilization Corporation, Burley Tobacco Growers Cooperative Association, Larus and Brother Company, P. Lorillard, Marland Tobacco Growers Association, Philip Morris, R. J. Reynolds, Stephano Brothers, Tobacco Associates, and United States Tobacco Company. They worked out a payment schedule for Hill and Knowlton's fees and TIRC grants based on amount of cigarettes or tobacco produced per year.

19. "Licensed Beverage Industries," 39; "A Report and Recommendations," 18 June 1951, Box 97, Folder 1, JWH.

20. Goss to Hill, 30 August 1951, Box 99, Folder 8, JWH; Outline of Suggested Activities, 19 October 1951, Box 99, Folder 8, JWH; Forwarding Memorandum from Edwin F. Dakin to Planning Committee, 1954, Box 110, Folder 2, JWH (hereafter Dakin Memo).

21. Dakin Memo. Hill wrote that there was never any thought that formation of the TIRC would "shut off the critics nor that it necessarily should" (Hill, *Corporate Public Relations*, 137).

22. Hill to Clarence Cook Little, 15 July 1954, Box 111, Folder 9, JWH; Little to Hill, 9 July 1954, Box 111, Folder 9, JWH; A. M. Rochlen to Hill, 25 February 1954, Box 45, Folder 7, JWH.

23. Background Material on the Cigarette Industry Client, 15 December 1953, Box 110, Folder 6, JWH; "Suggested Statement concerning Lawsuit for Companies to Issue," W. T. Hoyt to Hill, 25 February 1954, Box 110, Folder 10, JWH. Brown and Williamson

for one did not begin research on the health effects of smoking until about 1952 (Glantz et al., *Cigarette Papers*, 31).

In contrast to the American approach, in January 1954 the eight largest British companies chose to donate £250,000 over seven years to the Medical Research Council in London, leaving it to the council to decide which organizations should be funded to study the smoking and cancer connection (J. Wix and Sons, Ltd., "Memo to Chairman," 15 January 1954, Box 23, Folder 11, JWH). In 1956 they created the Tobacco Manufacturers' Standing Committee, modeled on the TIRC, and in 1962 they opened a laboratory for jointly sponsored industry research and changed their name to the Tobacco Research Council (Glantz et al., *Cigarette Papers*, 47).

24. For a complete account of tobacco trust investigations, see Tennant, *The American Cigarette Industry*. "Cigarette Makers Warned against Concerted Action," 1.

25. Document 1902.05, B&W. On the history of the papers, see Glantz et al., *Cigarette Papers*, 6–11. Among the public relations agents working for tobacco companies were Tommy Ross and Ben Sonnenberg (Darrow to Hill, 11 May 1955, Box 23, Folder 6, JWH).

26. "Analysis of Mail" received following publication of TIRC's announcement ad, n.d., Box 110, Folder 12a, JWH; Brecher et al., *The Consumers Union Report*, 115, 118. For a complete list of SAB members see Glantz et al., *Cigarette Papers*, 37–39.

27. Hill and Knowlton to T. V. Hartnett, 31 July 1954, Box 110, Folder 7, JWH; news release for 8 November 1954, Box 110, Folder 3, JWH. TIRC grants totaled $2.2 million in the first four years (Hill, *Corporate Public Relations*, 136).

28. Memo to T. V. Hartnett, 31 July 1954, Box 110, Folder 7, JHW; Dakin Memo. Rhoads was Dr. Cornelius P. Rhoads, director of the Sloan-Kettering Institute for Cancer Research, where Wynder et al.'s 1953 research had been conducted.

29. Goss to Publicity Department, 8 January 1954, Box 110, Folder 10, JWH; Hill and Knowlton to T. V. Hartnett, Report of Activities through 31 July 1954, Box 110, Folder 7, JWH. TIRC doctors gradually took a more activist stance (see, for example, schedule for "Conference: Relation of Use of Tobacco . . . ," 28–29 January 1955, Box 3, Folder 126, EAG).

30. Goss to Publicity Department, 8 January 1954, Box 110, Folder 10, JWH; Darrow to Hill, 19 April 1955, Box 23, Folder 6, JWH; Hill and Knowlton to T. V. Hartnett, Report of Activities through 31 July 1954, Box 110, Folder 7, JWH. Reprint of Leonard Engel, "Do We Have to Give Up Smoking?," *Harper's* 10 December 1954, Box 25, JWH (mailed to all doctors under sixty-five, journalists, and "other public opinion leaders"); and "Editorial Comment on Tobacco and Health," reprints of newspaper editorials sent to editors 20 August 1954, Box 109, Folder 12, JWH; "A Scientific Perspective on the Cigarette Controversy," n.d., Box 111, Folder 7, JWH; Goss to Hill and staff, 22 July 1954, Box 111, Folder 1, JWH; Neuberger, *Smoke Screen*, 23–26.

31. Fritschler, *Smoking and Politics*, 18. By the 1960s the companies themselves used mouse skin painting to test components for carcinogenicity in their search for a "safe" cigarette (Glantz et al., *Cigarette Papers*, 108).

32. White, *Merchants of Death*, 30; Wynder to Graham, 4 December 1953, Box 103, Folder 762, EAG.

33. "Report Links Smoking to Lung Tissue Change," 8; Whelan, *Smoking Gun*, 23. The TIRC had donated just over $838,000 by December 1955 and $2.2 million by January 1957 (TIRC news releases, Box 55, Folder 17, Evjue Papers). Document 1920.01, B&W; Hilts, *Smoke Screen*, 15.

34. "A Frank Statement," 4 January 1954, Box 108, Folder 12, JWH; Wynder and

Cornfield, "Cancer of the Lung in Physicians," 441–44; Ochsner, *Smoking and Cancer*, 52.

35. Hill and Knowlton to T. V. Hartnett, Report of Activities through 31 July 1954, Box 110, Folder 7, JWH.

36. "Filter Tips Don't Filter Much," 68; Ochsner, *Smoking and Cancer*, 54. Along with product innovation, manufacturers also began seeking new markets for their products. Cigarette exports, for example, began a steady climb in 1955 (Miles and Cameron, *Coffin Nails*, 94, 97, 101, 121).

37. Neuberger, *Smoke Screen*, 94–95; Ochsner, *Smoking and Cancer*, 55; O'Brien, *Cigarets*, 23.

38. Tareyton ad in American Tobacco Company, *"Sold American!,"* 138–39; Pall Mall ad in *Time* 64 (27 September 1954), 51; L&M ad in *Time* 63 (25 January 1954), 5. Friedman, *Public Policy*, 30; Miles and Cameron, *Coffin Nails*, 82.

39. Seldin, *The Golden Fleece*, 122; Dakin Memo. Philip Morris ad in *Life* 36 (18 January 1954), emphasis and ellipses in original.

40. J. J. D. to Hill, 14 December 1953, Box 110, Folder 10, JWH; "Advertising of Cigarettes," 652–53; "'AMA Journal' Stops Taking Cigaret Ads," 1, 93. *Ad Age* editorials: "Word from the Tobacco Companies," 12; "Did You Order This, Doctor?," 12; and "The Chant of the Tobacco Men," 12.

41. Ochsner, *Smoking and Cancer*, 56.

42. "Price of Cigarettes," 333; "Cigaret Manufacturers Should Try Again," 69.

43. Wootten, "Cigarette Sales 2% under 1952," 34; "New Attacks Hit Cigarets," 27; "Can Cigars & Tobacco Take Advantage of Cigaret Trouble?" 25; "Cigarets Are Heading into a King-Size Race," 24; and "Cigaret Makers Ignore Cancer Data," 32.

44. "Analysis of Press Coverage on Tobacco Controversy," and R. L. Paterson to Hill, 5 March 1954, Box 109, Folder 1, JWH; Miller, "Smoking Up a Storm," 20–22.

45. "Cigarettes Found to Raise Death Rate," 1.

46. Kaplan, "Full Cancer Data on Tobacco Urged," 4; "Doctors Puff Away," 4.

47. Blakeslee, "Survey Shows Cigarette Smokers Die Sooner," 1; "Cancer, Heart Death Link," 1; "Smokers' Death Survey Called 'Preliminary,'" 4; "Tobacco Group Urges Further Cancer Study," 9.

48. Program of TIRC, 9 September 1954, Box 111, Folder 2, JWH; TIRC Activities for August and September, 7 October 1954, Box 111, Folder 2, JWH; "Program of Tobacco Industry Research Committee," n.d., Box 111, Folder 1, JWH; Carl Thompson to Hill, 9 September 1954, Box 111, Folder 1, JWH; Goss to Hill, Littin, Hoyt, and Darrow, 8 June 1954, Box 111, Folder 1, JWH.
During this period, the industry did not attempt to use its advertising dollars to influence press coverage of the issue. However, a substantial literature documents more recent attempts to censor or journalists' self-censoring of news about smoking to insure continued revenue from tobacco advertising (Weis and Burke, "Media Content and Tobacco Advertising," 59–69; Smith, "Magazines' Smoking Habit," 29–31; and Jacobson and Amos, "When Smoke Gets in Your Eyes," 99–137).

49. Krieghbaum, *Science and the Mass Media*, 3; Lewenstein, "'Public Understanding of Science,'" 48–49; Ochsner, *Smoking and Cancer*, 72.

50. Farago, *Science and the Media*, 10.

51. Bayley, *Joe McCarthy and the Press*, 75; "Tobacco Industry Research Committee," 1175.

52. Cohn, *News and Numbers*, 6; Burnham, *How Superstition Won*, 239. The situation is little changed today. "If you talk to people in the working press, in particular the

science writers," according to PR consultant Chester Burger, "they'll just look at you if you mention the Tobacco Institute and laugh. It has zero credibility. But it still gets quoted because when they print articles attacking tobacco and cancer, they feel fairness requires that they quote the other side of the story, and so they still go to the Tobacco Institute" (Burger interview).

53. Hill to George F. Hamel, 4 January 1966, Hamel Papers; Document 19002.01, B&W; Glantz et al., *Cigarette Papers*, 71–74; Hilts, *Smoke Screen*, 24–26. H&K routinely kept client information such as resignations confidential, so it occurred without public fanfare.

54. Kluger, *Ashes to Ashes*, 229.

55. Mapes to George L. Stearns, 29 August 1947, Box 104, Folder 3, JWH; Glantz et al., *Cigarette Papers*, 289–90.

56. Document 2112.04 and Document 2215.01, B&W.

57. Since 1958 the Tobacco Institute, also founded through Hill and Knowlton, has handled the public relations function for the industry, while the TIRC, renamed the Council for Tobacco Research—USA in 1964, continued to sponsor research on smoking and related fields. The institute was created to provide a more vocal lobbying arm when regulations against tobacco were proposed in several states ("Tobacco's Smoking Gun?," 25; Freedman and Cohen, "Smoke and Mirrors," 1).

58. Hilts, "Tobacco Chiefs Say Cigarettes Aren't Addictive," A1.

59. Document 1816.05, B&W; Strum, "Judge Cites Possible Fraud," 1, 7; Klaidman, "Blowing Smoke," 10–11; Hilts, *Smoke Screen*, 153–54; Thorn, "Tobacco Wars," 31–32.

60. Neither the public relations idea nor the research idea was new. In 1950 Parker McComas of Philip Morris warned that the industry "urgently needs an industry-wide public relations program as an effective antidote to the sensation-seeking articles on tobacco, Government attacks and heavy taxation" ("Attacks Deplored on Use of Tobacco," 41). Dr. Herman Hillboe, New York health commissioner, proposed that manufacturers invest "a few million dollars of their advertising budgets in research," arguing the money "would never be missed because so much is spent" (Weaver, "Health Chief Asks Lung Cancer Study," 37). Notes from meeting of 28 December 1953, Richard Darrow, Box 109, Folder 14, JWH; Dick Darrow to Carl Thompson, 17 August 1954, Box 111, Folder 1, JWH.

61. Brecher et al., *Consumers Union Report*, 113. Graham to Charles Cameron, 10 January 1956, Box 3, Folder 25, EAG; Hill and Knowlton to William T. Evjue, 6 May 1955, Box 55, Folder 17, Evjue Papers.

62. Document 2101.07, B&W; Hilts, *Smoke Screen*, 17; Janis and Feshbach, "Effects of Fear-Arousing Communications," 78–92; Sperber, *Murrow*, 497; Harlow, *Social Science in Public Relations*, 71.

63. Miles and Cameron, *Coffin Nails*, 37; U.S. Department of Health and Human Services, *Reducing the Health Consequences*, 189–90; Gerstein and Levison, *Reduced Tar and Nicotine Cigarettes*, 11; "Tide Leadership Panel," 31; "Most Admen Are Changing," 17–18.

Chapter Seven

1. Burt and Taines, "Public Relations in Foreign Markets," 64.

2. John W. Hill, "Problems of American Business Abroad," 1954, Box 39, Folder 11, JWH; Hill, *Making of a Public Relations Man*, 196.

3. Ghertman and Allen, *Introduction to the Multinationals*, 7–8; Tugendhat, *The*

Multinationals, 10; Jones, *Evolution of International Business*, 30, 36, 44; Kean, *Public Relations Man Abroad*, 140.

4. Tugendhat, *The Multinationals*, 11, 26; Donaldson, *Ethics of International Business*, 30; Ramu, *Multinational Firms*, 66. On GATT, see 61 Stat. (5) A3 and (6) A1365, 4 Bevans 639. The Hickenlooper amendment [Pub.L. 88–633, Pt. III, § 301 (d) (4)] to the Foreign Assistance Act of 1961 passed on 7 October 1964.

5. Gilpin, *U.S. Power*, 139–44; Tugendhat, *Multinationals*, 27; Wilkins, *Maturing of the Multinational*, 287, 290–91; Kean, *Public Relations Man Abroad*, 4.

6. Vernon, *Manager in the International Economy*, 205, table 10-1. By 1957 2,800 U.S. companies had stakes in 10,000 direct investment enterprises abroad (Wilkins, *Maturing of the Multinational*, 341). Jones, *Evolution of International Business*, 46; Tugendhat, *The Multinationals*, 24; Hill, *Making of a Public Relations Man*, 195–96.

7. Cutlip, *The Unseen Power*, discusses some international clients of various agencies before World War II; see especially chapters on Wright, Lee, and Byoir. Both Hill and Byoir tried to solicit Puerto Rico when its contract with Wright expired in 1950 (Hill to George E. Allen, 9 March 1950, Box 1, Folder 6, JWH). Bernays, "Emergence of the Public Relations Counsel," 305; Dale Cox to Hill, 8 April 1953, Box 23, Folder 10, JWH; Moskowitz, "Industrials and Ad Agencies," 49; Random, "Agencies Move," 60, 62.

An example of the inaccuracies in the historiography on international PR due to a lack of information is an article on Barnet & Reef Associates, which claims that the agency "pioneered in providing worldwide public relations programming through an extensive network of leading practitioners." However, the agency was founded in 1958, four years after H&K's network was already in place (Reed and Hardy, "Pioneering International Public Relations," 12).

8. John W. Hill, "International Public Relations—Hope and Reality," *Public Relations Journal* (December 1957), 14, Box 39, Folder 11, JWH. This was a great period of change for Hill personally, especially in the moderation of his political views. This was apparently a common experience for European travelers following the war (Pool, Keller, and Bauer, "Influence of Foreign Travel," 172–73).

9. Hill, *Making of a Public Relations Man*, 192; Hamel, "John W. Hill," 69; "Clients of Hill and Knowlton, Inc. and Affiliates," 1955, Box 5, Folder 2, JWH; Hill to Harry S. Cooper, 3 March 1954, Box 23, Folder 11, JWH; see also, client list, 1950, Box 7, Folder 2, JWH, and Memorandum on Hill & Knowlton, Inc., n.d. [1951], Box 99, Folder 8, JWH; "Texas Co. Retains Hill & Knowlton," 36; "Public Relations Program Prepared for the Republic of Colombia," 6 June 1949, Box 93, Folder 6, JWH; Hill to Goss and King, 30 January 1953, Box 23, Folder 10, JWH. No indication that Byoir actually opened an office was found in the course of this study.

10. Hill to Goss and King, 30 January 1953, Box 23, Folder 10, JWH; Hill, *Making of a Public Relations Man*, 190; Hill to Tom Clark, 20 February 1953, Box 23, Folder 10, JWH.

11. Memoir, Box 4, Folder 8, 146-C, MJ; Hill, *Making of a Public Relations Man*, 190–92.

12. "Summary Report," 20 April 1954, Box 6, Folder 5, MJ; Jackson, "East of Suez," 3; Hill to W. F. Bramstedt, 4 January 1954, Box 5, Folder 6, MJ; "Caltex," n.d., Box 5, Folder 6, MJ.

13. "Persons Interviewed in Indonesia," 22 March 1954, Box 92, Folder 4, JWH.

14. "Report on Public Relations Study for Ceylon," 1 March 1954, Box 5, Folder 9, MJ.

15. "Summary Report: Public Relations Survey," 20 April 1954, Box 6, Folder 5, MJ.

16. "Specific problems . . . ," n.d., Box 6, Folder 3, MJ; draft article, 9 June 1954, Box 6, Folder 5, MJ.

17. "Summary Report," 20 April 1954, Box 6, Folder 5, MJ.

18. "Summary Report," 20 April 1954, Box 6, Folder 5, MJ; draft article, 9 June 1954, Box 6, Folder 5, MJ; "Specific Problems . . . ," n.d., Box 6, Folder 3, MJ; Cook, *The Declassified Eisenhower*, 185–88; Ambrose, *The President*, 192–97.

19. "Summary Report," 20 April 1954, Box 6, Folder 5, MJ.

20. Hill to Emerson M. Butterworth, 18 May 1955, Box 92, Folder 2, JWH; Hill to Velmans, 21 September 1955, Box 24, Folder 8, JWH.

21. Hill, "International Public Relations," Box 39, Folder 11, JWH.

22. Hill, *Making of a Public Relations Man*, 189, 192; Hill to Campbell-Johnson, 17 September 1953, Box 24, Folder 3, JWH; O. M. Gale to Wm. G. Werner, 30 March 1954, Box 104, Folder 14, JWH; McIntyre, "European Press Many Things," 20; "Hill & Knowlton to Join Four European Concerns," 40; Hill to Jock Henderson, 27 December 1954, Box 23, Folder 11, JWH; news release for 12 July 1954, Box 27, Folder 12, JWH; Hill, *Making of a Public Relations Man*, 191–92; Darrow to George E. McCadden, 17 August 1954, Box 22, Folder 3, JWH.

Affiliates added later were Italpublic in Italy; the Buro für Auslandsinformation in Germany; Cockfield, Brown and Company in Canada; Lennart Lagebrant in Sweden; Marcel Yoel, Interpress in Greece; Bendix Bech-Thostrup in Denmark; Edmundo Lassalle Latin American Operations in Central and South America and Mexico; BSR in Lebanon; and W. L. Green Public Relations in New Zealand.

23. Hill to Goss and King, 30 January 1953, Box 23, Folder 10, JWH. Hill estimated the agency would have to carry the overseas office for at least one year, if not two, which meant at least $20,000, plus another trip to Europe by Hill in 1954.

24. Hill to Goss and King, 30 January 1953, Box 23, Folder 10, JWH; King to Hill, 4 February 1953, Box 23, Folder 10, JWH. By establishing a network in Europe and working through Loet Velmans, H&K contradicted the general trend identified by public relations scholars who argue that public relations ideas and terms were exported to Europe primarily through Great Britain; Hazelton and Kruckeberg, "European Public Relations Practice," 368.

25. Hill to Bauer, 5 February 1954, Box 24, Folder 2, JWH; Campbell-Johnson to Hill, 23 February 1954, JWH; Hill to Hollander, 7 September 1955, Box 24, Folder 5, JWH; Hill to H&K, 26 March 1954, Box 23, Folder 11, JWH. Campbell-Johnson, Ltd., continued to work for the industry for several years, issuing "Smoking and Health Monthly Report," a summary of media coverage, to British American Tobacco (Document 1014.01, B&W).

26. Hill to D. J. Koeleman, 25 January 1955, Box 94, Folder 11, JWH.

27. "Memorandum to the Staff," 8 September 1954, Box 112, Folder 11, JWH.

28. Memorandum on Associates' Meeting, 2 April 1955, Box 24, Folder 1, JWH. Hill and Knowlton, Inc., *Handbook on International Public Relations*, vols. 1 and 2: Eric Cyprès, "Belgium," 1:4–5; Gerald W. Schroder, "West Germany," 1:182; Eric White Associates, "Malaysia," 2:118.

29. Hill and Knowlton, Inc., *Handbook on International Relations*, vols. 1 and 2: Eric White Associates, "Australia," 2:4; Alan Campbell-Johnson and John Foley, "The United Kingdom," 1:150–52; Grant, *Propaganda and the Role of the State*, 248.

30. John J. Slocum to Hill, 26 February 1954, Box 23, Folder 11, JWH; Velmans to Hill, 13 October 1954, Box 22, Folder 3, JWH.

31. Hansjürgen Schubert to Hill, 13 March 1953, Box 23, Folder 10, JWH. Velmans also reported that other agencies, like Selvage, Lee and Chase, had likewise been unable to attract German business (Velmans to Hill and Goss, 15 January 1954, Box 24, Folder 6, JWH). "Franck Bauer et Associes," n.d., Box 24, Folder 2, JWH.

32. Cyprès to Hill, 9 July 1958, Box 57, Folder 12, JWH; P. B. Smith to Bauer, 27 De-

cember 1955, Box 104, Folder 14, JWH; Velmans to Hill, 14 January 1956, Box 104, Folder 14, JHW; Hill to Bauer, 18 April 1956, Box 104, Folder 14, JWH; Hill to Cyprès, 9 November 1956, Box 104, Folder 14, JWH.

33. William A. Durbin, "How to Serve Clients Abroad," in Hill and Knowlton, Inc., *Current Thoughts*, 32; Hill to Velmans, 18 October 1955, Box 24, Folder 1, JWH; Hill to Campbell-Johnson, 7 December 1955, Box 24, Folder 1, JWH; Velmans to Hill, 24 September 1955, Box 24, Folder 8, JWH.

34. Hill to Moens, 9 February 1956, Hill to Cyprès, 27 September 1956, and Hill to Moens, 4 October 1956, Box 112, Folder 5, JWH.

35. World Congress of Public Relations, *Public Relations in the Service of Social Progress*, 209–10, 212; Rydell, *World of Fairs*, 193.

36. Hamel, "John W. Hill," 195–96; Hill to Alan Campbell-Johnson, 17 April 1958, Box 57, Folder 12, JWH; Hill to Velmans, 6 May 1958, Box 57, Folder 12, JWH. "N.V." means "Naamlooze Venootschap" (limited liability company); the company was officially formed in 1956. Wise, "Hill & Knowlton's World," 100; interview transcript, 1957, Box 39, Folder 7, JWH; Burson interview. See also, "J. Carlisle MacDonald Joins New Company," *American Metal Market*, 18 September 1956, Box 102, Clips (2), AISI; and Velmans, Foreword to the thirtieth anniversary edition of Hill's *Making of a Public Relations Man*.

International business continued to grow through the 1980s, but during the 1990s the three largest international public relations firms began to lose money (Levin, "Global PR Efforts on the Wane," 28).

37. "Public Relations in the Service of Social Progress," 215, 225–34. In 1960 John Hill received the "Knight of the Order of Leopold" decoration from Belgium in recognition of the firm's promotion of the Brussels World Fair (*Editor and Publisher*, Box 42, Biographical Clippings, JWH). Hill and Knowlton, Inc., *Handbook on International Public Relations*.

38. Reed and Hardy, "Pioneering International," 13. Barnet and Reef was merged into Harshe, Rotman and Druck in 1964.

39. Ball, "Relations of the Multinational," 64; Behrman, *U.S. International Business*, 94; Jones, *Evolution of International Business*, 292; Boddewyn and Kapoor, "External Relations," 436.

40. Robinson, *International Business Policy*, 139; Brannen and Hodgson, *Overseas Management*, 13; Kean, *Public Relations Man Abroad*, 12.

41. Hill, *Corporate Public Relations*, 148; Dinerman, "Image Problems for American Companies Abroad," 137; Kean, *Public Relations Man Abroad*, 145.

42. Whyte, *Is Anybody Listening?*, 82–84, 102–6.

43. Hill, "I Predict," 63; Hill, "Future of Corporate Public Relations," 15; Trento, *Power House*, 93–94.

44. Botan, "International Public Relations," 151; "Report on Public Relations Study for Ceylon," 1 March 1954, Box 5, Folder 9, MJ. A survey conducted in the mid-1960s indicated that among 100 member companies of the National Foreign Trade Council, the members that conducted active public relations programs abroad had all sought the services of nationals to help (William A. Durbin, "A Look at International Public Relations," in *Public Relations: Speeches by Executives of Hill and Knowlton*, 51).

45. Mapes to Goss, 14 December 1948, Box 57, Folder 5, JWH.

46. Quoted in Darrow, Forrestal, and Cookman, *Dartnell Public Relations Handbook*, 180.

47. Jones, *Evolution of International Business*, 3; Hill, *Corporate Public Relations*, 153–54; draft article, 9 June 1954, Box 6, Folder 5, MJ.

48. Fayerweather, *International Business Management*, 111; "A Survey of Caltex Group Publications," 5 September 1955, Box 92, Folder 6, JWH.

49. "A Credo," Box 5, Folder 6, MJ.

50. Hill, "Problems of American Business Abroad," 1954, Box 39, Folder 11, JWH.

51. "A Survey of Caltex Group Publications," 5 September 1955, Box 92, Folder 6, JWH; Banks, *Multicultural Public Relations*, 113.

Chapter Eight

1. Trento, *Power House*, 327, 329; "Industry Ranking for H&K," Box 6, Folder 10, MJ; Goodell, "What Hill & Knowlton Can Do," 75; "Too Much Flak," 42; Lipman, "Hill & Knowlton Adds Lobbyist Wexler," B8.

2. Hamel, "John W. Hill," 55; Burson interview.

3. Harty, *Hucksters in the Classroom*, 63–68; Hill, *Making of a Public Relations Man*, 148; John W. Hill, "Public Relations in a Shrinking World," in Hill and Knowlton, Inc., *Current Thoughts*, 6; Carl Thompson, "Warning Flags (Still) Wave," in Hill and Knowlton Executives, *Critical Issues*, 108; John G. Mapes, "Computers," in Hill and Knowlton, Inc., *Current Thoughts*, 18–29.

During the 1959 controversy, H&K, the union, the companies, and the government issued over 200 news releases and about 150 booklets and reports. The agency borrowed a page from advertising agencies in using copy testing; executives wanted to know how effectively they had reached employees in such materials. Many words management used were misunderstood by the steelworkers, and H&K recommended replacements: "compute" should be "figure," and "take precedence," "come first" (Hill, "What We Learned in the Steel Negotiations," 6–7, 10).

4. Manning, personal correspondence; Chase interview; Gray, personal correspondence, 15 April 1993; Burger interview; Burson interview.

5. Hill to Mapes, 16 May 1952, Box 7, Folder 3, JWH; O'Dwyer, "H&K Has History of Turmoil," 1, 30–32. The "troika" of Bill Durbin, Charles Puzzo, and Velmans ran the agency for a short time after Darrow died in 1976. Durbin retired in 1980 and Puzzo in 1981 (news release, 28 August 1984, Box 5, Folder 7, MJ).

6. Hamel, "John W. Hill," 70–71.

7. Marcus, *National Government*, 961–62; Hill, *Making of a Public Relations Man*, 121. The Phillips decision, 347 U.S. 672, 74 S.Ct. 794, was handed down on 7 June 1954.

8. Ross, *Image Merchants*, 184; "Preliminary Outline of Public Relations Program Recommendations" and "The NGORC Program for 1955–56," Box 103, Folder 4, JWH; "Information and Aids Kit for Local Programs," Box 103, Folder 2, JWH; advertisements, Box 102, Folder 13, JWH; Hill to Max D. Howell, 4 January 1955, Box 102, Folder 11, JWH; Steve Smoke to staff, 31 January 1955, Box 69, Folder 12, JWH; "Rough Cost Estimates," 4 November 1954, Box 103, Folder 4, JWH; Hill, *Making of a Public Relations Man*, 123–25.

9. News release, June 1956, Box 103, Folder 3, JWH; H.R. 6645; "Veto of Bill to Amend the Natural Gas Act," *Public Papers of the Presidents of the United States: Dwight D. Eisenhower, 1956*, 256; Hamel, "John W. Hill," 113–17; Hill, *Making of a Public Relations Man*, 120, 124. See also, U.S. Senate, *Oil and Gas Lobby Investigation*.

10. Hamel, "John W. Hill," 107–13; Harris, *Real Voice*, 55.

11. Goss, "Witness for the Prosecution," 432.

12. Libertella, "The Steel Strike of 1959," 232, 235–36.

13. Hoerr, *And the Wolf Finally Came*; Lally, "Steel's Public Image," 8 November

1962, Box 102, Public Relations (2), AISI; Hill, *Making of a Public Relations Man,* 82–83.

14. Hill, *Making of a Public Relations Man,* 147, 154; Richard W. Darrow, "For Public Relations," in Hill and Knowlton, Inc., *Public Relations;* Darrow, "Public Relations," in Hill and Knowlton, Inc., *Current Thoughts,* 189.

15. Collected publications of the executives: Hill and Knowlton, Inc., *Handbook on International Public Relations,* vols. 1, 2, *Stock Exchange,* and *Current Thoughts;* Hill and Knowlton Executives, *Critical Issues;* Youth and Education Department, *Youth and Careers in Education.*

16. Trento, *Power House,* 89–91.

17. "Personal Chemistry Clicked," 15; Rigg, "PR Agency Caught in Turmoil,"1; Mattelart, *Advertising International,* 179.

18. Dilenschneider, *Power and Influence;* Goodell, "What Hill and Knowlton Can Do," 44.

19. Feder, "Hill & Knowlton Chief," C1; Dilenschneider, *Power and Influence,* xxv; Goodell, "What Hill and Knowlton Can Do," 75.

20. Richard W. Darrow, "Where Else," in Hill and Knowlton, Inc., *Current Thoughts,* 15.

21. Riegle, "Hill and Knowlton, Inc.," 20–21.

22. De Witt, "Balancing Influence and Integrity," C1; Dilenschneider, "'We Don't Do Coups,'" 41; Dilenschneider, *Power and Influence,* 31, 38; McCauley, "H&K Keeps Pro-Life Account," 33.

23. Trento, *Power House,* 358, 361; Behar, "Thriving Cult," 50–51, 55, 57; "WPP/Lilly Suit Settled," B5.

24. "Bishops Hire PR Firm," 394; "Bishops under Fire," 24.

25. "When a PR Firm Could Use a PR Firm," 44; "Bishops under Fire," 24; Trento, *Power House,* 364.

26. Lipman, "Hill & Knowlton's PR Tactics," B4; "H&K Leads PR Charge," 11–12; Pratt, "Hill & Knowlton's Two Ethical Dilemmas," 288; Rowse, "Flacking for the Emir," 20; Miller, "Sheik of Few Words," A8; MacArthur, *Second Front,* 46, 49.

The $11 million budget was very large. By comparison, other H&K foreign accounts registered with the government according to the Federal Agents Registration Act spent the following in the first six months of 1989: Bermuda Department of Tourism, $447,268, Mazda Motor Corporation, $820,169, the Republic of Turkey, $595,838, and, for eleven months, Indonesia, $2.2 million ("FARA Fees and Expenses," 1).

27. Rowse, "Flacking for the Emir," 20, 22; Bleifuss, "Flack Attack," 73; Trento, *Power House,* 380; "H&K Leads PR Charge," 11–12; "PR Firm to Push Kuwaitis' Message," B2; Lee, "Kuwait's Campaign," A1; MacArthur, *Second Front,* 50; "VNR Top Ten," 14.

The Kuwaiti group unexpectedly ended its contract with H&K in January, although it continued to pay the other public relations and lobbying firms it had retained, including the Rendon Group, for media relations; Neill & Co., lobbyists; and Pintak/Brown International, another public relations firm (Price, "Free Kuwait Group," A4; Lee, "Kuwait's Campaign on the PR Front," A1). Rumor suggested that the client was upset with H&K's blatant self-promotion throughout the campaign.

28. Bilski, "Witnesses to Terror," 32; "Dismantling a Country," 26; Rowse, "Flacking for the Emir," 21.

29. Rowse, "Flacking for the Emir," 20; Trento, *Power House,* 380; Beyer, "Iraq's Power Grab," 16, 19; Campbell, *Politics without Principle,* 15.

30. Elliot, "Dispute in the Public Relations Industry," D8; Strong, "Portions of the Gulf War," 12.

31. A notable exception was "Massacre of the Innocents?," 114; MacArthur, "Remember Nayirah," A11; "H&K Defends Credibility," 9; Strong, "Portions of the Gulf War," 12.

32. MacArthur, "Remember Nayirah," A11; "Deception on Capitol Hill," A10; Eidson, "P.R. Firm Had No Reason," A28; Krauss, "Congressman Says Girl Was Credible," A11.

33. See, for instance, Rowse, "How to Build Support for War," 28.

34. "H&K Defends Credibility," 10; "Deception on Capitol Hill," A10. See also Priest, "Kuwait Baby-Killing Report Disputed," A7; Rowse, "How to Build Support," 29; MacArthur, Second Front, 62, 73–74.

35. De Witt, "Balancing Influence," C1; "Too Much Flak," 42; Trento, Power House, 369, 372; Mundy, "Is the Press Any Match?," 33; Lipman, "H&K's PR Tactics," B4.

36. "PR Problem at Hill and Knowlton," 50; "Bishops Hire PR Firm," 394.

37. Lipman, "Hill & Knowlton Drops Dilenschneider," B4; "PR Problem at Hill and Knowlton," 50; "Too Much Flak," 42.

38. Trento, Power House; Gray, personal correspondence, 30 November 1997; Brophy, "Gray Eminence," 102–3; Clifford, "Power House," 37; "Shift at Top," D3.

39. Lipman, "H&K's PR Tactics," B4; Trento, Power House, 331.

40. Newsom, "PR Practitioners Question Client Choice," 4; McCauley, "H&K Keeps Pro-Life Account," 32; De Witt, "Balancing Influence," C1; Gray interview.

41. "The 1991 Public Relations Agency Report Card," 19–26; "Tilting at Windmills," 8; "1992 PR Fee Income," 18; "1992 DC-Area Fee Income," 36; "1992 Chicago-Area Fee Income," 40; "1992 Fee Income of PR Firms according to Areas of Specialization," 48; Sellers, "Do You Need Your Ad Agency?," 148.

42. Feder, "Hill and Knowlton Chief," C1; Hamel, "John W. Hill," 61–62; Bird, "Hill & Knowlton Sues," B4; Lee, "PR Firm Loses Bid," F1.

43. "Too Much Flak," 42.

44. Lee, "Image Conscious," E1; quoted in Roschwalb, "Hill & Knowlton Cases," 273; Lipman, "H&K Drops Dilenschneider," B4.

45. Skolnik, "Emerging Firm of the '90s," 23; Elliott, "Hill & Knowlton Forms a Unit," D5; El-Faizy, "It's No Occident," 13; McCartin, Carter, Turner, and Brandao, "Hill and Knowlton," 1.

46. "PR Operations," A13; Parker-Pope, "Hill & Knowlton Polishes Its Own Image," B1.

Chapter Nine

1. Hill, Making of a Public Relations Man, 149.

2. Harris, Right to Manage, 193.

3. Whyte, Is Anybody Listening?, vii; "Public Relations," 100.

4. Goss, "How to Reduce Business' Credibility Gap," 398; Hill, "Function of Public Relations," in Hill and Knowlton Executives, Critical Issues, 16; draft of introduction for anniversary book (never completed), Box 41, Folder 6, JWH.

5. Tedlow, Keeping the Corporate Image, 204–5; Ryerson, "Old Challenges in Steel's Public Relations," address before the AISI, Public Relations Session, 26 May 1954, Box 102, Public Relations (1), AISI; Hill, "Public Relations and the Trade Association," 44–45.

6. Tedlow, Keeping the Corporate Image, 204–5.

7. Marchand, "Fitful Career," 151.

Manuscript Collections

Independence, Missouri
Harry S. Truman Library
   American Insitute of Public Opinion Papers
   George P. Baker Oral History (1974)
   John D. Clark Papers
   Harold L. Enarson Papers
   John C. Houston Papers
   J. Howard McGrath Senatorial Records
   Charles Murphy Oral History (1970)
   Charles Murphy Papers
   President's Air Policy Commission Papers
   Charles Sawyer Papers
   John R. Steelman Oral History (1963)
   David Stowe Oral Histories (1963, 1976, 1989)
   David Stowe Papers
   W. Stuart Symington Papers
   Harry S. Truman Papers, Official File
   President's Secretaries' File
   White House Bill File
   Horace Weihmiller Papers

Madison, Wisconsin
State Historical Society of Wisconsin
   Bruce Barton Papers
   William T. Evjue Papers
   George F. Hamel Papers
   John W. Hill Papers
   James Irwin Papers
   Merrick Jackson Papers
   Hans von Kaltenborn Papers
   Alexander Wiley Papers
   Wisconsin Creameries Association Annual Convention and Annual Reports
   Wisconsin Creameries Association Newsletters

Wisconsin Legislative Reference Bureau
    Newspaper Clipping Files

New York, New York
Columbia University Oral History Collection
    Roger Blough Oral History (1975)
    John Brophy Oral History (1955)
    Ira C. Eaker Oral History (1974)
    Eugene E. Wilson Oral History (Naval History Project, 1962)

San Francisco, California
University of California
    Brown and Williamson Papers (accessed through http://www.library.ucsf.edu./
        tobacco)

St. Louis, Missouri
Washington University Medical Library
    Evarts A. Graham Papers

Washington, D.C.
Archives of the Catholic University of America
    Philip Murray Papers
Library of Congress
    Robert A. Taft Papers

Wilmington, Delaware
Hagley Museum and Library
    All-American Aviation, Inc., Papers
    American Iron and Steel Institute Papers
    Boeing-Vertol Division Papers

Personal Interviews and Correspondence

Chester Burger, 1 March 1993, New York City
Harold Burson, telephone interview, 29 March 1993
Howard Chase, 20 May 1993, New York City
Robert K. Gray, personal correspondence, 15 April 1993 and 30 November 1997
Robert K. Gray, telephone interview, 23 June 1993
Farley Manning, personal correspondence, 1 May 1993

Government Publications

President's Air Policy Commission. *Survival in the Air Age*. Washington, D.C.: U.S.
    Government Printing Office, 1948.
Public Papers of the Presidents of the United States: Dwight D. Eisenhower, 1956.
    Washington, D.C.: U.S. Government Printing Office, 1958.
Public Papers of the Presidents of the United States: Harry S. Truman, 1945. Wash-
    ington, D.C.: U.S. Government Printing Office, 1961.

Public Papers of the Presidents of the United States: Harry S. Truman, 1952. Washington, D.C.: U.S. Government Printing Office, 1966.

U.S. Bureau of the Census. *Historical Statistics of the United States*. Bicentennial Edition, Part 1. 12 vols. Washington, D.C.: Bureau of the Census, 1976.

U.S. Congress. House. Committee on Agriculture. *Oleomargaine Tax Repeal Hearings*. 80th Congress, 2d session, 8–12 March 1948.

U.S. Congress. House. Subcommittee on the Study of Monopoly Power of the Committee on the Judiciary. *Study of Monopoly Power*. 81st Congress, 2d Session, 1950.

U.S. Congress. Senate. Congressional Aviation Policy Board. *National Aviation Policy*. Report 949, 80th Congress, 2d session, 1948.

U.S. Congress. Senate. Finance Committee. *Oleomargarine Tax Repeal Hearings*. 80th Congress, 2d session, 1948.

U.S. Congress. Senate. Special Subcommittee to Investigate Political Activities, Lobbying, and Campaign Contributions. *Oil and Gas Lobby Investigation*. 84th Congress, 2d Session, 1956.

U.S. Congress. Senate. Subcommittee of the Committee on Education and Labor. *Violations of Free Speech and Rights of Labor*. 75th Congress, 2d Session, 1938.

U.S. Department of Agriculture. *Agricultural Statistics*. Washington, D.C.: U.S. Government Printing Office, 1953.

U.S. Department of Commerce. *Statistical Abstract of the U.S.*, 85th ed. Washington, D.C.: U.S. Government Printing Office, 1964.

U.S. Department of Health and Human Services. *Reducing the Health Consequences of Smoking: 25 Years of Progress, A Report to the Surgeon General*. Rockville, Md.: U.S. Department of Health and Human Services, 1989.

Newspaper, Trade, and Magazine Articles and Published Pamphlets

"Advertising of Cigarettes, The." *Journal of the American Medical Association* 13 (30 October 1948): 652–53.

"Aftermath of a Massacre." *New Republic* 92 (22 September 1937): 174.

"Aggressive Plan, An." *Hoard's Dairyman* 94 (10 January 1949): 24.

"Air Policy." *Tide* 22 (12 March 1948): 57–58.

"'AMA Journal' Stops Taking Cigaret Ads." *Advertising Age* 24 (9 November 1953): 1+.

"Attacks Deplored on Use of Tobacco." *New York Times* (28 March 1950): 41.

"Awards Made for PR." *Tide* 24 (5 May 1950): 56.

Baldwin, Hanson W. "What Air Power Can—and Cannot—Do." *New York Times Magazine* (30 May 1948): 5–7+.

"Battle for Britain's Steel." *Fortune* 38 (December 1948): 88–90.

Behar, Richard. "The Thriving Cult of Greed and Power." *Time* 137 (6 May 1991): 50–57.

"Betrayal of Air Power, The." *Aviation Week* 48 (5 April 1948): 50; (12 April 1948): 54; (19 April 1948): 66.

Beyer, Lisa. "Iraq's Power Grab." *Time* 136 (13 August 1990): 16–24.

"Big Tobacco Stocks Rally; Darr Disputes Cancer Talks." *Raleigh News and Observer* (11 December 1953): 1.

Bilski, Andrew. "Witnesses to Terror." *Macleans* (22 October 1990): 32.

Bird, Laura. "Hill & Knowlton Sues Ex-Aides, Shakes Up Its Washington Office." *Wall Street Journal* (28 August 1992): B4.

"Bishops Hire PR Firm." *Christian Century* 107 (18 April 1990): 394.

"Bishops under Fire, The." *Newsweek* 115 (23 April 1990): 24.

Blakeslee, Alton L. "Survey Shows Cigarette Smokers Die Sooner Than Non-Smokers." *St. Louis Post-Dispatch* (21 June 1954): 1.

Bleifuss, Joel, "Flack Attack," *Utne Reader* (January–February 1994): 72–79.

"Bold Decision Turns Tide of Battle on Oleo Yellow." *Hoard's Dairyman* 93 (25 March 1948): 260.

Bonney, Walter T. "Aviation Public Relations." *Air Affairs* 3 (Winter 1950): 576–88.

Bowen, Croswell, and George R. Clark. "Reputation by Sonnenberg." *Harper's* 200 (February 1950): 39–49.

Brophy, Beth. "The Gray Eminence." *Forbes* 129 (18 January 1982): 102–3.

Broun, Heywood. "L'Affaire Sokolsky." *New Republic* 95 (3 August 1938): 360–61.

Burt, John C., and Beatrice Green Taines. "Public Relations in Foreign Markets." *Printers' Ink* 214 (22 February 1946): 27–29+.

"Butter." *Nation* 166 (8 May 1948): 491.

"Butter Institute." *Tide* 21 (28 November 1947): 52.

"Butter or Oleomargarine—Who Needs Protection?" *Hoard's Dairyman* 93 (10 April 1948): 317.

"Butter-Oleo Battle Re-engaged." *American Butter and Cheese Review* 10 (November 1948): 4.

"Can Cigars & Tobacco Take Advantage of Cigaret Trouble?" *Tide* 28 (31 July 1954): 25.

"Can Wage Board Survive Dispute over Steel Case?" *U.S. News and World Report* 32 (4 April 1952): 69–70+.

"Cancer, Heart Death Link to Cigarets Found in Study." *Chicago Daily Tribune* (22 June 1954): 1.

"Cancer in Heavy Smokers." *Science News Letter* 57 (3 June 1950): 343.

Carr, C. C. "Translating the American Economic System." *Public Relations Journal* 5 (June 1949): 1–4.

"Chant of the Tobacco Men, The." *Advertising Age* 25 (11 January 1954): 12.

Cheney, Richard. "Some Facts about Steel Profits." *Steelways* 8 (May 1952): 1–3.

"Cigaret Makers Ignore Cancer Data, Dr. Ingraham Says." *Advertising Age* 20 (4 November 1957): 32.

"Cigaret Manufacturers Should Try Again." *Christian Century* 71 (January 1954): 69.

"Cigarets Are Heading into a King-Size Race This Fall." *Tide* 28 (17 July 1954): 24.

"Cigarette Makers Warned against Concerted Action." *Raleigh News and Observer* (1 January 1954): 1.

"Cigarettes Found to Raise Death Rate in Men 50 to 70." *New York Times* (22 June 1954): 1.

Clifford, Garry. "The Power House." *People* 38 (5 October 1992): 37+.

Conn, Harry. "Steel: A Myth Exposed." *New Republic* 125 (17 December 1951): 14–15.

———. "Steel: The Price of Peace." *New Republic* 127 (28 July 1952): 8–9.

"Corporate Profits Understated." *Labor Research Association Economic Notes* 20 (June 1952): 6–7.

"Corporation, The." *Fortune* 13 (March 1936): 59–67+.

Cort, John C. "The Church and the Steel Crisis." *Commonweal* 56 (23 May 1952): 169–71.

Crowell, Evelyn Miller. "The Editorial Slant on Steel." *New Republic* 87 (August 5, 1936): 377–79.

"'Dairy Depression' Seen in Oleo Bill." *New York Times* (4 March 1949): 11.

Dales, Douglas. "Ending of Oleo Tax Raises Use of Fats." *New York Times* (24 September 1950): 79.

Damon, Ralph S. "Airline Outlook." *Air Affairs* 3 (December 1950): 459–63.

De Seversky, Alexander P. "The U.S. Air Force in Power Politics." *Air Affairs* 2 (Winter 1949): 477–90.

De Witt, Karen. "Balancing Influence and Integrity." *New York Times* (10 September 1991): C1.

"Deception on Capitol Hill." *New York Times* (15 January 1992): A10.

"Did You Order This, Doctor?" *Advertising Age* 24 (21 December 1953): 12.

"'Digest' Tobacco Diatribe Turned into Viceroy Ad." *Advertising Age* 21 (2 January 1950): 1+.

"Dismantling a Country." *Newsweek* (1 October 1990): 26.

"Doctors Puff Away." *New York Times* (23 June 1954): 4.

Drepperd, Carl W. "Begin Selling 'Free Enterprise' in the Kindergarten." *Printers' Ink* 204 (13 August 1943): 20+.

Eidson, Thomas E. "P.R. Firm Had No Reason to Question Kuwaiti's Testimony." *New York Times* (17 January 1992): A28.

Eisenhower, Dwight D. "Liberty Is at Stake." *Vital Speeches of the Day* 27 (17 January 1961): 228–30.

El-Faizy, Monique. "It's No Occident PR Firms Fill Asian Void." *Crains New York Business* (12 April 1993): 13.

Elliot, Stuart. "A Dispute in the Public Relations Industry." *New York Times* (14 May 1992): D8.

———. "Hill & Knowlton Forms a Unit to Direct Public Relations Efforts toward Gay Men and Lesbians." *New York Times* (23 June 1995): D5.

"Emergency Advertising." *Printers' Ink* 166 (12 April 1934): 43.

"Expansible Industry or Mothball Fleet?" *Aviation Week* 48 (3 May 1948): 50.

"FARA Fees and Expenses." *O'Dwyer's PR Service Report* 4 (January 1990): 1.

"Favor Passage." *Wisconsin Food Dealer* 40 (June 1949): 14.

Feder, Barnaby J. "Hill & Knowlton Chief Makes an Abrupt Exit." *Wall Street Journal* (27 September 1991): C1.

"Fight Fraud." *Hoard's Dairyman* 93 (10 March 1948): 210.

"Filter Tips Don't Filter Much, AMA Cigaret Research Discloses." *Advertising Age* 24 (3 August 1953): 68.

Freedman, Alix, and Laurie P. Cohen. "Smoke and Mirrors." *Wall Street Journal* (11 February 1993): 1.

Friedman, Saul. "The Rand Corporation and Our Policy Makers." *Atlantic Monthly* 212 (September 1963): 61–68.

"Fun with Margarine." *Fortune* 37 (February 1948): 124.

Girdler, Tom M. *The C.I.O. versus American Democracy*. Cleveland, Ohio: Republic Steel Corporation, 1937.

"Girdler Repeats His Biggest 'No' and Steel Union Orators Go to a Funeral." *News Week* 9 (12 June 1937): 14–15.

Golden, L. L. L. "Survival Lessons." *Saturday Review* 52 (9 August 1969): 49.

Goodell, Jeffrey. "What Hill & Knowlton Can Do for You (And What It Couldn't Do for Itself." *New York Times Magazine* (9 September 1990): 44+.

Goss, Bert C. "How to Reduce Business' Credibility Gap: Government Industry Relations." *Vital Speeches of the Day* 32 (24 March 1966): 396–98.

Grace, Eugene E. "Industry and the Public." *Vital Speeches of the Day* 2 (1 August 1936): 678–82.

Grafton, Samuel. "Propaganda from the Right." *American Mercury* 34 (March 1935): 257–66.

Gridley, Don. "Weaknesses of Strike Copy." *Printers' Ink* 178 (11 March 1937): 86–89.

"H&K Defends Credibility after Baby Story Exposé." *O'Dwyer's PR Services Report* 6 (February 1992): 1+.

"H&K Leads PR Charge in Behalf of Kuwait Cause." *O'Dwyer's PR Services Report* 5 (January 1991): 1+.

Hammond, Mary K. "The Steel Strike of 1952." *Current History* 23 (November 1952): 285–90.

"Harvard Medic Says TIRC Has Ignored Cancer Evidence." *Advertising Age* 28 (14 October 1957): 20.

Heilbroner, Robert L. "Public Relations: The Invisible Sell." *Harper's* 214 (June 1957): 23–31.

Hill, John W. "Can We Afford Ignorance?" *Editor and Publisher* 82 (26 February 1949): 19+.

———. "Challenge to Industry Is to Communicate with People." *Editor and Publisher* 85 (16 February 1952): 25.

———. "Corporation Lawyers and Public Relations Counsel." *Business Lawyer* 14 (April 1959): 587–608.

———. "Corporations—The Sitting Ducks." *Public Relations Quarterly* 22 (Summer 1977): 8–10.

———. "Education for a Public Relations Career." *Public Relations Journal* 14 (August 1958): 14–15+.

———. "The Future of Corporate Public Relations." *Public Relations Journal* 21 (September 1965): 10–13.

———. "I Predict: A Severe Test for Public Relations during 1958." *Printers' Ink* 261 (27 December 1957): 62–63.

———. "Industry's Iron Curtain." *Public Relations Journal* 2 (November 1946): 3–9.

———. "International Public Relations—Hope and Reality." *Public Relations Journal* 13 (December 1957): 11–14.

———. "The Making of a Public Relations Counselor." *Public Relations Journal* 20 (June 1964): 22–25.

———. "Public Relations and the Trade Association." *American Trade Association Executives Journal* 7 (October 1955): 43–49.

———. "Public Relations Development in Europe." *PR* 3 (April 1958): 16.

———. "What We Learned from the Steel Negotiations." *Public Relations Journal* 16 (August 1960): 6–10.

———. "Where Company Public Relations Must Do Its Basic Job: In the Home Community." *Printers' Ink* 262 (3 January 1958): 57–58.

Hill, John W., and Albert L. Ayars. "More Money for Our Colleges—And Where It's Coming From." *Saturday Review* 38 (30 July 1955): 7–10+.

Hill, John W., and J. E. Payne. "Scientists Can Talk to the Layman." *Science* 117 (17 April 1953): 403–5.

Hill and Knowlton, Inc. *Public Relations Speeches by Executives of Hill and Knowlton, Inc.*, n.d. [1964?].

"Hill & Knowlton to Join Four European Concerns." *New York Times* (13 July 1954): 40.

Hilts, Philip J. "Tobacco Chiefs Say Cigarettes Aren't Addictive." *New York Times* (15 April 1994): A1.

"Hour of Decision Has Arrived, The." *Hoard's Dairyman* 94 (25 March 1949): 262.

"How Potent Is the Legion?" *Aviation Week* 47 (14 July 1947): 7.

"In a Rabbit's Eye." *Time* 59 (18 February 1952): 96−97.

"Industrial War, The." *Fortune* (16 November 1937): 166−68.

"Industry's Public Relations Job." *Conference Board Business Record* 2 (March 1945): 75−79.

"Iron & Steel Program." *Tide* 22 (16 July 1948): 50.

Irwin, James W. "Tell the Public Why America's Future Depends upon Free Enterprise!" *Printers' Ink* 204 (17 September 1943): 17−18+.

Jackson, Merrick. "East of Suez." *Public Relations Journal* 10 (August 1954): 3−5.

Johnston, Eric A. "Free Enterprise Now Faces Crisis and Opportunity." *Printers' Ink* 207 (14 April 1944): 19−20+.

"Just as Good." *New Yorker* 26 (18 March 1950): 23−24.

Kaplan, Morris. "Full Cancer Data on Tobacco Urged." *New York Times* (23 June 1954): 4.

Krauss, Clifford. "Congressman Says Girl Was Credible." *New York Times* (12 January 1992): A11.

"Labor Relations and Public Relations." *Conference Board Management Record* 11 (July 1949): 304−5.

"Latest on Oleo." *Hoard's Dairyman* 93 (25 April 1948): 350.

Lazarsfeld, Paul F. "Who Influences Whom—It's the Same for Politics and Advertising." *Printers' Ink* 211 (8 June 1945): 32+.

Lee, Gary. "Kuwait's Campaign on the PR Front." *Washington Post* (29 November 1992): A1.

———. "Image Conscious: Howard Paster Brings a Low-Key Approach to Hill and Knowlton." *Washington Post* (5 October 1992): E1.

———. "PR Firm Loses Bid to Curb Ex-Employees." *Washington Post* (25 September 1992): F1.

Lee, Ivy. "The Problem of International Propaganda." Address to a private group, London, 3 July 1934.

Lee, John C. "Public Relations in the Aircraft Industry." *Public Relations Journal* 2 (May 1946): 9−11.

Leviero, Anthony. "Truman Asks Millions Jobs, Extension of Rent Curbs, More Buying Power for '49." *New York Times* (8 January 1949): 1.

Levin, Gary. "Global PR Efforts on the Wane." *Advertising Age* 65 (16 May 1994): 28.

"Licensed Beverage Industries: Girding for a Big PR Battle." *Tide* 28 (30 January 1954): 39−40.

"Lifting of Margarine Tax Fails to Cut Butter Sales So Far." *Tide* 25 (16 March 1951): 11−12+.

Lindow, A. H. "Creamery Operation Is a Profession." *National Butter and Cheese Journal* 39 (December 1948): 38−39.

Link, Henry C. "How to Sell America to Americans." *Public Relations Journal* 3 (July 1947): 3−7+.

Lipman, Joanne. "Hill and Knowlton Adds Lobbyist Wexler." *Wall Street Journal* (3 August 1990): B8.

———. "Hill & Knowlton Drops Dilenschneider." *Wall Street Journal* (27 September 1991): B4.

———. "Hill & Knowlton's PR Tactics Face New, Intensified Criticism." *Wall Street Journal* (7 January 1992): B4.

"Lung Cancer Views Aired." *Raleigh News and Observer* (10 December 1953): 1.

MacArthur, John R. "Remember Nayirah, Witness for Kuwait?" *New York Times* (6 January 1992): A11.

McCartin, Tom, Ken Carter, Lydia Paredes Turner, and Atala Brandao. "Hill and Knowlton, Dallas Sets Precedent, Brings African American, Hispanic Firms under One Roof." *Business Wire* (20 March 1991): 1.

McCauley, Kevin. "H&K Keeps Pro-Life Account Despite Heavy Opposition." *O'Dwyer's PR Service Report* 4 (June 1990): 31+.

McIntyre, Robert B. "European Press Many Things to H&K Executives." *Editor and Publisher* 96 (23 March 1963): 20+.

"Management Looks at Public Relations." *Conference Board Business Record* 10 (December 1953): 450–53.

Mapes, John G. "Computers in Public Relations Practice." *Public Relations Quarterly* 12 (Spring 1967): 28.

"Margarine Loses Again." *Newsweek* 31 (29 March 1948): 62.

"Margarine Survey." *Tide* 22 (30 July 1948): 41.

"Margarine Tax Fight, The." *Milwaukee Journal* (9 March 1948): 14.

"Margarine Taxes." *Business Week* (2 February 1946): 43–44.

"Margarine vs. Butter, A Good Fight to Get In On." *Life* 24 (8 March 1948): 32.

"Massacre of the Innocents?" *Nation* (4 February 1991): 114.

Men Who Make Steel, The. New York: American Iron and Steel Institute, May 1936.

Miller, Judith. "Sheik of Few Words Gets Message Across." *New York Times* (1 October 1990): A8.

"More on the Margarine Fight." *American Butter and Cheese Review* 11 (January 1949): 4.

"More on Oleo-Butter." *American Butter and Cheese Review* 10 (December 1948): 4–5.

"More on Public Relations." *American Milk Review* 11 (April 1949): 32–33+.

Morris, John D. "House Votes to Repeal Oleo Taxes, 260 to 106, after Stormy Session." *New York Times* (29 April 1948): 1.

Moskowitz, Milton. "Industrials and Ad Agencies Find Export Field in Ferment." *Industrial Marketing* 43 (December 1958): 49–50.

"Most Admen Are Changing Their Smoking Habits—Or Quitting." *Tide* 28 (27 February 1954): 17–18.

Mundy, Alicia. "Is the Press Any Match for Powerhouse P.R.?" *Columbia Journalism Review* 31 (September–October 1992): 27–34.

"New Attacks Hit Cigarets as Industry PR Gets Underway." *Tide* 28 (3 July 1954): 27.

Newsom, Doug. "PR Practitioners Question Client Choice and Representation." *PR Update* (March 1992): 4.

"1991 Public Relations Agency Report Card, The." *Inside PR* 11 (July 1991): 19–26.

"1992 Chicago-Area Fee Income." *O'Dwyer's PR Service Report* 8 (May 1993): 40.

"1992 DC-Area Fee Income." *O'Dwyer's PR Service Report* 8 (May 1993): 36.

"1992 Fee Income of PR Firms according to Areas of Specialization." *O'Dwyer's PR Service Report* 8 (May 1993): 48.

"1992 PR Fee Income of 50 Firms Supplying Documentation to O'Dwyer's PR Service Report Directory of PR Firms." *O'Dwyer's PR Service Report* 8 (May 1993): 18.

"No Margarine Compromise." *New York Times* (8 March 1949): 24.

"No Shortage Here." *CIO News* 15 (18 February 1952): 3.

"'Nobody Wins a Strike,'" *Printers' Ink* 171 (30 May 1935): 92.

Norr, Roy. "Cancer by the Carton." *Reader's Digest* 61 (December 1952): 7–9.

Ochsner, Alton. "The Case against Smoking." *Nation* (23 May 1953): 432.

O'Dwyer, Jack. "H&K Has History of Turmoil in Top Executive Changes." *O'Dwyer's PR Service Report* 5 (November 1991): 1+.

"Oleo Lobby Has Launched Another Bitter Attack." *Hoard's Dairyman* 93 (25 February 1948): 143.

"Oleo Tax Repealer Dies." *American Butter Review* 10 (July 1948): 2.

Parker-Pope, Tara. "Hill & Knowlton Polishes Its Own Image." *Wall Street Journal* (19 February 1997): B1+.

"Personal Chemistry Clicked, The." *Fortune* 101 (10 March 1980): 15–16.

"PR Comics." *Tide* 21 (5 December 1947): 58.

"PR Firm to Push Kuwaitis' Message." *USA Today* (28 August 1990): 2B.

"PR Men Give Pro & Cons on Steel Case." *Tide* 26 (9 May 1952): 42–43.

"PR Operations Associated with Ad Agencies Documenting Fees." *O'Dwyer's Directory of Public Relations Firms* (1996): A13.

"PR Problem at Hill and Knowlton, The." *Business Week* (2 September 1991): 50.

Price, Joyce. "Free Kuwait Group Ends PR Contract." *Washington Times* (15 February 1991): A4.

"Price of Cigarettes, The." *Commonweal* 60 (9 July 1954): 333.

Priest, Dana. "Kuwait Baby-Killing Report Disputed." *Washington Post* (7 February 1992): A7.

"Public Relations: A Communication System Ripens." *Printer's Ink* 273 (25 November 1960): 66–68.

"Public Relations: Its Uses for Industry." *Time* 63 (10 May 1954): 100.

"Quizzing Randall." *U.S. News and World Report* 32 (9 May 1952): 98–99.

Ramsey, D. C. "Aircraft Industries Association." *Air Affairs* 3 (Autumn 1949): 160–77.

Randall, Clarence B. "Free Enterprise Is Not a Hunting License." *Atlantic Monthly* 189 (March 1952): 38–41.

———. "Steel: The World's Guinea Pig." *Atlantic Monthly* 190 (December 1952): 31–34.

Random, Mark. "Agencies Move to Be in on Ground Floor of European Common Market." *Advertising Age* 30 (27 April 1959): 43+.

"Report Links Smoking to Lung Tissue Change: Tie to Cancer Seen." *Wall Street Journal* (Midwest edition) (3 June 1955): 8.

"Report to Board on Public Opinion Shows Problems Faced by Industry." *NAM News* 17 (15 October 1949): 8–10.

"Republic Steel." *Fortune* 12 (December 1935): 76–83+.

Rigg, Cynthia. "PR Agency Caught in Turmoil at JWT." *Crains New York Business* 3 (2 February 1987): 1.

Riis, Roger William. "How Harmful Are Cigarettes?" *Reader's Digest* 56 (January 1950): 1–11.

"Rise of 54% in Manufacturing Products." *Labor Research Association Economic Notes* 16 (May 1948): 5.

Rowse, Arthur E. "Flacking for the Emir." *Progressive* 55 (May 1991): 20–22.

———. "How to Build Support for War." *Columbia Journalism Review* 31 (September–October 1992): 28–29.

Rudge, Fred. "Two-Way Communications during Negotiations and Strikes." *Public Relations Journal* 6 (January 1950): 12–13+.

"Seizure Order, The." *New York Times* (10 April 1952): 28.

Sellers, Patricia. "Do You Need Your Ad Agency?" *Fortune* 128 (15 November 1993): 147–48+.

"Shall We Have Airplanes?" *Fortune* 37 (January 1947): 77–81+.

Shelton, Willard. "Fair Offer on Steel." *Nation* 174 (29 March 1952): 293–94.

———. "Steelworkers Will Fight." *Nation* 174 (24 May 1952): 501.

"Shift at Top of P.R. Firm." *New York Times* (24 October 1992): D3.

Skolnik, Rayna. "The Emerging Firm of the '90s." *Public Relations Journal* 49 (March 1993): 20–25.

Smith, R. C. "The Magazines' Smoking Habit." *Columbia Journalism Review* 16 (January–February 1978): 29–31.

"Smoke Gets in the News." *Life* 35 (21 December 1953): 20–21.

"Smoke Screen." *Time* 55 (17 April 1950): 102.

"Smokers' Death Survey Called 'Preliminary' by Tobacco Group." *St. Louis Post-Dispatch* (22 June 1954): 4.

"Smoking and Health." *Science* (7 June 1957): 1129–33.

"Smoking and Mortality." *Scientific American* 191 (August 1954): 37–38.

"Smoking Mice Live Normal Span." *U.S. News and World Report* 28 (3 February 1950): 22–23.

"Smoking Tobacco." *Journal of the American Medical Association* 143 (17 June 1950): 696.

Sokolsky, George E. "The CIO Turns a Page." *Atlantic Monthly* 160 (September 1937): 309–17.

———. "Creeds and Faiths." *New York Herald Tribune* (20 December 1937): 14.

———. "Giants in These Days." *Atlantic Monthly* 157 (June 1936): 691–700.

"Sokolsky Makes Reply." *New York Times* (22 July 1938): 12.

"Steel." *Commonweal* 26 (July 9, 1937): 284–85.

"Steel and the Press." *New Republic* 126 (5 May 1952): 5–6.

"Steel Output Drops to 12½% in Strike." *Steel Facts* (June 1952): 1–2.

"Steel Panel Is Revival of Discredited Procedure." *NAM News* 17 (23 July 1949): 14.

"Steel PR Men Bombard the Press and Public." *Tide* 26 (2 May 1952): 37.

"Steel Profits: How High?" *U.S. News and World Report* 32 (11 April 1952): 22–23.

"Steel Seizure Presents Congress with Its Greatest Issue of the Year." *Congressional Digest* 31 (May 1952): 129–30.

"Steel Takes Its Case to the Public." *Tide* 26 (25 April 1952): 30.

"Steel: What Next, Mr. President?" *New Republic* 126 (21 April 1952): 3.

"Strike Copy in Seattle." *Printers' Ink* 171 (16 May 1935): 80.

Strong, Morgan. "Portions of the Gulf War Were Brought to You By. . . ." *TV Guide* (22 February 1992): 11–13.

Strum, Charles. "Judge Cites Possible Fraud in Tobacco Research." *New York Times* (8 February 1992): 1+.

Sweeney, Vincent D. *The United Steelworkers of America: Twenty Years Later, 1936–1956* United Steel Workers of America, 1956.

"T-H Can't Be Rejiggered; It Must Be Repealed." *CIO News* 15 (21 April 1952): 7.

"Tax Gouge." *Wisconsin Food Dealer* 41 (January 1950): 8.

"Texas Co. Retains Hill & Knowlton." *Tide* 26 (5 September 1952): 36.

Thompson, Robert E. S. "C.I.O. Expanding on Two Big Fronts." *New York Times* (27 June 1937): E7.

Thorn, J. Dale. "Tobacco Wars: Public Relations on Trial." *Strategist* 3 (December 1997): 28–32.

"Tide Leadership Panel: A Few Significant Facts about the Smoking Habits of Advertising Executives." *Tide* 31 (22 March 1957): 31.

"Tilting at Windmills." *Washington Monthly* 24 (March 1992): 8.

"Tobacco Group Urges Further Cancer Study." *Chicago Daily Tribune* (23 June 1954): 9.

"Tobacco Smoking and Longevity." *Science* 87 (4 March 1938): 216–17.

"Tobacco's Smoking Gun?" *Harper's* 276 (June 1988): 25–26.

"Too Much Flak Downs a Flack." *Time* 38 (7 October 1991): 42.

"Truman and Steel." *Life* 32 (21 April 1952): 32.

"Two Air Policy Boards." *Aviation Week* 47 (July 28, 1947): 50.

"Two New PR Firms." *Tide* 24 (22 September 1950): 58–59.

"Unilever I: The Heritage." *Fortune* 36 (December 1947): 88–92+.

"Unilever III—The Conversion" *Fortune* 37 (February 1948): 74–81+.

"Unilever's Africa." *Fortune* 37 (January 1948): 57–65+.

"Up Butter and at 'Em." *American Milk Review* 12 (January 1950): 22.

"U.S. Corporate Management." *Fortune* 7 (June 1933): 47–51+.

"U.S. Oleo Tax Nearer Repeal." *Milwaukee Journal* (8 March 1950): 4.

"U.S. Produces More Oleo than Butter." *Farm Journal* 72 (June 1948): 46.

"U.S. Steel Corporation, The: II." *Fortune* 13 (April 1936): 126–36.

"U.S. Treasury Urges Repeal of Federal Margarine Taxes." *Milwaukee Journal* (8 March 1948): 1.

Vine, Vernon. "It's a Showdown—Butter vs. Oleo." *Farm Journal* 72 (May 1948): 43–45.

"VNR Top Ten, The." *Columbia Journalism Review* 29 (March–April 1991): 14.

Vorse, Mary Heaton. "Big Steel and the Little Man." *Nation* 174 (21 June 1952): 603–5.

"Washington Outlook." *Business Week* (26 July 1948): 6.

Weaver, Warren Jr. "Health Chief Asks Lung Cancer Study." *New York Times* (3 June 1953): 37.

Wells, Ken. "Remain Silent and Die." *Public Relations Journal* 4 (October 1948): 9–12.

"What Socialized Steel Means." *U.S. News and World Report* 30 (29 September 1950): 24–25.

"When a PR Firm Could Use a PR Firm." *Business Week* (14 May 1990): 44.

"Where Do We Go From Here?" *Hoard's Dairyman* 95 (25 February 1950): 142.

Whitmore, Eugene. "Public Relations—A Two-Way Street." *American Business* (May 1946): 20–1+.

"'Who Can Win?'" *Printers' Ink* 171 (30 May 1935): 16.

"Wildest Blue Yonder Yet, The." *Fortune* 38 (March 1948): 94–99+.

"Will Strikes Bring Socialism?" *U.S. News and World Report* 32 (18 April 1952): 15–17.

Wilson, Eugene E. "The Moral Edge." *Air Affairs* 3 (Winter 1950): 541–47.

Wise, T. A. "Hill and Knowlton's World of Images." *Fortune* 76 (1 September 1967): 98–101+.

"Wooing the Eggheads for Alcoa." *Business Week* (19 December 1953): 115–18.

Wootten, Harry M. "Cigarette Sales 2% under 1952." *Printers' Ink* 246 (15 January 1954): 34–37+.

"Word from the Tobacco Companies." *Advertising Age* 24 (7 December 1953): 12.

"WPP/Lilly Suit Settled." *Wall Street Journal* (6 July 1994): B5.

"Yellow Belongs to Butter." *Hoard's Dairyman* 94 (25 February 1949): 142.

"Your Letters Will Decide Yellow Oleo Issue." *Hoard's Dairyman* 94 (10 April 1949): 304.

Journal Articles and Book Chapters

Arkin, Aaron, and David H. Wagner. "Primary Carcinoma of the Lung." *Journal of the American Medical Association* 106 (22 February 1936): 587–91.

Auerbach, Jerold S. "The La Follette Committee: Labor and Civil Liberties in the New Deal." *Journal of American History* 51 (December 1964): 435–59.

Ball, George W. "The Relations of the Multinational Corporation to the 'Host' State." In *Global Companies: The Political Economy of World Business*, edited by George W. Ball, 64–69. Englewood Cliffs, N.J.: Prentice-Hall, 1975.

Ball, Richard A., and J. Robert Lilly, "The Menace of Margarine: The Rise and Fall of a Social Problem." *Social Problems* 29 (June 1982): 488–98.

Baughman, James L. "Classes and Company Towns: Legends of the 1937 Little Steel Strike." *Ohio History* 87 (Spring 1978): 175–92.

———. "*See It Now* and Television's Golden Age, 1951–58." *Journal of Popular Culture* 15 (Fall 1981): 106–15.

Bernays, Edward L. "Emergence of the Public Relations Counsel: Principles and Recollections." *Business History Review* 45 (Autumn 1971): 296–316.

Bernstein, Irving. "Economic Impact of Strikes in Key Industries." In *Emergency Disputes and National Policy*, edited by Irving Bernstein, Harold L. Enarson, and R. W. Fleming, 24–45. New York: Harper and Brothers, 1955.

Bernstein, Marvin H. "Political Ideas of Selected American Business Journals." *Public Opinion Quarterly* 17 (Summer 1953): 258–67.

Blumenthal, Frank H. "Anti-Union Publicity in the Johnstown 'Little Steel' Strike of 1937." *Public Opinion Quarterly* 3 (October 1939): 676–82.

Boddewyn, J., and Ashok Kapoor. "The External Relations of American Multinational Enterprises." *International Studies Quarterly* 16 (December 1972): 433–53.

Botan, Carl. "International Public Relations: Critique and Reformulation." *Public Relations Review* 18 (Summer 1992): 149–59.

Boyer, William W. "Policy Making by Government Agencies." *Midwest Journal of Political Science* 4 (November 1960): 267–88.

Broders, A. C. "Squamous-Cell Epithelioma of the Lip." *Journal of the American Medical Association* 74 (6 March 1920): 656–64.

Burger, Chester. "Credibility: When Public Relations Works." In *Perspectives in Public Relations*, edited by Raymond Simon, 306–12. Norman: University of Oklahoma Press, 1966.

Calfee, John. "Cigarette Advertising Regulation Today: Unintended Consequences and Missed Opportunities?" *Consumer Research Annual* (1986): 264–68.

"Cigaret Habit." *Journal of the American Medical Association* 138 (25 December 1948): 1287.

"Cigaret Habit." *Journal of the American Medical Association* 138 (27 November 1948): 1008.

Cutlip, Scott M. "The Tobacco Wars: A Matter of Public Relations Ethics." *Journal of Corporate Public Relations* 3 (1992–93): 26–31.

Davison, W. Phillips. "The Third-Person Effect in Communication." *Public Opinion Quarterly* 47 (Spring 1983): 1–15.

Dexter, Lewis Anthony. "What Do Congressmen Hear: The Mail." *Public Opinion Quarterly* 20 (Spring 1956): 16–27.

DiBacco, Thomas V. "Draft the Strikers (1946) and Seize the Mills (1952): The Business Reaction." *Duquesne Review* 13 (Fall 1968): 63–75.

Dilenschneider, Robert L. "'We Don't Do Coups.'" *Gannett Center Journal* (Spring 1990): 35–46.

Dinerman, Helen. "Image Problems for American Companies Abroad." In *The Corporation and Its Publics: Essays on the Corporate Image*, edited by John W. Riley Jr., 137–58. New York: John Wiley and Sons, 1963.

Doll, Richard, and A. Bradford Hill. "A Study of the Aetiology of Carcinoma of the Lung." *British Medical Journal* (1952): 1271–86.

———. "Smoking and Carcinoma of the Lung." *British Medical Journal* (1950): 739–48.

Enarson, Harold L. "The Politics of an Emergency Dispute: Steel, 1952." In *Emergency Disputes and National Policy*, edited by Irving Bernstein, Harold L. Enarson, and R. W. Fleming, 46–74. New York: Harper and Brothers, 1955.

Fones-Wolf, Elizabeth. "Industrial Recreation, the Second World War, and the Revival of Welfare Capitalism, 1934–1960." *Business History Review* 60 (Summer 1986): 232–57.

Freeman, Joshua. "Delivering the Goods: Industrial Unionism during World War II." *Labor History* 19 (Fall 1978): 570–93.

Friedell, H. L., and L. M. Rosenthal. "The Etiologic Role of Chewing Tobacco in Cancer of the Mouth." *Journal of the American Medical Association* 116 (10 May 1941): 2130–35.

Grace, Edwin J. "Tobacco Smoking and Cancer of the Lung." *American Journal of Surgery* 60 (June 1943): 361–64.

Goss, Bert C. "Witness for the Prosecution." *Journal of the American Pharmaceutical Association*, n.s., 3 (August 1963): 412–13+.

Gras, N. S. B. "Shifts in Public Relations." *Bulletin of the Business Historical Society* 19 (October 1945).

Green, William. "The Taft-Hartley Act: A Critical View." *Annals of the American Academy of Political and Social Science* 274 (March 1951): 200–205.

Griffith, Robert. "Old Progressives and the Cold War." *Journal of American History* 66 (September 1979): 334–47.

———. "The Selling of America: The Advertising Council and American Politics, 1942–1960." *Business History Review* 57 (Autumn 1983): 388–412.

Hammond, E. Cuyler, and Daniel Horn. "The Relationship between Human Smoking Habits and Death Rates: A Follow-Up Study of 187,766 Men." *Journal of the American Medical Association* 155 (7 August 1954): 1316–28.

Harbison, Frederick H., and Robert C. Spencer. "The Politics of Collective Bargaining: The Postwar Record in Steel." *American Political Science Review* 48 (September 1954): 705–20.

Harrison, Larry. "Tobacco Battered and Pipes Shattered: A Note on the Fate of the First British Campaign against Tobacco Smoking." *British Journal of Addiction* 81 (1986): 553–58.

Hazelton, Vincent, and Dean Kruckeberg. "European Public Relations Practice: An Evolving Paradigm." In *International Public Relations: A Comparative Analysis*, edited by Hugh M. Culbertson and Ni Chen, 367–77. Mahwah, N.J.: Lawrence Erlbaum, 1996.

Hilgartner, Stephen, and Charles L. Bosk. "The Rise and Fall of Social Problems: A Public Arenas Model." *American Journal of Sociology* 94 (July 1988): 53–78.

Irons, Peter H. "American Business and the Origins of McCarthyism: The Cold War Crusade of the United States Chamber of Commerce." In *The Specter: Original*

Essays on the Cold War and the Origins of McCarthyism, edited by Robert Griffith and Athan Theoharis, 72–89. New York: New Viewpoints, 1974.

Irwin, James W. "Winning Better Relations with the Community." In *Your Public Relations*, edited by Glenn Griswold and Denny Griswold, 170–92. New York: Funk and Wagnalls, 1948.

Jacobson, Bobbie, and Amanda Amos. "When Smoke Gets in Your Eyes: Cigarette Advertising Policy and Coverage of Smoking and Health in Women's Magazines." In *Smoking Out the Barons: The Campaign against the Tobacco Industry*, edited by the British Medical Association, Public Affairs Division, 99–137. New York: John Wiley and Sons, 1986.

Janis, Irving L., and Seymour Feshbach. "Effects of Fear-Arousing Communications." *Journal of Abnormal and Social Psychology* 48 (1953): 78–92.

Klaidman, Stephen. "Blowing Smoke." Woodrow Wilson International Center for Scholars Media Studies Project, 1989 Essay Contest Winner.

Kornhauser, Arthur. "Are Public Opinion Polls Fair to Organized Labor?" *Public Opinion Quarterly* 10 (Winter 1946–47): 484–500.

Lombard, Herbert L., and Carl R. Doering. "Cancer Studies in Massachusetts: Habits, Characteristics and Environment of Individuals with and without Cancer." *New England Journal of Medicine* 198 (26 April 1928): 481–87.

McCombs, Maxwell, and Donald Shaw, "The Agenda-Setting Function of Mass Media." *Public Opinion Quarterly* 36 (Summer 1972): 176–87.

McLeod, Jack, Zhongdang Pan, and Dianne Rucinski. "Levels of Analysis in Public Opinion Research." In *Public Opinion and the Communication of Consent*, edited by Theodore L. Glasser and Charles T. Salmon, 55–85. New York: Guilford, 1995.

Marchand, Roland. "The Fitful Career of Advocacy Advertising: Political, Protection, Client Cultivation, and Corporate Morale." *California Management Review* 29 (Winter 1987): 128–56.

―――. "The Inward Thrust of Institutional Advertising: General Electric and General Motors in the 1920s." *Business and Economic History* 18 (1989): 188–96.

Miller, Karen. "National and Local Public Relations Campaigns during the 1946 Steel Strike." *Public Relations Review* 21 (Winter 1995): 305–23.

―――. "Smoking Up a Storm: Public Relations and Advertising in the Construction of the Cigarette Problem, 1953–1954." *Journalism Monographs* 136 (December 1992).

Mingos, Howard. "Birth of an Industry." In *The History of the American Aircraft Industry*, edited by G. R. Simonson, 25–69. Cambridge, Mass.: MIT Press, 1968.

"Mortality of Doctors in Relation to Their Smoking Habits, The." *Journal of the American Medical Association* 156 (25 September 1954): 449–50.

Mrozek, Donald J. "The Truman Administration and the Enlistment of the Aviation Industry in Postwar Defense." *Business History Review* 48 (Spring 1974): 73–94.

Ochsner, Alton, Paul T. DeCamp, M. E. DeBakey, and C. J. Ray. "Bronchogenic Carcinoma: Its Frequency, Diagnosis and Early Treatment." *Journal of the American Medical Association* 148 (1 March 1952): 691–97.

Pabst, W. R., Jr. *Butter and Oleomargarine: An Analysis of Competing Commodities*. Studies in History, Economics and Public Law No. 427 (New York: Columbia University, 1937).

Phelps, Orme W., and John E. Jeuck. "Criticisms of the National Labor Relations Act." *Journal of Business* 12 (January 1939): 30–50.

Pollay, Richard W. "Propaganda, Puffing and the Public Interest." *Public Relations Review* 16 (Fall 1990): 39–54.

Pool, Ithiael de Sola, Suzanne Keller, and Raymond A. Bauer. "The Influence of Foreign Travel on Political Attitudes of American Businessmen." *Public Opinion Quarterly* 20 (Spring 1956): 161–75.

Pratt, Cornelius B. "Hill and Knowlton's Two Ethical Dilemmas." *Public Relations Review* 20 (Fall 1994): 277–94.

Prechel, Harland. "Steel and the State: Industry, Politics and Business Policy Formation, 1940–1989." *American Sociological Review* 55 (October 1990): 648–68.

Price, Vincent. "On the Public Aspects of Opinion: Linking Levels of Analysis in Public Opinion Research." *Communication Research* 15 (December 1988): 659–79.

Reed, John M., and Sarah Hardy. "Pioneering International Public Relations: The Story of Barnet & Reef Associates." *International Public Relations Review* 14 (1991): 12–15.

Roschwalb, Susanne A. "The Hill and Knowlton Cases: A Brief in Controversy." *Public Relations Review* 20 (Fall 1994): 267–76.

Rossiter, Clinton L. "The President and Labor Disputes." *Journal of Politics* 11 (February 1949): 93–120.

Schilling, Warner R. "The Politics of National Defense: Fiscal 1950." In *Strategy, Politics and Defense Budgets*, edited by Walter R. Schilling, Paul Y. Hammond, and Glenn H. Snyder, 30–105. New York: Columbia University Press, 1962.

"Smoking Tobacco." *Journal of the American Medical Association* 143 (17 June 1950): 696.

Snegireff, Leonid S., and Olive M. Lombard. "Survey of Smoking Habits of Massachusetts Physicians." *New England Journal of Medicine* 250 (June 1954): 1042–45.

Sofchalk, Donald G. "The Chicago Memorial Day Incident: An Episode of Mass Action." *Labor History* 6 (Winter 1965): 3–43.

Stebbins, Phillip E. "Truman and the Seizure of Steel: A Failure in Communication." *Historian* 34 (November 1971): 1–21.

Stratton, Samuel S. "Public Relations in Steel." *Public Opinion Quarterly* 1 (April 1937): 107–11.

Suchman, Edward, Rose K. Goldsen, and Robin M. Williams Jr. "Attitudes toward the Korean War." *Public Opinion Quarterly* 17 (Summer 1953): 171–84.

Taft, Robert A. "The Taft-Hartley Act: A Favorable View." *Annals of the American Academy of Political and Social Science* 274 (March 1951): 195–99.

"Tobacco Industry Research Committee." *Journal of the American Medical Association* 155 (24 July 1954): 1175.

Tousley, Rayburn D. "Marketing." In *Margarine: An Economic, Social and Scientific History, 1869–1969*, edited by J. H. van Stuyvenberg, 227–79. Liverpool: Liverpool University Press, 1969.

Velmans, Loet. Foreword to the thirtieth anniversary edition of *The Making of a Public Relations Man* by John W. Hill. New York: Passport Books, 1993.

Vogel, David. "Why Businessmen Distrust Their State: The Political Consciousness of American Corporate Executives." *British Journal of Political Science* 8 (January 1978): 45–78.

Weis, William L., and Chauncey Burke. "Media Content and Tobacco Advertising: An Unhealthy Addiction." *Journal of Communication* 36 (Autumn 1986): 59–69.

Wyant, Rowena. "Voting via the Senate Mailbag." *Public Opinion Quarterly* 5 (Fall 1941): 359–82.

Wynder, Ernest L., and Jerome Cornfield. "Cancer of the Lung in Physicians." *New England Journal of Medicine* 248 (12 March 1953): 441–44.

Wynder, Ernest L., and Evarts A. Graham. "Tobacco Smoking as a Possible Etiologic

Factor in Bronchiogenic Carcinoma." *Journal of the American Medical Association* 143 (27 May 1950): 329–36.

Wynder, Ernest L., Evarts A. Graham, and Adele B. Croninger. "Experimental Production of Carcinoma with Cigarette Tar." *Cancer Research* 13 (December 1953): 855–64.

Books

Abromeit, Heidrun. *British Steel: An Industry between the State and the Private Sector.* Warwickshire: Berg Publishers, 1986.

Aircraft Industries Association of America. *Aircraft Year Book for 1948.* Washington, D.C.: Aircraft Industries Association of America, 1948.

———. *Aircraft Year Book for 1949.* Washington, D.C.: Lincoln Press, 1949.

Ambrose, Stephen E. *The President.* Vol. 2 of *Eisenhower.* New York: Simon and Schuster, 1984.

American Iron and Steel Institute. *AISI Yearbook: 1948.* New York: J. C. Dillon, 1949.

———. *Steel's Competitive Challenge.* New York: AISI, 1961.

American Tobacco Company. *"Sold American!" The First Fifty Years, 1904–1954.* N.p.: American Tobacco Company, 1954.

Bailey, Stephen K., and Howard D. Samuel. *Congress at Work.* New York: Henry Holt, 1952.

Banks, Stephen P. *Multicultural Public Relations: A Social-Interpretive Approach.* Thousand Oaks, Calif.: Sage, 1995.

Baughman, James L. *The Republic of Mass Culture: Journalism, Filmmaking, and Broadcasting in America since 1941.* Baltimore: Johns Hopkins University Press, 1992.

Bayley, Edwin R. *Joe McCarthy and the Press.* New York: Pantheon Books, 1981.

Behrman, Jack. *U.S. International Business and Governments.* New York: McGraw-Hill, 1971.

Bernays, Edward L. *Biography of an Idea: Memoirs of Public Relations Counsel Edward L. Bernays.* New York: Simon and Schuster, 1965.

———. *Public Relations.* Norman: University of Oklahoma Press, 1952.

Bernstein, Irving. *Turbulent Years: A History of the American Worker, 1933–1941.* Boston: Houghton Mifflin, 1970.

Bilstein, Roger E. *Flight in America, 1900–1983: From the Wrights to the Astronauts.* Baltimore: Johns Hopkins University Press, 1984.

Blackman, John L., Jr. *Presidential Seizure in Labor Disputes.* Cambridge, Mass.: Harvard University Press, 1967.

Bluestone, Barry, Peter Jordan, and Mark Sullivan. *Aircraft Industry Dynamics: An Analysis of Competition, Capital, and Labor.* Boston: Auburn House, 1981.

Borowski, Harry R. *A Hollow Threat: Strategic Air Power and Containment before Korea.* Westport, Conn.: Greenwood Press, 1982.

Bottoms, Bill. *The VFW: An Illustrated History of the Veterans of Foreign Wars of the United States.* Rockville, Md.: Woodbine House, 1991.

Brannen, Ted R., and Frank X. Hodgson. *Overseas Management.* New York: McGraw-Hill, 1965.

Brecher, Ruth, Edward Brecher, Arthur Herzog, Walter Goodman, Gerald Walker, and the Editors of Consumer Reports. *The Consumers Union Report on Smoking and the Public Interest.* Mount Vernon, N.Y.: Consumers Union, 1963.

Bristol, Lee H., Jr., ed. *Developing the Corporate Image: A Management Guide to Public Relations*. New York: Charles Scribner's Sons, 1960.

Brody, David. *Labor in Crisis: The Steel Strike of 1919*. Philadelphia: J. B. Lippincott, 1965.

———. *Steelworkers in America: The Nonunion Era*. Cambridge, Mass.: Harvard University Press, 1960.

Broughton, Averell. *Careers in Public Relations: The New Profession*. New York: E. P. Dutton, 1943.

Burgoyne, Arthur G. *The Homestead Strike of 1892*. Pittsburgh: University of Pittsburgh Press, 1979.

Burnham, John C. *How Superstition Won and Science Lost: Popularizing Science and Health in the United States*. New Brunswick, N.J.: Rutgers University Press, 1987.

Campbell, David. *Politics without Principle: Sovereignty, Ethics, and the Narratives of the Gulf War*. Boulder, Colo.: Lynne Rienner Publishers, 1993.

Chandler, Alfred D., Jr. *The Visible Hand: The Managerial Revolution in American Business*. Cambridge, Mass.: Harvard University Press, 1977.

Chandler, Lester V. *America's Greatest Depression, 1929–1941*. New York: Harper and Row, 1970.

Cleveland, Reginald M., and Frederick P. Graham, eds. *The Aviation Annual of 1946*. Garden City, N.Y.: Doubleday, 1946.

Cohen, Bernard C. *The Press and Foreign Policy*. Princeton, N.J.: Princeton University Press, 1963.

Cohen, Lizabeth. *Making a New Deal: Industrial Workers in Chicago, 1919–1939*. New York: Cambridge University Press, 1990.

Cohn, Victor. *News and Numbers: A Guide to Reporting Statistical Claims and Controversies in Health and Other Fields*. Ames: Iowa State University Press, 1989.

Congress of Industrial Organizations. *Proceedings of the First Constitutional Convention*. Pittsburgh: Congress of Industrial Organizations, 1938.

———. *Proceedings of the 14th Constitutional Convention*. Pittsburgh: Congress of Industrial Organizations, 1952.

Cook, Blanche Wiesen. *The Declassified Eisenhower: A Divided Legacy*. Garden City, N.Y.: Doubleday, 1981.

Corn, Joseph C. *The Winged Gospel: America's Romance with Aviation, 1900–1953*. New York: Oxford University Press, 1983.

Council on Wage and Price Stability. *A Study of Steel Prices*. Washington, D.C.: Council on Wage and Price Stability, 1975.

Cutlip, Scott M. *The Unseen Power: Public Relations, a History*. Hillsdale, N.J.: Lawrence Erlbaum, 1994.

Darrow, Richard W., Dan J. Forrestal, and Aubrey O. Cookman. *Dartnell Public Relations Handbook*. Chicago: Dartnell Corporation, 1967.

Davis, Vincent. *Postwar Defense Policy and the U.S. Navy, 1943–1946*. Chapel Hill: University of North Carolina Press, 1966.

Dilenschneider, Robert L. *Power and Influence: Mastering the Art of Persuasion*. New York: Prentice-Hall, 1990.

Doenecke, Justus D. *Not to the Swift: The Old Isolationists in the Cold War Era*. Lewisburg, Pa.: Bucknell University Press, 1979.

Donaldson, Thomas. *The Ethics of International Business*. New York: Oxford University Press, 1989.

Donovan, Robert J. *Tumultuous Years: The Presidency of Harry S Truman, 1949–1953*. New York: W. W. Norton, 1982.

Elder, Charles D., and Rober W. Cobb. *The Political Uses of Symbols*. New York: Longman, 1983.

Ewen, Stuart. *PR! A Social History of Spin*. New York: Basic Books, 1996.

Farago, Peter. *Science and the Media*. New York: Oxford University Press, 1976.

Fayerweather, John. *International Business Management: A Conceptual Framework*. New York: McGraw-Hill, 1969.

Fones-Wolf, Elixabeth A. *Selling Free Enterprise: The Business Assault on Labor and Liberalism, 1945–1960*. Urbana: University of Illinois Press, 1994.

Friedman, Kenneth Michael. *Public Policy and the Smoking-Health Controversy: A Comparative Study*. Lexington, Mass.: D. C. Heath, 1975.

Fritschler, A. Lee. *Smoking and Politics: Policymaking and the Federal Bureaucracy*. New York: Appleton-Century-Crofts, 1969.

Gaddis, John Lewis. *The Long Peace: Inquiries into the History of the Cold War*. New York: Oxford University Press, 1987.

Galambos, Louis, and Joseph Pratt. *The Rise of the Corporate Commonwealth: U.S. Business and Public Policy in the Twentieth Century*. New York: Basic Books, 1988.

Galbraith, John Kenneth. *American Capitalism: The Concept of Countervailing Power*. Boston: Houghton Mifflin, 1952.

Gerstein, Dean R., and Peter K. Levinson, eds. *Reduced Tar and Nicotine Cigarettes: Smoking Behavior and Health*. Washington, D.C.: National Academy Press, 1982.

Ghertman, Michel, and Margaret Allen. *An Introduction to the Multinationals*. London: Macmillan Press for the Institute for Research and Information on Multinationals, 1984.

Gilpin, Robert. *U.S. Power and the Multinational Corporation*. New York: Basic Books, 1975.

Gitlin, Todd. *The Whole World Is Watching: Mass Media in the Making and Unmaking of the New Left*. Berkeley: University of California Press, 1980.

Glantz, Stanton A., John Slade, Lisa A. Bero, Peter Hanauer, and Deborah E. Barnes. *The Cigarette Papers*. Berkeley: University of California Press, 1996.

Goldstein, Laurence. *The Flying Machine and Modern Literature*. Bloomington: Indiana University Press, 1986.

Gordon, Colin. *New Deals: Business, Labor, and Politics in America, 1920–1935*. New York: Cambridge University Press, 1994.

Grant, Mariel. *Propaganda and the Role of the State in Inter-War Britain*. Oxford: Clarendon Press, 1994.

Green, James R. *World of the Worker: Labor in Twentieth-Century America*. New York: Hill and Wang, 1980.

Grunig, James E., and Todd Hunt. *Managing Public Relations*. New York: Holt, Rinehart and Winston, 1984.

Hamby, Alonzo L. *Beyond the New Deal: Harry S. Truman and American Liberalism*. New York: Columbia University Press, 1973.

Harlow, Rex. *Social Science in Public Relations*. New York: Harper and Brothers, 1957.

Harris, Howell John. *The Right to Manage: Industrial Relations Policies of American Business in the 1940s*. Madison: University of Wisconsin Press, 1982.

Harris, Richard. *The Real Voice*. New York: Macmillan, 1964.

Harty, Sheila. *Hucksters in the Classroom: A Review of Industry Propaganda in Schools*. Washington, D.C.: Center for Study of Responsive Law, 1979.

Heal, David W. *The Steel Industry in Post War Britain*. North Pomfret, Vt.: David and Charles, 1974.

Henderer, F. Rhodes. *Public Relations Practices in Six Industrial Corporations*. Pittsburgh: University of Pittsburgh Press, 1956.

Herken, Gregg. *The Winning Weapon: The Atomic Bomb in the Cold War, 1945–1950*. New York: Vintage Books, 1982.

Herling, John. *Right to Challenge: People and Power in the Steelworkers Union*. New York: Harper and Row, 1972.

Hill and Knowlton Executives. *Critical Issues in Public Relations*. Englewood Cliffs, N.J.: Prentice-Hall, 1975.

Hill and Knowlton, Inc. *Current Thoughts on Public Relations*. New York: M. W. Lads, 1968.

———. *Handbook on International Public Relations*. Vol. 1. New York: Frederick A. Praeger, 1967.

———. *Handbook on International Public Relations*. Vol. 2. New York: Frederick A. Praeger, 1968.

———. *The Stock Exchange, the SEC, and Your Financial Public Relations*. New York: Hill and Knowlton, 1971.

Hill, John W. *Corporate Public Relations: Arm of Modern Management*. New York: Harper and Brothers, 1958.

———. *The Making of a Public Relations Man*. New York: David McKay, 1963.

Hilts, Philip J. *Smoke Screen: The Truth behind the Tobacco Industry Cover-Up*. Reading, Mass.: Addison-Wesley, 1989.

Hinton, Harold B. *Air Victory: The Men and the Machines*. New York: Harper and Brothers, 1948.

Hoerr, John P. *And the Wolf Finally Came: The Decline of the American Steel Industry*. Pittsburgh: University of Pittsburgh Press, 1988.

Hogan, William T. *Economic History of the Iron and Steel Industry in the United States*. Lexington, Mass.: Lexington Books, 1971.

Hooks, Gregory. *Forging the Military-Industrial Complex: World War II's Battle of the Potomac*. Urbana: University of Illinois Press, 1991.

Hunziker, Otto F. *The Butter Industry*. LaGrange, Ill.: n.p., 1920.

Jones, Geoffrey. *The Evolution of International Business*. New York: Routledge, 1996.

Katz, Elihu, and Paul F. Lazarsfeld. *Personal Influence*. Glencoe, Ill.: Free Press, 1955.

Kean, Geoffrey. *The Public Relations Man Abroad*. New York: Frederick A. Praeger, 1968.

Kelley, Stanley, Jr. *Professional Public Relations and Political Power*. Baltimore: Johns Hopkins University Press, 1956.

Kelly, Fred C. *Miracle at Kitty Hawk*. New York: Farrar, Straus and Young, 1951.

Kennett, Lee. *A History of Strategic Bombing*. New York: Charles Scribner's Sons, 1982.

Kluger, Richard. *Ashes to Ashes: America's Hundred-Year Cigarette War, the Public Health, and the Unabashed Triumph of Philip Morris*. New York: Alfred A. Knopf, 1996.

Krieghbaum, Hillier. *Science and the Mass Media*. New York: New York University Press, 1967.

Krooss, Herman E. *Executive Opinion: What Business Leaders Said and Thought on Economic Issues, 1920s–1960s*. Garden City, N.Y.: Doubleday, 1970.

Lazarsfeld, Paul F., Bernard Berelson, and Hazel Gaudet. *The People's Choice*. New York: Columbia University Press, 1948.

Lee, Ben S., ed. *Aviation Facts and Figures*. Washington, D.C.: Lincoln Press, 1956.

Lee, Ivy. *Publicity: Some of the Things It Is and Is Not*. New York: Industries Publishing, 1925.

Leuchtenberg, William E. *Franklin D. Roosevelt and the New Deal, 1932–1940*. New York: Harper and Row, 1963.

Lichtenstein, Nelson. *Labor's War at Home: The CIO in World War II*. New York: Cambridge University Press, 1982.

MacArthur, John R. *Second Front: Censorship and Propaganda in the Gulf War*. New York: Hill and Wang, 1992.

McCullough, David. *Truman*. New York: Simon and Schuster, 1992.

McQuaid, Kim. *Uneasy Partners: Big Business in American Politics, 1945–1990*. Baltimore: Johns Hopkins University Press, 1994.

Marchand, Roland. *Advertising the American Dream: Making Way for Modernity, 1920–1940*. Berkeley: University of California Press, 1986.

Marcus, Kenneth Karl. *The National Government and the Natural Gas Industry, 1946–56: A Study in the Making of National Policy*. New York: Arno Press, 1979.

Marcus, Maeva. *Truman and the Steel Seizure Case: The Limits of Presidential Power*. New York: Columbia University Press, 1977.

Mattelart, Armand. *Advertising International: The Privatisation of Public Space*. Translated by Michael Chanon. New York: Routledge, 1991.

Miles, Robert H., and Kim Cameron. *Coffin Nails and Corporate Strategies*. Englewood Cliffs, N.J.: Prentice-Hall, 1982.

Millis, Walter, ed. *The Forrestal Diaries*. New York: Viking Press, 1951.

Mills, C. Wright. *The Power Elite*. New York: Oxford University Press, 1959.

Nelson, Daniel. *American Rubber Workers and Organized Labor, 1900–1941*. Princeton, N.J.: Princeton University Press, 1988.

Neuberger, Maurine. *Smoke Screen: Tobacco and the Public Welfare*. Englewood Cliffs, N.J.: Prentice-Hall, 1963.

O'Brien, Edward J. *Cigarets: Slow Suicide!* New York: Exposition Press, 1968.

Ochsner, Alton. *Smoking and Cancer: A Doctor's Report*. New York: Julian Messner, 1954.

Olasky, Marvin N. *Corporate Public Relations and American Private Enterprise: A New Historical Perspective*. Hillsdale, N.J.: Lawrence Erlbaum, 1987.

Patterson, James T. *Mr. Republican: A Biography of Robert A. Taft*. Boston: Houghton Mifflin, 1972.

Polenberg, Richard. *War and Society: The United States, 1941–1945*. Philadelphia: J. B. Lippencott, 1972.

Pollard, Robert A. *Economic Security and the Origins of the Cold War, 1945–1950*. New York: Columbia University Press, 1985.

Powers, George. *Cradle of Steel Unionism: Monongahela Valley, Pa*. East Chicago, Ind.: Figueroa Printers, 1970.

Rae, John B. *Climb to Greatness: The American Aircraft Industry, 1920–1960*. Cambridge, Mass.: MIT Press, 1968.

Ramu, S. Shira. *Multinational Firms: Strategies & Environments*. New Delhi, India: Sultan Chand & Sons, n.d.

Rand Corporation. *Rand 25th Anniversary Volume*. Santa Monica, Calif.: Rand Corporation, 1973.

Raucher, Alan R. *Public Relations and Business, 1900–1929*. Baltimore: Johns Hopkins University Press, 1968.

Reardon, Steven L. *The Formative Years, 1947–1950*. Vol. 1 of *History of the Office of the Secretary of Defense*. Washington, D.C.: Office of the Secretary of Defense, 1984.

Riepma, S. F. *The Story of Margarine*. Washington, D.C.: Public Affairs Press, 1970.

Robinson, Richard D. *International Business Policy*. New York: Holt, Rinehart and Winston, 1964.

Ross, Irwin. *Image Merchants*. New York: Doubleday, 1959.

Ruble, Kenneth D. *Land O'Lakes: Farmers Make It Happen*. Minneapolis, Minn.: Land O'Lakes, 1973.

Rydell, Robert W. *World of Fairs: The Century-of-Progress Expositions*. Chicago: University of Chicago Press, 1993.

Sawyer, Charles. *Concerns of a Conservative Democrat*. Carbondale: Southern Illinois University Press, 1968.

Schwitzer, M. K. *Margarine and Other Food Fats: Their History, Production and Use*. London: Leonard Hill, 1956.

Seldin, Joseph. *The Golden Fleece: Selling the Good Life to Americans*. New York: Macmillan, 1963.

Sevareid, Eric. *In One Ear*. New York: Alfred A. Knopf, 1952.

Sherry, Michael S. *Preparing for the Next War: American Plans for Postwar Defense, 1941–45*. New Haven: Yale University Press, 1977.

Smith, Bruce L. R. *The RAND Corporation: Case Study of a Nonprofit Advisory Corporation*. Cambridge, Mass.: Harvard University Press, 1966.

Sperber, A. M. *Murrow: His Life and Times*. New York: Freundlich Books, 1986.

Steel Case Research Committee. *The Steel Case: Industry Statements Presented to the Steel Panel of the National War Labor Board*. N.p.: Steel Case Research Committee, 1944.

Stein, Herbert. *The Fiscal Revolution in America*. Chicago: University of Chicago Press, 1969.

Stephenson, Howard, and Wesley Fiske Pratzner. *Publicity for Prestige and Profit*. New York: McGraw-Hill, 1953.

Sussman, Leila. *Dear FDR: A Study of Political Letter-Writing*. Totowa, N.J.: Bedminster Press, 1963.

Sutton, Francis X., Seymour E. Harris, Carl Kaysen, and James Tobin. *The American Business Creed*. New York: Schocken Books, 1962.

Sweeney, Vincent D. *The United Steelworkers of America: Twenty Years Later, 1936–1956*. N.p.: United Steelworkers of America, 1956.

Taylor, Frank J., and Lawton Wright. *Democracy's Air Arsenal*. New York: Duell, Sloan and Pearce, 1947.

Tedlow, Richard S. *Keeping the Corporate Image: Public Relations and Business, 1900–1950*. Greenwich, Conn.: JAI Press, 1988.

Temin, Peter. *Lessons from the Great Depression*. Cambridge, Mass.: MIT Press, 1989.

Tennant, Richard B. *The American Cigarette Industry*. New Haven: Yale University Press, 1950.

Trento, Susan B. *The Power House: Robert Keith Gray and the Selling of Access and Influence in Washington*. New York: St. Martin's Press, 1992.

Troyer, Ronald J., and Gerald E. Markle. *Cigarettes: The Battle over Smoking*. New Brunswick, N.J.: Rutgers University Press, 1983.

Tugendhat, Christopher. *The Multinationals*. London: Eyre & Spottiswoode, 1971.

United Steelworkers of America. *Proceedings of the Sixth Constitutional Convention*. Pittsburgh: United Steelworkers of America, 1952.

United Steelworkers of America Education Department. *Then and Now: The Road Be-*

tween. The Story of the United Steelworkers of America. N.p.: United Steelworkers of America, 1974.

Vaizey, John. *The History of British Steel.* London: Weidenfeld and Nicolson, 1974.

Vander Muelen, Jacob A. *The Politics of Aircraft: Building an American Military Industry.* Lawrence: University Press of Kansas, 1991.

van Stuvenberg, J. H., ed. *Margarine: An Economic, Social and Scientific History, 1869–1969.* Liverpool: Liverpool University Press, 1969.

Vernon, Raymond. *Manager in the International Economy.* 2d ed. Englewood Cliffs, N.J.: Prentice-Hall, 1972.

Watson, George Jr. *The Office of the Secretary of the Air Force, 1947–1965.* Washington, D.C.: Center for Air Force History, 1993.

Whelan, Elizabeth M. *A Smoking Gun: How the Tobacco Industry Gets Away with Murder.* Philadelphia: George F. Stickley, 1984.

White, Larry C. *Merchants of Death: The American Tobacco Industry.* New York: Beech Tree Books, 1988.

Whyte, William H., Jr. *Is Anybody Listening? How and Why U.S. Business Fumbles When It Talks to Human Beings.* New York: Simon and Schuster, 1952.

Wilkins, Mira. *The Maturing of the Multinational Enterprise: American Business Abroad from 1914 to 1970.* Cambridge, Mass.: Harvard University Press, 1974.

World Congress of Public Relations. *Proceedings of the First World Congress of Public Relations: Public Relations in the Service of Social Progress.* Brussels: World Congress of Public Relations, 1958.

Yergin, Daniel. *Shattered Peace: The Origins of the Cold War and the National Security State.* Boston: Houghton Mifflin Company, 1977.

Youth and Education Department. *Youth and Careers in Education.* New York: Hill and Knowlton, 1971.

Zahavi, Gerald. *Workers, Managers, and Welfare Capitalism: The Shoeworkers and Tanners of Endicott Johnson, 1890–1950.* Urbana: University of Illinois Press, 1988.

Zieger, Robert H. *American Workers, American Unions, 1920–1985.* Baltimore: Johns Hopkins University Press, 1986.

——. *The CIO, 1935–1955.* Chapel Hill: University of North Carolina Press, 1955.

Theses and Dissertations

Bennett, Robert James. "Carl Byoir, Public Relations Pioneer." M.A. thesis, University of Wisconsin, 1968.

Hamel, George F. "John W. Hill, Pioneer of Public Relations." M.S. thesis, University of Wisconsin, 1966.

Hartmann, Susan M. "President Truman and the 80th Congress." Ph.D. diss., University of Missouri, 1966.

Howard, Martha C. "The Margarine Industry in the United States: Its Development under Legislative Control." Ph.D. diss., Columbia University, 1951.

Lewenstein, Bruce V. "'Public Understanding of Science' in America, 1945–1965." Ph.D. diss., University of Pennsylvania, 1987.

Libertella, Anthony Frank. "The Steel Strike of 1959: Labor, Management, and Government Relations." Ph.D. diss., Ohio State University, 1972.

Sofchalk, Donald Gene. "The Little Steel Strike of 1937." Ph.D. diss., Ohio State University, 1961.

Stalker, John Nellis. "The National Association of Manufacturers: A Study in Ideology." Ph.D. diss., University of Wisconsin, 1950.

and natural gas program, 174; and
pharmaceutical industry program, 175;
on credibility gap, 191

Gourmet, 71

Grace, Eugene, 15

Graham, Evarts A., 123, 124, 126–27,
133

Gray, Robert Keith, 170, 180, 183, 184,
185

Great Britain: nationalization of steel,
55

Griffith, Robert, 54

Group Attitudes Development Corporation, 96, 164, 173

Growden, Gordon A., 66, 96

Grunig, James, 27

Hahn, Paul M., 128

Hammond, Cuyler, 125, 127, 133

*Handbook on International Public Rela-
tions*, 162

H&K Marketing Services Corporation,
173

Harlow, Rex, 145

Harris, John Howell, 56, 190

Harris-Fulbright bill, 174

Hartnett, Timothy, 132, 134

Hearst, William Randolph Jr., 140

Hedley, Thomas, 152

Hewitt-Robins, 72

Hickenlooper amendment, 151

Hilgartner, Stephen, 35

Hill, Bradford, 123, 133

Hill, John Wiley, 1, 4, 9, 54; relationship
with traditionalist clients, 3; public
relations philosophy, 3, 9, 25–27, 191;
professional ethics, 4–5; early career,
9, 20; conservatism, 9, 22; on New
Deal, 12; in La Follette hearings, 18;
photographs of, 21, 39, 171; executive
demeanor, 22; participation in policy
making of corporate clients, 22–23;
red-baiting, 24; attitudes toward big
labor and big government, 24, 25; concept of public opinion, 25, 115; relationship with leading industrialists,
27–28; and steel industry's community
relations program, 60–61, 63; and
margarine controversy, 75, 88–89;
response to takeover of steel mills,

100; support for Taft-Hartley, 106;
on effects of steel campaign, 113; on
tobacco industry campaign, 129–30,
141–42; growing interest in international public relations, 149–50,
156; lifelong interest in international
affairs, 152; on role of public relations
in cold war, 163, 164; on international
public relations, 165, 166; strategy
for long-term success, 170–73; on
improved public opinion of business,
191–92

Hill, Katherine Jameson, 10

Hill, T. Wiley, 10

Hill and Knowlton, Inc., 1, 21; main goal,
3; conservative point of view, 3–4;
effect on public opinion, 4; approach to
public relations, 9; founding of, 9–12;
work for Greater Akron Association,
18; work for Avco Manufacturing,
19–20; expansion, 19–21; Washington
office, 20–21; emergence as major public relations firm, 22–28; product publicity, 23; anti-Communist subtext of
materials, 24; and chemical industry,
129; and liquor industry, 129; women's
program, 164; conservative personnel
policies, 164–65; refusal of political
and religious accounts until 1987,
178; impact on media discussion, 189–
90; impact on postwar America, 189–
94; impact on political discussion, 190;
impact on public discourse, 190–91;
impact on government-industry
accommodation, 192; impact on climate of intolerance, 192–93

—air power campaign, 32, 33, 34–35;
seeking federal air policy, 35–38; gar-
nering media support, 38–41; reaching
interested public organizations, 41–44;
coordinating campaign, 44–45; effects
of campaign, 45–50

—international expansion, 149–50,
151–52; public relations audit for
Caltex, 153–56, 164, 165–66, 167;
network of associated public relations
firms, 156–57, 160; opening of international headquarters, 157–58; early
overseas accounts, 158–61; multiple
agenda in international work, 163–67;